Bobby Owsinski's

Social Media Promotion For Musicians

The Manual For Marketing Yourself, Your Band, And Your Music Online

Social Media Promotion For Musicians
The Manual For Marketing Yourself, Your Band, And Your Music Online
by Bobby Owsinski

Published by:
Bobby Owsinski Media Group
4109 West Burbank, Blvd.
Burbank, CA 91505

ISBN 978-1-4803-8735-5

Please note that much of this publication is based on personal experience and anecdotal evidence. Although the author and publisher have made every reasonable attempt to achieve complete accuracy of the content in this Guide, they assume no responsibility for errors or omissions. Also, you should use this information as you see fit, and at your own risk. Your particular situation may not be exactly suited to the examples illustrated herein; in fact, it's likely that they won't be the same, and you should adjust your use of the information and recommendations accordingly.

Any trademarks, service marks, product names or named features are assumed to be the property of their respective owners, and are used only for reference. There is no implied endorsement if we use one of these terms.

Finally, nothing in this book is intended to replace common sense, legal, medical or other professional advice, and is meant to inform and entertain the reader.

To buy books in quantity for corporate use or incentives, call 818.588.6606 or email office@bobbyowsinski.com.

Introduction

Through the years, the capabilities of an artist or band has developed in a variety of areas far beyond just the music they create. Not only do we live in an age where the resources and technical power available to the musician for creating music is far greater than ever before, but he or she also has new abilities in developing an audience for that music as well. In fact, an artist, producer, engineer, manager, publisher, record label exec or any other creative person can now reach out directly to his fans, followers, customers or clients, and they're able to reach right back.

What this means is that it's now possible to communicate, promote, sell to and generally keep in touch with your audience without the need for a middleman like was needed in the past. In order to do that, you need to use the many online tools available to you, like the various social media networks (Facebook, Twitter, YouTube, Google+ and the like) coupled with a website, blog and email list among other things. The problem is that all these tools at our disposal can be virtually useless, not to mention time-consuming, without a strategy.

The whole premise of what I outline in *Social Media Promotion For Musicians*, and augment in the Music 3.0 blog, is the use of social media for promotion, not just personal use. Personal use is casual while promotional use is professional, and that makes a big difference when it comes to your online approach and mindset. You're not just reaching out to your family and friends, you're communicating with fans and clients (although some may also be your family and friends). There's a right way to do it, and there's a lot more that goes into it than meets the eye.

When it comes to using social media for promotion, the general idea is to keep the discourse professional (although it's okay to vary from that occasionally), provide your clients and fans with the latest information about your professional life, and measure how well that exchange of information takes place. The measurement part is at once the easiest and the toughest of the three. There's a lot of data available to you from all sorts of sources that you can't get from traditional media, but evaluating that info to see just how well you're doing isn't always easy.

Likewise, there's a timing issue to social media that's many times overlooked. It's not only important how you communicate, but when you do it as well. For every online communication method, there are certain times during the day and week that you'll most effectively reach the most people in and out of your network. This is one of the main issues in social media promotion and you'll find quite a bit about the latest studies in this book that can prove quite helpful to your online strategy.

Of course, the more information you have, the more efficient you become, which is important if you're a creative person of any type. One of the problems with social media is that it can be a runaway train of time and energy if you're not careful. Hopefully the information you find in this book will help you have more time to do the thing you do best and probably enjoy the most - create.

Social Media Promotion For Musicians looks at every area of your online life and shows you how to use it as a promotional tool. You'll learn the ins and outs of services and features that you didn't even know existed, and you'll learn exactly how to use them to your benefit, as well as the latest concepts in using social media for promotion.

So settle back and enjoy the book. You'll find a lot of information in this one place that you won't find anywhere else, and hopefully you'll find it most helpful to your career.

1

It's Called Promotion

There are a lot of books and articles that you can read that will provide some excellent information about using just about any social media service available online today. The trouble is, casually using a social network is not using it for promotion. Let's say that again:

Using Is Not Promotion

Promotion requires a much different set of tactics, which we'll cover in depth as we go along in the book. Not only are the methods different, but so is the mindset, since we're not talking about any kind of promotion, we're talking self-promotion, which can be singularly uncomfortable for many people.

The Meaning Of Self-Promotion

I grew up in a small town in rural Pennsylvania (population around 5,000) in a middle class family that believed in hard work as the means to get ahead in life. In my family (as well as many others in the area), you never boasted nor talked about yourself with undue self-satisfaction unnecessarily. If you were commended or received an award, it was expected that people would discover the fact through the natural buzz of people personally interacting, so there was no need to ever broadcast it yourself. To put it simply, self-promotion was the ultimate dirty word because it was somehow connected with an expanded ego.

Self-promotion doesn't have to be ego-induced bragging though, and that's exactly what I mean in the context of your online presence. It doesn't require you posting how great you are, trying to sell yourself, or an exhibition of any kind of elevated self-esteem. Most of us hate that kind of behavior online or offline anyway, and the results are mostly negative as a result.

No, self-promotion using social media is about three things: communicating, interacting, and measuring. It's more about telling your fans, friends and followers what you're doing and who you're working with, rather than how cool you are because of those facts. It's about letting your fans, clients and customers know you're still around before you're forgotten. It's about informing them that your new music is being released instead of trying to sell it to them. It's all about context. It's not about you as much as it is about the information about you. That's the first part of self-promotion.

The second part of self-promotion is about them - your friends, fans, followers, clients and customers. It's about you soliciting their opinions, answering their questions, listening to their views, and asking for their help. It's not about you, it's about *us*. We all move forward on this journey together. They move with you because there's something they really like about you or identify with (hopefully your music). You help keep the process moving by providing as much information as you can about your journey along the way.

The last part of self-promotion is measurement. This is something that could never be accomplished before in the detail it's done online today. Every measurement about your audience is increasing granular, and that can either cause analysis paralysis or provide a better picture of just who all those fans and followers are. The measurement stats can show how many times a page on your site was visited, how long the viewer stayed, who viewed your post on any social network, how the person found it, where they live, and what computer operating system they use, among many other things. It can get scary how much we can learn about a fan or follower, or can be learned about us.

Although this sounds ominous, the bottom line is that the more we know about our fans and followers, the easier it is to give them what they want, nothing more or less. There are certain things they might love about you, but if you're unaware of what those thing are, you're likely posting the wrong content, which can lead to follower attrition. The measurement tools are easily available and they're mostly free, it's just up to you to use them in order to take advantage of their power.

Why Fan Data Matters

It's difficult to read a tech-related story these days without a reference to user data, metadata, or the latest popular term "Big Data" (large data sets controlled by mostly large companies), but there are a number of good reasons why this has become a major concern for artists, bands and businesses everywhere.

The biggest reason is that the more data you have about your fans and customers, the more you can take advantage of it for promotion as a result. That's because we're moving into a new era of marketing and promotion.

The future of marketing is micro-targeting.

The more you know about your fans, the easier it will be to send them only the information that they care about. Why inform a fan in St. Louis that you're doing a gig in Boston? There might be a time that you'd make that information available (if you're as big as Dave Matthews perhaps), but a few days before the show you just want to concentrate locally, and micro-targeting allows you to do that. What if you have a piece of merch that's aimed at your female fans in cold weather territories? Do you think the dudes care much about it? Do you think your female fans in Florida and Texas care much about it? Micro-targeting allows you to adjust your campaign accordingly.

And it makes measurement easier too. With a more precise user sample, it's much easier to tell if and how a campaign is actually working. If you shotgun a post to 3,000 fans and 15 respond, it looks like a response rate of only .5%, but if that same campaign was more precisely aimed at only 30 of those fans and you found that 12 responded, that's a whopping

40%. In the first example with a .5% response, you'd think that your campaign had a serious flaw in it. In the more targeted second example, we can see that the same campaign worked smashingly well. It all depends on targeting the right fans in the first place.

The old advertising days of "50% of advertising works. We just don't know which 50%," may soon be over, thanks to micro-targeting and better measurement techniques. It's all part of social self-promotion.

A Personal Story

Throughout this book I'll be giving you some personal experiences that I've had with social media promotion. The first I'd like to provide can be found below in Figure 1.1, which is a picture of me on ABC's 20/20 news show. Right after the second Obama inauguration, I was asked to come on the show as their "music and recording expert" to provide a definitive answer to whether Beyonce lip-synced the "National Anthem."

Figure 1.1: Bobby Owsinski on ABC's 20/20

I received about three minutes of national media airtime in front of nearly two million people, but that's not the significant part of the story. No, the story really was how I was asked to do the show. It turns out that Chris Connelly, the show's host, is a fan of my Big Picture music production blog. He found my blog through my posts on Twitter. When the opportunity arose on a story that he felt I could contribute to, he had his producer reach out to me to be on the show.

None of this would had ever happened if I didn't have a blog, nor would it have happened if I didn't frequently tweet about the blog posts. In other words, if it wasn't for social media, I never would've gotten the exposure on traditional media. It's one of the best examples of how social media promotion can work.

Social Media Promotion And The Music World

The reason why self-promotion can work in the music world today is because the basic structure of the music business has changed so much in the last decade. The Internet in all its forms has imposed many unexpected changes that many of the industry old guard consider a disaster, but everyone else considers a revolution. No longer are the record label gatekeepers needed as the business has truly changed in several ways.

The music business that we know today really started in a period that lasted from the 1950s until the early 1980s in the stage called *Music 1.0* that has more or less remained in place for nearly 60 years (see Figure 1.2).

Figure 1.2: The business structure of Music 1.0

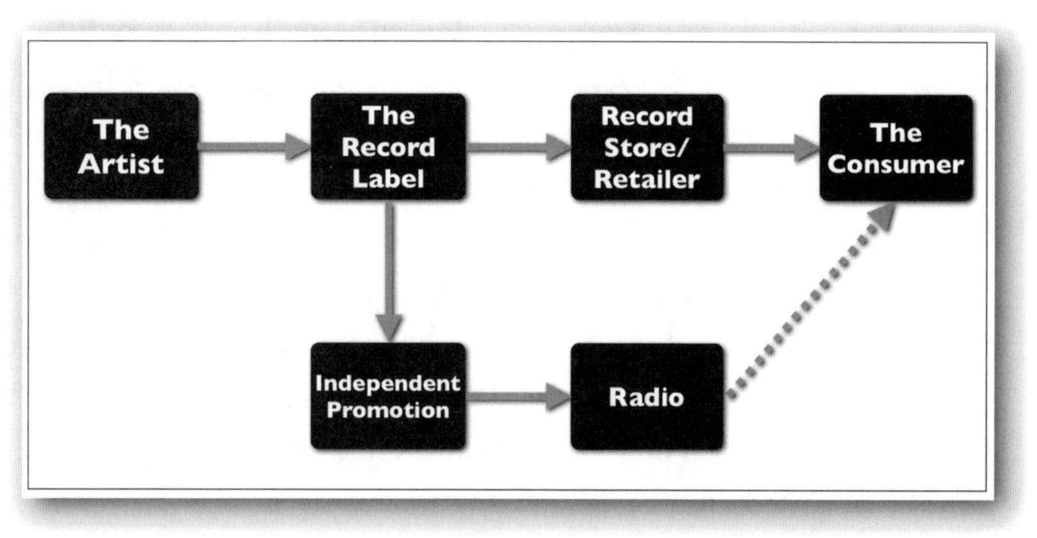

As you can see, the artist is signed to the label, who creates and manufactures the product, then sells it to the record store. In the meantime, the record label uses their own promotion department or independent promoters to persuade radio to play their releases, which the fan hears, and hopefully goes to the record store to buy. In this case, the record label is the center of the music business world, and the artist is removed from any contact with that consumer and fan, except for maybe an official fan club.

The music business evolved to *Music 1.5,* which began in 1982 with the creation of the CD format. The CD quickly became a new high-profit revenue stream, thanks in part to the introduction of MTV, which became an unexpected new avenue for promotion. This lead to ever-increasing sales that provided mountains of cash and profits, which brought a new-found respect from Wall Street, and before you knew it, four of the six major labels that were previously independently controlled were purchased by multi-national conglomerates. As a result of the new corporate ownership, an artist's image and the company's quarterly profits became more of a factor than the actual music, a trend that continues with large labels even today.

The day that the first MP3 digital music file was shared was the first day of *Music 2.0* (sometime around 1994). Although no one knew it at the time, this would soon become the disruption that would lead to the most major evolution in music business history, although at first it had little impact on overall sales. It wasn't long before record labels of all sizes became concerned about piracy, as record sales began to fall, and it became apparent the music industry needed to respond to the digital threat. Ironically, it was the computer industry that stepped in as its savior in 2001. While different digital-music services presented a wide range of alternatives to the labels to get paid for a download, Apple Computer's iTunes proved to be the business model that managed to actually monetize digital music and make it a true source of revenue. The revolution was now underway as the era of *Music 2.5* began.

The Current Music Business Structure

Today we live in the fifth generation of the music business called *Music 3.0*. It's a world where for the first time an artist can communicate, interact, market and sell directly to her audience, and they can communicate right back. This is something that true fans lust for, with no bit of trivia too small, and it's what makes Music 3.0 so powerful.

The biggest change that came with Music 3.0 is in its structure, since the middlemen is now cut out of the loop (see Figure 1.3). The artist and the fan are now directly in touch on any and every level they choose to be, from creation to promotion to marketing to sales. But merely staying in touch with a fan can be as fleeting as it sometimes is with friends or family. True fans, just like friends and family, want regular communication, and whether artists know it or not, so do they.

Figure 1.3: The business structure of Music 3.0

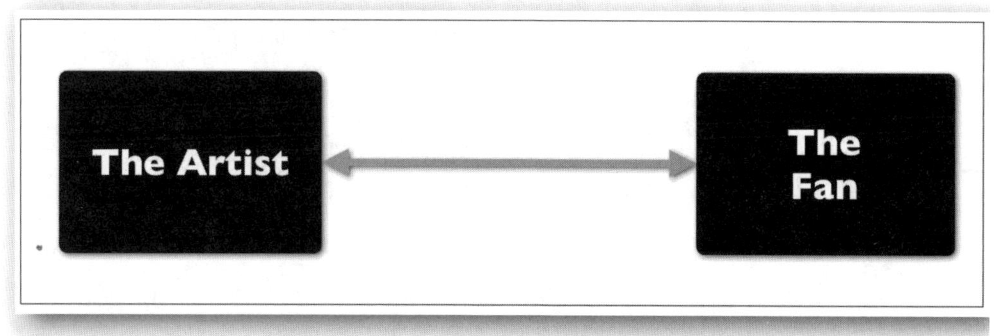

Music 3.0 allows the artist to promote and market directly to the fan. If you can reach the fan, you can make him aware of your products (music, gig tickets, and merchandise). If you can reach the fan, you can sell directly to them (although "offer them a product" is a more accurate way of putting it). Most importantly, Music 3.0 allows you to have a dialog with the fan in order to help you understand how to better fine tune the sales and marketing aspect of your business. What does the fan want? Just ask him. Does the fan want to be alerted when you come to town? Does the fan want a remixed version of a song? Would the fan be interested in a premium box set? By just asking, the fan will gladly let you know. And this is the essence of Music 3.0 - communication between the fan and the artist, or the ability of the artist to self-promote.

The New Audience

Another factor in Music 3.0 is that the audience has become niche oriented. From Brazilian marching band to Mandarin madrigal, if an artist searches long enough, he will find an audience. But although stratification of the audience means more opportunities for more artists, it also means that the possibility of a huge multi-million-selling breakout hit is diminished as fewer people are exposed to a single musical genre than ever before. Nearly gone are the days when a television appearance or heavy-rotation radio or MTV airplay can propel an artist to platinum-level success.

While remnants of the old Music 1.0 structure still exist (record labels, brick-mortar record stores, terrestrial radio, MTV, and so on) and can even be useful to the Music 3.0 artist, they will probably never again be the primary driving factor in the success of any artist. In a roundabout way, they never really were (the music is always the defining factor), although their influence was admittedly higher in the past.

It's said that a record label never signed an act because of its music; the label signed the act for the number of fans it either already had or had the potential of developing. If you had lines around the block waiting to see you play, the music didn't matter to the label, because you had an audience that was willing to buy it. And so it is with Music 3.0, only now you can develop that audience in a more efficient way and actually make a living with a limited but rabid fan base.

As stated before, it's the first time where there's no middleman if an artist choses not to have one. It's the first time that an artist can reach out directly to his fans, and they can reach back just as easily. It's an ecosystem that thrives on communication, and has a whole new set of rules for doing business as a result. It's an era finally adjusted for self-promotion - if you know how to do it.

Online Word Of Mouth

Social networks are now part of the fabric of our lives. Regardless of your age and where you live in the world, chances are that you've recently participated in a social network in some way. If we just look at the major social networks, we find that they have an enormous number of users as evidenced in Figure 1.4.

Figure 1.4: The major social networks

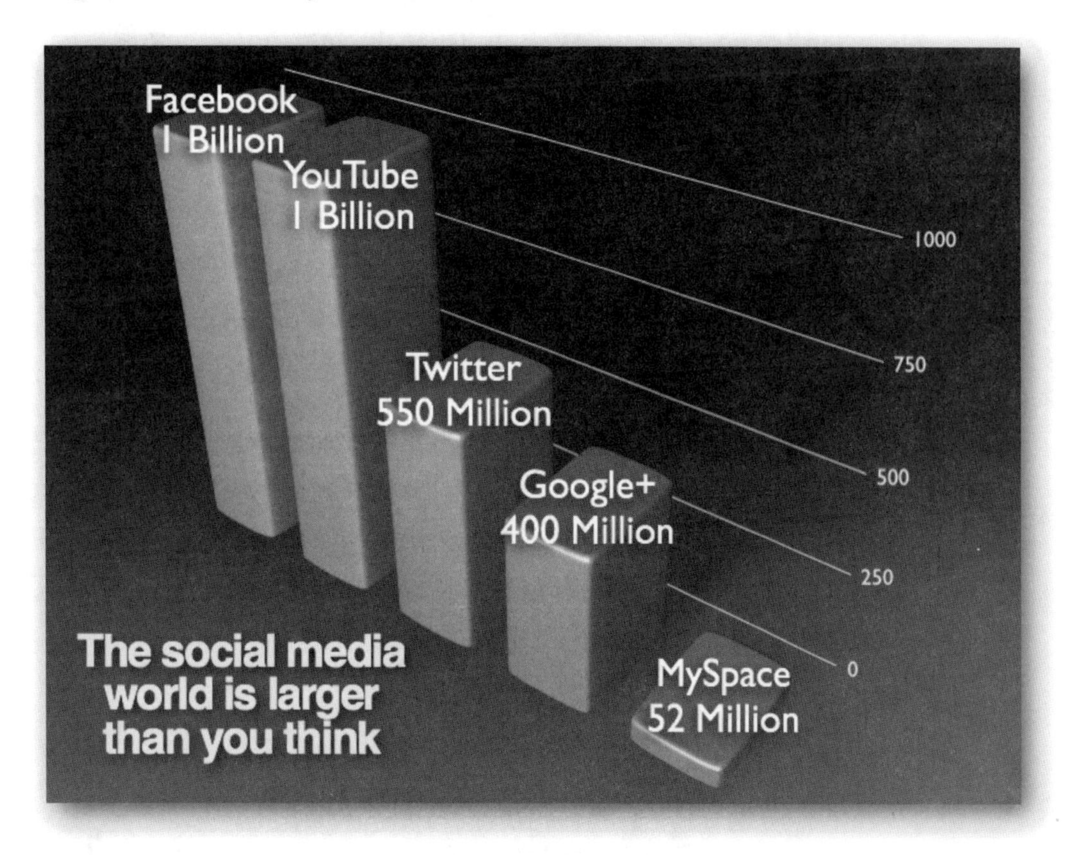

As you can see, both Facebook and YouTube have over a billion users, which means that if they were countries, either one could be the third largest in the world! MySpace is included as a reference, since at one time it was the most visited site on the Internet (yes, even more than Google for a bit) with more than 100 million active users at its peak.

Facebook is really the 800 pound gorilla in the social network world at the moment though, and the average user has an average of 190 Facebook friends. This piece of info is important since it's been estimated by a Pew Internet and American Life study that there are a total of more than 140 *billion* Facebook friends in all, and that any single user has access to over 156 thousand other people just by virtue of friends of friends. Think of the promotional possibilities just within your near sphere of influence as a result!

That tiny bit of info goes to prove a point. *Social media is really online word-of-mouth*. This is important because it's been long established that word-of-mouth is the most effective form of advertising and promotion, and some new research from Nielsen backs the premise up yet again. In its most recent "Global Trust In Advertising Survey," the research company determined that:

- 92% of consumers trust word-of-mouth recommendations from friends and family above all else, compared to only 14% who trust advertising.
- Online consumer reviews were the second most trusted form of advertising at 70%, which was an increase of 15% in the last four years.

What this boils down to is that word of mouth always has been, and still is the most trusted form of promotion available, regardless of whether it's in-person or online. The only difference is that it's so much more powerful when done online.

Imagine having a face-to-face conversation with one of your friends and saying, "Dude, I am so happy with this new project that I've been working on with Dave Grohl. I put a lot of work into it, but it was worth it because I think it's coming out great." Somewhere down the road, that friend might then say to one of his friends, "I heard that John (you) was working on a pretty cool project with Dave Grohl and it's coming out great," who then tells another friend, who tells another friend. Before you know it, each friend has told anywhere from three to five friends (according to a study by Ford Motor Company done in 1986), depending upon how relevant and juicy the news was.

Now imagine posting the same news on Facebook, Twitter or any social network. You've now multiplied that reach by hundreds or thousands. Not only will your fans and followers repost your news online, but they'll probably physically tell their friends as well. This goes to show what a massive force-multiplier social media can be when it comes to promotion, especially when you consider the 190 average friends that each of your Facebook friends have.

The Theory of 22

While people may tell three to five friends about any good news, that same Ford study also found that something negative can spread even further. Ford found that a person with a complaint will tell an average of 22 people! Something that's merely displeasing may be communicated to only between five and ten.

This is why it's important that you learn to promote online the correct way, since any misstep can quickly get out of control and can potentially do more harm than good. This is one of the few cases where sometimes you're lucky if you're simply ignored.

That said, when it comes to marketing just about anything (including you and your music), social media should be a priority since it's an effective yet inexpensive platform for getting the word out that consumers deem credible.

8 Advantages Of Social Media Over Traditional Media

Social media holds quite of number of advantages over traditional media when it comes to promotion. It's the hub around which the online wheel that we live in today turns, and the following (inspired by marketing guru Simon Mainwaring) provides some of the reasons why.

1. Cost: Beyond your time and production costs, social media promotion is almost free. Traditional media has a high barrier to entry cost-wise.

2. Intimacy: Fans crave a personal interaction with the artist, band or brand and now it's possible. Traditional media broadcasts to thousands or millions of people at once, which is far less intimate.

3. Targeting: A large portion of the audience that traditional advertising reaches doesn't care about your message, which is a waste of money. Social media is able to target only the people that will respond to what you have to offer.

4. Nimbleness: Social media promotion allows you to respond to any changes in the market instantly, while traditional media requires a larger infrastructure that can't move as quickly.

5. Measurement: Social media has a variety of tools that can provide all sorts of data that's just not possible with traditional media.

6. Potential Growth: While a viral hit is unpredictable, just about any promotion has at least the chance of seeing exponential growth in a short period of time. Traditional media requires a significant investment to grow, and has nowhere near the possibilities provided by something gone viral.

7. Participation: Social media allows artist to fan, and fan to fan, interaction to take place, while traditional media does not.

8. Proximity: Social media allows communication and interaction anywhere in the world. Traditional media is limited to the areas of the media buy.

We're lucky to live in a time where self-promotion is so inexpensive and easy. Once again, the biggest trick is knowing how to do it. Those tricks will be revealed as you read on.

Your Social Media Strategy

Most artists or bands use social media totally randomly. They create a Facebook page because that's what everyone does. They tweet because they heard Lady Gaga or Cold Play does that too. They create a Tumblr blog or join Pinterest because they've been told it's the latest thing. The problem is that because there's no overall strategy for dealing with social media, it takes a lot of time to keep up with everything, and the more time you have to spend online, the less time you have for the fun things like creating.

But another problem with having no strategy is that social media becomes much less effective as a promotional tool as well. That's why this chapter looks at your overall online strategy, not just for social media. In the end, it's all tied together.

It's A Big Social Media World

By now everyone knows how powerful other social networks besides Facebook can be, but usually the only ones thought of are Twitter and, more recently, Google+. There are a lot more than just those three though, and quite a few have very formidable numbers. According to Pingdom.com, these are the networks that have at least 1 million *daily* views.

1. Facebook - 310 M
2. Orkut - 51 M
3. Qzone - 37 M
4. Twitter - 22 M
5. Odnoklassniki - 9.3 M
6. LinkedIn - 8.0 M
7. vKontakte 8.0 M
8. Badoo - 8.0 M
9. Mixi -7.0 M
10. Flickr - 4.9 M
11. Hi5 - 4.2 M
12. MySpace - 4.0 M
13. Nasza Klasa - 4.0 M
14. Tuenti - 3.9 M
15. Hyves - 3.0 M
16. Renren - 3.0 M
17. Tagged - 2.6 M
18. Taringa! - 2.5 M
19. Cyworld - 2.2 M
20. Netlog - 2.1 M
21. LiveJournal - 2.0 M
22. Kaixin001 - 2.0 M

23. Wer-kennt-wen - 2.0 M
24. Sonico - 1.5 M
25. Douban - 1.5 M
26. MeinVZ - 1.5 M
27. Skyrock - 1.4 M
28. deviantART - 1.3 M
29. iWiW - 1.1 M

As you can see, there are plenty that you probably don't recognize, mostly because they're popular in an area of the world other than North America, but that doesn't mean they're any less powerful in getting your message across.

TIP: *When determining your social strategy, ask your fans if there's another network that they visit often, and be prepared to jump in if the answer is yes.*

The Problems And The Solutions

It's probably no surprise that four out of five Internet users regularly visit social networks and blogs, and as you're probably well aware, it takes a fair amount of time to participate in only the largest ones, let alone any of the other alternatives. In fact, the average person:

- posts 90 pieces of Facebook content per month
- spends 23 minutes a day on Twitter
- watches 124 videos equaling 3.75 hours of video on YouTube a month

That's plenty of time right there that probably isn't as productive as you'd like it to be. The last chapter discussed how just using a social network wasn't enough; you have to know how to use it for promotion. Now you can see that there's an additional problem, this one regarding time. It's possible to spend so much time maintaining your social media accounts that you never have time for anything else.

The solution, of course, is to have a total online strategy, and there are three reasons why this is important:

- **Efficiency**: so you spend less time online for the same results or better.

- **Effectiveness**: your fan base increases and you're better at giving them what they want.

- **Message Control**: you have total control of your brand and how it's presented

Attaining any one of these items makes it worth the effort to develop a strategy, but put all three together and it becomes a no-brainer. The problem is that there are so many online social sites and services, not to mention your main website, blog, music and video hosting site, that it's easy to get confused or sidetracked by the sheer breadth of it all. Luckily, there's help.

The Big Picture

There are a lot of online elements that every artist, band or brand has to be involved in these days in order to be an effective online marketer. It's pretty easy to get confused and either not know where to begin, or throw yourself scattershot at all of them, which usually means that your efforts will be ineffective when it comes to promotion. If we just look at the major components, it looks something like this:

Your website
Your email list
Facebook and Google+ posts
Twitter
Music releases
YouTube video posts
Blog posts

Throw in any of the 100+ additional networks available and it's no wonder why artists, bands and music execs become bewildered by it all. We can make things a bit simpler by separating these components so they fall into one of three categories; content, interaction and tactics. If we break all this out, it looks like this:

Content: the places online where you place the material that you generate, like information about your band, music, videos, or blog posts.

Interaction is all the social networks where you might interact with your fans and followers. These include:

- Your website
- Your mailing list
- Your blog
- Your videos on Youtube and other video sites
- Your music files on Soundcloud or other music hosting sites

Interaction: the places where you regularly communicate with your fans, followers, clients and customers. These include:

- Facebook
- Twitter
- Google+
- Pinterest
- Bookmarking
- Any other social network

Tactics: everything required to define and refine who you are and your position in the online world. These include:

- Branding
- Strategy
- Measurement

All this gets more interesting when we put into the form of a Venn chart as in Figure 2.1 and watch how the categories intersect.

Figure 2.1: A Venn chart of your online presence.

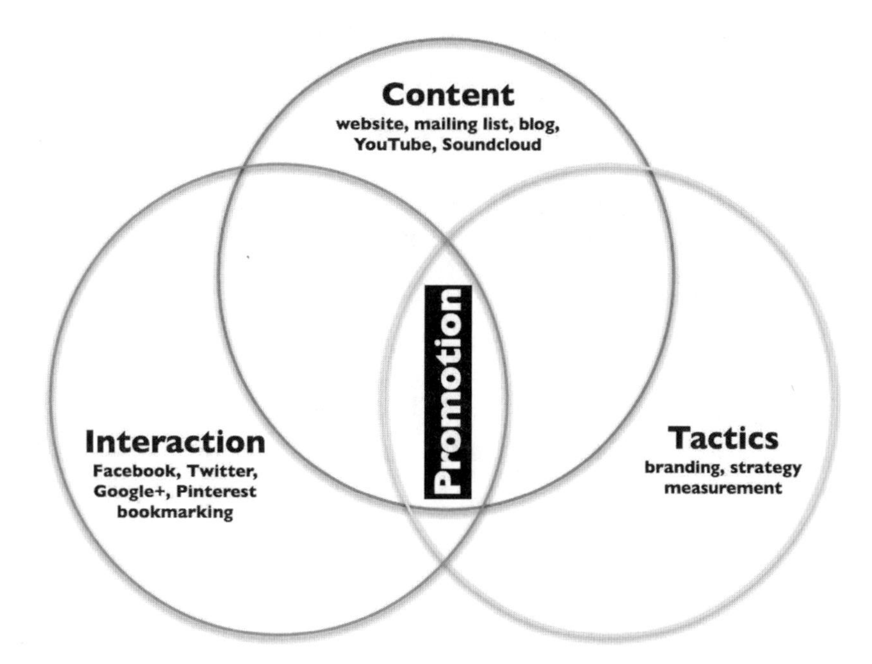

As you can see, where all three category circles cross, a new element pops up - promotion. This isn't possible without all three elements combined, which goes to show just how synergistic they all are. Use only one or two and you fall short; use all three and new possibilities for promotion arise. That's not the strategy though, only the general overview.

Developing Your Online Strategy

The biggest difficulty artists, bands, musicians, producers, songwriters, publishers and even record labels have when it comes to social media is that they don't have an online focus. They may have a website, but rely on Facebook for most of their traffic. Maybe it's a Tumblr or Wordpress blog that gets the most attention, with a Facebook page getting some consideration depending on the whim of the day. Even worse, maybe they have a website, Facebook page, blog, Twitter account, mailing list, Google+ account and more, and all get random attention. The problem is, until you have a single focal point online, you don't really have a strategy. That's where your website comes in as your primary online element.

Don't Depend On An External Site

Unfortunately, a website many times gets overlooked as an integral piece of your digital promotional life because there are so many other places that you can use as your online focal point. Having a Facebook page or Tumblr blog, or relying on another social network as your online central focus has a number of potential flaws, not the least is control of your message. Let's look at three scenarios where relying on a social media site as your main contact point can prove disastrous.

- **Scenario #1:** Our first scenario is a real-life example of a band I'll hypothetically call "The Unknowns," since one of the band members asked me not to reveal their true name. During the heyday of MySpace around 2004 the band was hot and eventually developed a following of over 900,000. This led to a number of record labels becoming interested (remember that they sign you for your audience, not your music), with the band eventually signing a big deal with one of the largest major labels at the time. The label immediately told the band to suspend their MySpace account because "we can do all that better in-house than you can." In typical record company fashion, the label ultimately did very little for the band's online presence. They did create a new slicker label-managed MySpace account, but they were not able to transfer any of the band's previous followers, thus leaving them with a presence that was far less than they had before they were signed. Of course, when The Unknown's album was released they had no way to alert those 900,000 followers since they didn't have any of their email addresses, and they didn't even have a website where their fans could go in order to discover the latest news about them. Needless to say, the album bombed and the band was dropped from the label. They never recovered that massive fan base that they had before they were signed.

The moral of the story is that if they had redirected those fans from their MySpace account to their website in order to harvest at least some of the email addresses, things might've turned out a lot differently, since they could have alerted their fans when the album was released. And that's the problem with relying on an external site that you don't control as your focal point online.

It's too easy for today's artist who only dabbles in social networking to get complacent and comfortable with the abilities of a single social network, but that can spell disaster for maintaining your fan base if you're not careful. As those artists who formerly depended upon MySpace now know, what's hot today can be ice cold tomorrow. But other negative scenarios also exist that can be far worse than the network falling out of favor.

This scenario was recently played out again early 2013 in a slightly different manner when MySpace relaunched an updated version of their site. Every single artist lost all of their followers, and every MySpace user lost their previous settings, and any affiliation with the artists they were following. All users had to reregister again, and all artists, regardless of how popular they were (even owner Justin Timberlake), started all over again with zero followers!

- **Scenario #2:** Let's say that you've cultivated a huge following on Facebook. What would happen if Facebook was purchased by EXXON (highly unlikely, but let's pretend), who decides that all it wants is the underlying technology of the network, and shuts the rest down? If you didn't capture the email addresses of all your followers, you'd lose them to the nothingness of cyberspace. Don't laugh - a scenario like this could happen, but most likely on another smaller network.

- **Scenario #3:** What would happen if Facebook (I'm picking on them because they're the big dog on the social block) changes its terms of service, and now charges you $.25 for every fan past 100? If you're lucky enough to have 8,000 fans, it's going to cost you $2,000 to continue. Or what if they decided to limit everyone's fan connections to 100? Both are unlikely, but something similar could happen, where suddenly you're unable to access that large fan base that you've worked so hard to develop.

The point of all of the above scenarios is that when you depend on a social network for your online presence, you're ceding control to an unknown, unseen force that can change it's will at any time with no regard to your online well-being. That's why it's imperative that you don't count on a single social network for your total online presence or even your social media presence. If you rely on an external network, sooner or later you're going to get burnt. It's the nature of the Internet to constantly change, and it's too early to get a feel for the life span of even of the largest sites and networks.

Just to illustrate the volatile nature of social networks, in 2005 MySpace was the most visited social network online with 100 million users. A mere five years later and it had dropped below 25 million, yet has recently doubled that number and is growing again. What this means is that you must pick and choose the social networks that you participate in wisely, and always engage in a number of networks in case one suddenly falls out of favor.

Relying On Too Many Sites

Another common mistake that artists sometimes make is having too many contact points (like their website, blog, Facebook, Tumblr and Reverb Nation, for example) all requiring separate updates. You can imagine how tough it is to keep every one of those sites updated regularly. Worse is the fact that it's confusing for the fan, who just wants a single place to visit. When you don't have a plan, it takes a lot of time to maintain your accounts and the updates and posts happen randomly or not at all, which can lead to follower attrition. Yet another problem is that you may be collecting email addresses from each site and they may all be going on different mailing lists.

The quick solution is to use one site (usually your website) as a your main focal point and use that to feed daily updates and info to all the others via RSS or social-media broadcast tools like Tweetdeck or Hootsuite.com (which we'll cover later in the book). This means that you only need to update a single site and all the others will be updated at the same time, although it's good practice to customize the post for each slightly.

The Center Of Your Online Universe

The second component of this management strategy would be to have all of your satellite sites (blog, Facebook, and so on) designed in such a way as to feed your social media viewers into your website (see Figure 2.2). At a bare minimum, the email registration of each satellite site should feed into the same list as your main site.

Figure 2.2: The center of your online universe

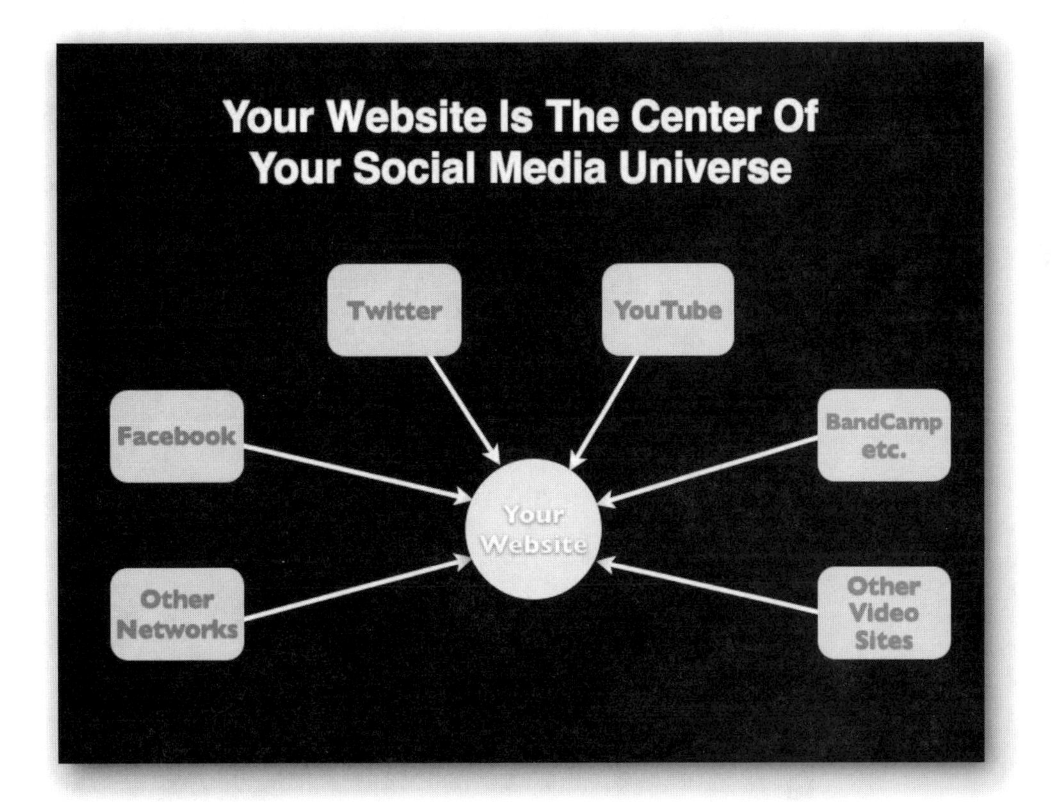

That's not to say that you don't want to communicate with fans or clients on Facebook, Twitter or your blog. It just means that whenever it's appropriate, you link them back to your site. You do this so they're always aware that the main information about you (like tour dates, video and song releases, contact and booking information, etc.) can be found there, and you can capture their email address for your mailing list so you can communicate directly to them without the randomness of a social network. As you'll see in Chapter 4, there's a host of additional reasons why having a strong website is important, even if it's not updated often. You may use other parts of your online presence more, but few are as effective for doing business.

The Steps To A Successful Online Strategy

Although you'll find plenty of detailed information in this book about most aspects of your online strategy, here are the six basic steps you'll need to take in order to prepare for online promotion.

1. Make your website your main online focal point. Make sure that all your important information is curated there and is easy for a site visitor to find. Chapter 4 will describe what a modern artist website needs to look like and how it should function.

2. Create accounts on the "Big 4" social networks (Facebook, Twitter, Google+ and YouTube). You can't be everywhere at once. Even if you could it would take so much time that you'd never have any time to make music, which is what we're trying to avoid. That said, in order to get the most out of social media promotion, you need the following:

- **A Facebook page.** Regardless of how you feel about Facebook, you still need a presence on it if for no other reason than it's easy proximity to lots of potential new fans. If you're just starting out, you might want to start with a personal page instead of a fan site though. It can be embarrassing to have a fan page with only a few followers, and a personal site is a way to gain some momentum before you make the leap. We'll cover the ins and outs of Facebook in Chapter 6.

- **A Twitter account.** The people that dismiss Twitter are the ones that aren't aware of how to use it for promotion. It's extremely powerful for attracting new fans and keeping your current ones instantly informed. We'll look at Twitter in Chapter 7.

- **A YouTube channel.** Videos are such a major part of any musician, artist or band's online presence that you really need your own channel to exploit them successfully. Chapter 9 will describe how.

- **A Google+ account.** Google+ is not yet an absolutely necessary network to participate in, but it's still growing and has a number of unique features that work particularly well for anyone in the music business. We'll delve into Google+ more in Chapter 10.

- **A look at other networks.** As I've pointed out previously, there are a ton of other social networks and a many of them might deserve your attention at some point. There comes a point in time where the amount of time invested versus the potential outcome just doesn't balance out, which is why you should probably stay with the previous four networks until you're really comfortable before you decide take on another one. The only exception to that would be if a big portion of your audience is on a particular network other than the "Big 4" (like Pinterest for example, which we'll look at in Chapter 11), then you might want to substitute that network for Google+.

3. Use a social media broadcast app for all your updates. An app like Tweetdeck or Hootsuite is one of the keys to streamlining the process that saves time and makes what you do online more efficient. We'll discuss these and other similar apps throughout the book.

4. Develop your social media sites so they all feed viewers into your main site. The key is to make sure that any viewer on any site is aware that you have a website and knows that it's the main repository of information about you.

5. Be sure that email list subscribers from all sites go to same master list. Different mailing lists don't do you much good if you have to create a separate newsletter blast for each one. We'll look at mailing lists and newsletters in Chapter 5.

6. Get third party help when you get to the point where you're overwhelmed. At some point social-media management gets too complex for the artist to maintain, and third-party help is needed. This is usually a good thing, since that means you've progressed to a point that things are so massive that you can't keep up. Furthermore, a company that specializes in social-media management can keep you current with new tools and techniques that you might not be aware of. Even when outside help arrives, remember that you're still the one that drives the bus. Be sure to take part in all strategy discussions, but leave the actual facilitation to the company you've hired.

Having a sound social strategy is the key to successful promotion. The upcoming chapters of this book will examine each of the above points in much more detail as you learn the ins and outs of how this is accomplished.

***TIP**: The order of importance of your online components is (1) website, (2) mailing list, (3) Facebook, (4) Twitter, (5) YouTube, (6) blog. The order of importance of numbers 3 to 6 may change, but your website and mailing list will always be the most important.*

✦

3

Developing Your Brand

Before you begin any promotion you have to know exactly what it is that you're promoting. In this case, the product is you, your music, and your image. Put them together and they become your "brand."

Whenever the word "brand" is spoken to musicians their eyes usually glaze over faster than an air guitar contest, and understandably so. Branding smacks of marketing, which is business, not art. Every musician wants to stay in their comfort zone, which is creating art, and that's the reason why they entered into the music business in the first place.

But it's called the music "business" for a reason. If you're playing music (or producing, engineering, publishing, songwriting, etc.) for any reason more than a hobby, commerce enters into the equation, and the more in-demand you are, the more money you'll make. Whether you know it or not, you are a brand. The problem is that most of us aren't aware what our brand, or any brand for that matter, really is.

What Is A Brand?

One of the things that an artist or band hears a lot these days is the need to promote "your brand" in order to get ahead in the current era of the music business. That's all well and good, but you can't promote your brand unless you know the definition of a brand in the first place. So what exactly is a brand?

A brand is a promise of quality and consistency.

Want a few good examples of a brand in every day life? How about MacDonald's for starters. No matter where in the world you go, you can always recognize a McDonald's franchise by the now-famous golden arches, and you know that a Big Mac will taste like a Big Mac. Beijing, Cleveland, Amsterdam, Sydney, Johannesburg, or Sao Paulo, it will always taste the same.

Then there's Coke. First you have the distinctive script logo and the signature shaped bottle, then you have the exact same taste from bottle to can to fountain (unless they get the syrup to carbonated water mixture slightly wrong). Once again, anywhere in the world, a Coke's a Coke. When Coke tried to change the formula in 1985, they unwittingly broke their brand and had to fight to get their customers back because the trust in the brand was damaged.

If we look to the world of electronics, there's Apple. First you have the identifying one-bite-of-the-apple logo that's so strong that you don't even need to have the name spelled out. Then no matter what product you purchase from Apple, you can expect a sleek high-tech design and an easy to understand user interface.

If we look to the world of music, there's Fender, which was the world's leading brand for guitars and guitar amplifiers until CBS bought them in 1965. Slowly but surely, the new owners broke the brand because they neither understood the market nor cared about the quality of the product. The once mighty Fender name became an insignia for ill-conceived products that didn't work nearly as well as they once did. It was only when management purchased the company from CBS in 1985 that Fender was able to gradually restore it's brand to where it is today, once again one of the great names in musical instruments.

Artist Branding

For an artist, a brand means a consistency of persona, and usually a consistency of sound. Regardless of what genre of music the artist delves into, the feel is the same and you can tell it's none other than that artist. Madonna has changed musical and fashion directions many times during her career but her brand remained consistent. Her post-feminist persona remained the same even as she changed to and from the "material girl." The Beatles tried a wide variety of directions, but you never once questioned who you were listening to. It was always fresh and exciting, yet distinctly them. The same goes for any of the legacy acts that have lasted 20+ years, which is why they lasted that long.

On the other hand, Neil Young almost killed his career with an electronic album called *Trans* that alienated all but his hardiest fans, and the well-respected voice of Sound Garden, Chris Cornell, may have done irreparable harm to his solo career thanks to his loop-based electronic pop album with Timbaland (*Scream*). Why did this happen? For both artists, the album no longer "felt" like them. Both Young and Cornell built their careers on organic music played with a band, and as soon as their music became regimented and mechanical, the consistency (and some say the quality) of their brands was lost. After *Trans*, Young returned to his roots and slowly built his brand back to superstar level over time, and recently Cornell went back to sing with Sound Garden, which could be a move to rebuild his rock credibility.

How do you determine what your brand is? It's easier said than done. In order for an artist to successfully promote their brand, they must have a great sense of self-awareness. You must know who you are, where you came from, and where you're going in terms of your music and your career. You must know what you like and don't like, and what you stand for and why. And you must have an inherent feel for your sound and what works for you, which is usually against the grain of a current trend unless you happen to be leading it.

***TIP**: Brand self-awareness sometimes differentiates a superstar from a star, and a star from someone who wants it really badly but never seems to get that big break.*

The Three Pillars Of A Successful Brand

One of the problems with the process of branding is that by being such an obvious goal, it can feel like a sell-out. That very well may be true in some cases were the branding is created more to manipulate an artist to fit into a trend rather than as a promotional strategy to build the artist's audience.

The problem is that whether you like it or not, if you're an artist, you're already a brand. It may not be a strong brand, but then again, it very well may be stronger than you think without any thought or effort on your part. What I want to outline here are the elements that make up a brand and how they're created.

So what are the pillars of building the brand? There are three:

- **Familiarity**: You can't have a brand unless your followers or potential followers are familiar enough with who you are. They don't even have to know what you sound like to be interested in you if you have a buzz and they've heard about you enough to want to check you out. Amanda Palmer, who more people know for her social media savvy than her music, fits into this category.

- **Likeability**: Your followers have to like you or something about you. It could be your music, or it could be your attitude or your image. You could even say how much you hate your fans and do everything to ridicule them, and that irreverent manner could be just the thing they like about you. It doesn't matter what it is, but there has to be something they like. Most artists fall into this category.

- **Similarity**: Your fans have to feel that either you represent them in a cause or movement (like a new genre of music), or that someday they can be you. Female Olympic athletes usually don't do well in this category because their sleek and muscular look is so far beyond what the ordinary girl or women can attain that they can't relate to them. On the other hand, young girls love Taylor Swift because they feel that she could be their best friend from next door.

If you have those three things along with a product that consistently maintains its quality (your music), you've got a brand. I wouldn't intentionally try to manufacture your brand so it absolutely complies with these pillars (people usually see right through that), but always keep in mind that this is how your audience views you, although none of them may even realize it.

Developing Your Brand

While the music that you play or create is totally up to you and outside the realm of this book, what we can deal with is the second part of the brand - your image. Here are some steps to take to refine your brand.

1. Make sure your brand image accurately portrays your music and personality. If you're a biker band, you probably don't want a website that's all pink and flowery. On the other hand, the pink works great for Katy Perry. Likewise, if you're an EDM artist you wouldn't want your site to show the woods and trees, although that could work well for an alt rock band from Minnesota or someone doing music for meditation.

2. Keep it honest and simple. Don't try to be who you're not, it's too hard to pull off. You are who you are and people will either love you for it or they won't. While you can concoct a backstory where you were taught a new form of music by aliens, then honed your technique in the jungles of Brazil, that just sets your brand up to fail if you really can't live up to the image that's been painted. Best to keep things simple and be honest about who and what you are and where you came from. If people like what you do and can relate to you, that will shine through and your fans will not only find it interesting enough, but will be totally fascinated as well.

3. Differentiate yourself. While it might seem tempting to proclaim that you're just like Coldplay, that doesn't immediately make you their equal in the eyes of the public. The fact of the matter is, there already is a Coldplay, why does the world need another one? It's their brand, not yours. The only way that a brand can be successful is to differentiate itself from the competition. A great example is the seminal punk band The Ramones, who decided that all their songs would be as short as possible and played without solos. There must be something that makes you unique in even a small way. If you can't find it, it may be time to go back to the drawing board.

4. Keep the look consistent. Consistency of product and image are the key to branding. That's why you need to use the same logo and fonts and have the same general look and feel across all your promo for it to be effective. That includes your website, press kit, blog, newsletter and all social media.

5. Create a remarkable logo. This is a requirement if you're planning to promote your brand. You need this for your website, social sites, merchandise, press kit, promo and on your stage during gigs. In short, it has to be part of everything you do. You may start promoting yourself without it, but it's a big plus if you already have a logo. It separates you from the newbies. Just as an example, here are a few unmistakable musician's logos in Figure 3.1.

If you're a musician without a band, a producer, songwriter or engineer, it doesn't mean that you must also have a logo as well (although it would be better), but at the very least, use the same font for your name on your blog, website, newsletter and anywhere else it might appear.

Figure 3.1: Recognizable Band Logos

6. Great photos are a necessity. You need first class photos for posters, merch, website, social networks, press kits, and a lot more if you want to build your brand. This is as important as the logo - you need a great photo in order to begin any kind of promotion. Have you ever seen a Facebook page or website of a major artist without an artist or band photo?

7. Give away samples. Learn this phrase well as it will be repeated throughout this book.

Your music is your marketing.

That means that you can't look at your music as your product. It may bring in some money eventually but not all that much in the grand scheme of things. Remember that 90 to 95% of the money that a major artist earns is *not* from recorded music. It's from concerts, merchandise, publishing and licensing.

***TIP**: Don't be afraid to give your music away. It's your best marketing tool and the best way to build your brand.*

8. Cool is never declared. You cannot proclaim how new and unique you are. If such a statement is in fact true, people will find out soon enough and tell the world. You can use quotes from other people, but telling the world that you think you're cool does not make it so.

These are not the only steps that you can take, but they'll take you a long way to creating a brand image that works for you.

Why A Trademark Can Be Important

If you've established your logo or a unique look to your brand, it can be quite beneficial to have it trademarked. The reason is that not only can it provide an additional income stream at some point, but it can also provide some protection as well. First, let's look at exactly what a trademark is.

A Trademark is any unique symbol, design, mark or words that distinguishes your product from others in the marketplace.

An example of a trademark could be the Nike swoosh, the design of the Coke bottle, or the McDonald's golden arches. These are all trademarks because you identify the design with their product without ever considering a similar product. The mark separates the brand from the competition around it.

Here's why having a trademark can be important. Let's say your band name is "Shooting Star" and you're based in Birmingham, Alabama. You begin to play a club circuit that leads you from Florida to Nashville and you're becoming pretty popular. If you've not trademarked the name "Shooting Star," there's nothing to prevent another band from taking the same name and calling up that club in Tallahassee you just played at a few weeks ago and booking a gig using the same name without telling them they're different. You may have used the name first, but unless it's trademarked, you have no legal recourse.

Another reason owning your trademark can be important is when you're signed to a record label. If at some point you have a falling out, there's no reason why the label can't put out an album of your outtakes to try to make some money without your knowledge (it's been done plenty of times before). If you owned your trademark however, they'd be legally forced to come to you to license the mark before they could either sell or promote the album.

Yet another reason is merch. If you become popular enough that merch emblazoned with your name has some value to it, there's nothing to stop a street vendor from running off a hundred T-shirts and selling them outside your gig before your fans even get inside the door to look at your official merch. They may still do it if you own your trademark, but at least you would have a legal recourse to have them cease and desist from selling them. If you don't own your trademark, you may be out of luck.

Acquiring A Mark

There are two ways to acquire a trademark; the cheap and easy way, and the expensive way. As with most things in life, you get what you pay for.

The easy way is to just start use the ™ trademark symbol on your branding. This is called a "common law" trademark, and all that's required is that you just begin using it before anyone else, as in the case of the band name. The problems with this are that you must continually use the mark without any breaks or the mark offers you little protection, your protection can be fairly limited even with a continuos mark and may even be restricted to a certain location, and you're not able to register for an international trademark.

The second way requires an official registration with the US Patent and Trademark Office (uspto.gov) and is indicated with an R in a circle like this - ®. It costs anywhere from $275 to $325, but is complicated enough that you probably want an attorney to submit the registration for you in order to ensure that you're properly protected. The value of a registered trademark is that it's the ultimate protection for your mark, and it then allows you to apply for a trademark in other countries as well.

Trademarks can be a complex area of the law where you definitely should have advice from an attorney, but it will give you the optimum protection and control that could turn into an income stream somewhere down the road.

I'm With The Brand

It seems that as music stars becomes more popular, so too does their desire to cash in on their fame through what's known as "brand extension." That used to be quite contrary to what many artists were about, preferring to not lend their image to anything not directly involved in their music, but today it's just a matter of fact. Just as an example, here's how a number of high-profile artists have extended their brands with products that aren't exactly tied to music.

- Aerosmith guitarist Joe Perry has his own line of hot sauce.
- The r&b singer Usher teamed up with Mastercard to launch a range of credit cards.
- Brit pop legend Cliff Richards, Boz Scaggs, Mick Hucknall (Simply Red), Dave Matthews, Mick Fleetwood, Les Claypool, Jonathan Cain (Journey), Maynard James Keenan (Tool, Perfect Circle), AC/DC, Olivia Newton John, David Coverdale (Whitesnake) and Lil Jon all produce their own wines.
- Justin Bieber has, curiously for a guy, his own line of nail polish called *One Less Lonely Girl*.
- Madonna opened the *Hard Candy Fitness* centre in Mexico City, the first of what she hopes will be a worldwide chain of gyms.
- Lady Gaga has released her own range of Heartbeat headphones.
- Beyoncé is now focusing on her clothing lines, *House of Dereon* and *I Am Sasha Fierce*.
- Jay-Z has non-musical business opportunities including the clothing label Rocawear, the New York nightclub 40/40, and a sports agency.

- 50 Cent, Eminem and Sean Combs (P. Diddy) all have their own clothing ranges, while Combs has also carved out an extra source of income for himself in promoting the vodka brand *Cîroc.*
- Katy Perry, Hillary Duff, Avril Lavigne, Mariah Carey, Britney Spears, Justin Bieber, Fergi, and host of other music celebs have their own fragrance lines.

This may or may not be the right way to go depending upon how you feel about commercialism in music, but some artists want to take advantage of every opportunity that their brand might bring, and consumer products are a way to go.

Brands And Social Media

Assuming that you maintain your brand integrity, here are few interesting facts from Atym Marketing Reseach about how social media plays into building that brand.

- 29% of Twitter users follow a brand.
- 39% have tweeted about a brand.
- 29% have retweeted about a brand.
- 58% of Facebook users have liked a brand.
- 42% have mentioned a brand in a status update.
- 41% have shared a link, video or story about a brand.
- 66% of people who have liked a brand have 100 or more Facebook friends.

The point of the stats above is that people who like brands are very active on social media and greatly influence others. That alone should be a good enough reason why social media should always be a main part of your brand building and overall marketing strategy.

4

Creating Your Killer Website

If you've read the previous chapters, you know how important a website can be to your branding and online strategy. That's said, just having a website that's not particularly well-conceived or designed can be only a few steps better than having none at all. It still takes the right elements and implementation to make a site effective.

The Elements Of A Successful Site

A website should be unique and individual when it comes to its design, and that means it should obviously reflect your brand and your music. That said, if we were to look at the ideal website we would find the following common elements:

The Site Name

The name of the site has to be easy to spell and remember, and it's best if it has a ".com" behind it rather than ".net," ".us," or other type of extension, although that's not absolutely necessary these days. Let's say that your band is called "The Unsigned." That means that the strongest URL would be "theunsigned.com." If that URL is not available, try some simple alternates like "theunsignedband.com," "unsignedband.com," or "unsignedtheband.com"

What you don't want is something that's so clever that people can't remember it, like "theun$igned.com." No matter how brilliant you think this is, you're going to have people confused on how to pronounce it, and you can't be sure that they'll actually type the $ sign into the search engine correctly when searching for your site.

Yet another problem is making it so long that it's unmemorable, like "theunsignedbandfrommaryland.com." You probably won't have much trouble registering the URL, but it won't matter because it's so long that it's difficult to read and way too difficult for someone to type correctly because it has so many characters.

The next problem is to make sure that the website URL doesn't present an unintentional double entendre. There are some classic bad ones that illustrate the point, like the website that displays the names of the agents that represent a certain celebrity called *Who Represents*. The URL is a different story as it reads "whorepresents.com." Then there's the site *Therapist Finder* who's URL reads "therapistfinder.com." Or the *Italian Power Generator* company who's URL reads "powergeneratorlia.com." Or the art designers with their "speedofart.com." Make sure you take a step back and read that URL before you commit to it so you won't be embarrassed later.

The Visual Design

The look of your site has to reflect your brand, as was discussed in Chapter 3. What that means is that there's no sense making it dark and menacing if you're a pop band, or making it flowery and colorful looking if you're an EDM artist. That said, here are a number of basic points to consider with your design.

1. Use the screen real estate wisely.

- Keep the most important content "above the fold," or at the top of the screen where the reader doesn't have to scroll down.
- Watch out for clutter. Achieve a balanced layout by designing no more than three focal points by using the "big, medium, small" strategy.
- Provide enough white space around elements so that they're visually distinguishable, but don't leave big areas of blank screen.

2. Specify fonts that are designed for the screen.

- Sans-serif fonts (those without the little tails on some of the characters) generally works the best (Verdana, Tahoma, Arial), although some serif fonts work okay (Georgia). Stay away from Times as it's designed for newspapers and can feel dated. Use any decorative font you want in a logo image, but stay away from browser decorative fonts (**Impact**, Comic Sans) that draw more attention than the copy itself.
- Only use two font families per page or site *at most*, and then only to contrast headings to text, or sidebar to main content.
- Format paragraphs and other content for the best readability

    - Use *text-align: left* for blocks of text.

    - Use *text-align: center* occasionally for a page heading or a special effect. but never for text blocks.

    - Use *text-align: right* to connect form labels with their data entry boxes or to connect left-hand captions to their associated images.

    - Use *text-align: justify* only if the column is wide enough so that it doesn't leave blocks of white space down the middle.

3. Avoid using fonts smaller than 10 point (depending on the font). One of the things that site visitors hate the most is having to zoom in to read something.

4. Fit the color scheme to the purpose of the site.

- A good bet is to select your colors based on your logo or an important image on the page.
- Like fonts, use one main color and one secondary color for a page or site; a third color might provide emphasis or contrast.
- Check for sufficient contrast between text and background, and also check that the contrast works for any color-blind visitors.
- Never use color alone to provide information.

5. Design For Mobile

Be sure that your site is built to display on a mobile browser. Don't forget that the world we now live in is a mobile one, and it's going to be even more so in the future. Make sure that your site looks good on a phone or tablet before confirming it as complete.

- Check the layout to be sure that everything shows up where you expect it on the screen.
- Check the readability of the text to be sure that the information on the site is useful to the visitor.

The Navigation

Many artist websites are quickly designed without much thought, and that makes the user experience somewhat less than elegant. Before you begin to design or redesign your site, consider these six tips to improve its navigation.

1. Keep it consistent. Consistent navigation from page to page in both how and where things appear on the site promotes ease of use and increases your visitor's ability to find relevant information more quickly.

2. Divide categories clearly. All categories must be clearly and visually defined, with category headings separated visually from sub-categories.

3. Keep the menu hierarchy to three. It's best to keep it to main idea, topic, and subtopic.

4. Make all navigation elements clickable links. All major category headings should be clickable links, even though you may have a drop-down menu with sub-categories.

5. Use accurate navigation titles. Visitors need a general idea of what they should find on a page even before they click on a navigation link.

6. Always test your site. Make sure that every link functions correctly before it goes live. This not only ensures a better user experience, but a better search ranking as well.

These are very simple points that will lead to a much better user experience, which is not only what we all want from a website, but one of the things that Google bases its search ranking on.

The Content

The content of your page is important in a number of ways. First, it's all the information that you want your site visitors to know, but it's also important from an SEO standpoint (Search Engine Optimization). Here are a couple of points to consider:

- **Make sure the site is based more on text than graphics.** Every picture tells a story, but it doesn't as far as the search engines are concerned. Even if the image or graphics is composed of all text, Google can't read it so it's ineffective for SEO purposes.

- **Keep your text to between 200 and 600 words.** Any fewer than 200 words and you might not have enough to get your point across, and any more than 600 and it becomes too much of a chore to read. From the SEO standpoint, Google loves more words as it's easier to extract how useful the information is to the visitor, and that's the most important attribute of modern search.

The Bio or About Page

This doesn't have to be your entire life's story. In fact, it's better that it's not. Leave the total history for the bio in your press kit. Two or three paragraphs that gives someone the overall picture of who you are and what you stand for is enough, with a link to the full bio if someone needs more info.

The Contact Page

It's hard to believe how many people overlook this section. Make sure that this link in very obvious. If people can't contact you, they can't book you. Make it easy for them and include not only your email address, but a phone number as well if you're not famous, since some people still prefer to just pick up the phone to make contact.

***TIP**: If you don't want people to call your personal phone, then get a Google Voice number, which will stay with you forever and dial any and all phones that you'd like.*

The Subscribe Page

As we talked about in the Chapter 2, the mailing list is the second most important part of your strategy, that's why it's especially important that your sign-up section is prominently displayed on every page (see Figure 4.1). The reason why is that you never know when someone will enter your site from a page other than your home landing page. You can't always be sure that they'll find their way back to the page that has the sign-up links, so just make it easy for them to sign up anywhere on your site. We'll discuss email lists more in Chapter 5.

Figure 4.1: The email sign-up section for Linkin Park

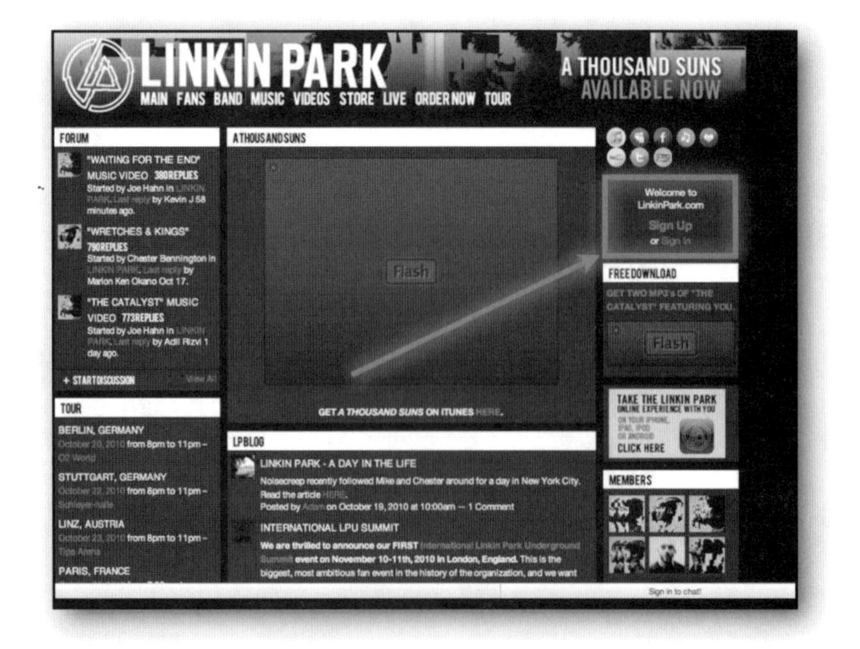

The Press Section

It's amazing that so many brands (which includes artists and bands as well as companies) don't have a proper "Press" section on their website that contains all the information that a journalist or blogger might need when writing a story. I speak from personal experience as a writer in that I'm always surprised with what I *can't* find on a typical site, instead of what I can.

Many brands think that just having a list of press releases is enough, but they're sadly mistaken (especially when the releases are not well organized to begin with, which is so sadly typical). You have to make available anything about your brand that you think a journalist might need, no matter how mundane, because sometimes the smallest item can make the biggest difference in how an article is written.

Here are some of the essential items that every website press section should have:

- **High resolution color and black and white photos that can be used for print.** Yes, print is slowly dying, but it's still with us and can have a huge impact in certain situations. You never know when you or your product will get a mention in a newspaper, magazine or book.
- **Low resolution color photos and graphics for websites and blogs.** A picture says a thousand words and you'd rather someone use one of yours on their blog or website than just supplying a link. Make it easy for them, but give them a variety to choose from.
- **Your logo.** It's surprising how often this is overlooked, but it's just as important as your photos and other graphics.
- **A biography.** Maybe you have an "About Us" or "About Me" section on the website or blog, but a more complete bio, or even a link to it from the press section, makes finding background info about you, your band or company a lot easier for the writer. The easier it is to find, the more likely it will be used.

- **Quotes from the media.** Great quotes about you or your product are also big with writers, since it adds credibility. Limit the quotes to those that are unique though. Ten quotes that all say the same, "You're the greatest," have a lot less impact than one, but it's OK to use several if they say the same thing in totally unique ways.
- **Links to any interviews.** Include links to any interviews that you might have done, either audio, video or just text. No need to post the entire interview on your site as a writer will probably not read it unless he needs some additional facts that he can't find anywhere else.
- **Scans of just three or four of your best press clippings**. Once again, less is more. Ten press clippings that say the same thing tend to actually diminish credibility. Three or four seems about the right number to have in order to give the writer sufficient information.
- **PDFs of adverts, promo flyers and posters.** This has a dual purpose in that its additional info for the writer but can also be used virally by fans. Many "superfans" will print these out and distribute them in their area if asked.
- **Web ready graphics and banners in a variety of sizes**. If you're doing any online campaigns (either advertising or fan-based viral), these can make it quite easy to be up and running in no time since everything is readily available.
- **Press releases.** These are only helpful for a writer if they contain enough background information on a particular subject so details are important. It's also easier for a writer if they're grouped by type (personnel, products, events, etc.) instead of by date.
- **Videos**: You need multiple types of videos - interview elements with the artist or entire band, and if it's a band, individual interviews as well, your most recent music videos, any music video that you consider a "hit," and a clip of a song from a show. It's best to make two versions available - one

with smaller web-ready files, and if you're an act that's breaking nationally, another version that's available in hi-res via FTP download.

- **Music**: Your songs can probably be found online already, but make it easy for whomever is reading by adding links so they can effortlessly find them. If you've done music for commercials or a soundtrack for a movie or television, include that as well but be sure that you have the right to do so before you post it.
- **Web Links**: Be sure to include links to any social media presence that you have on the web such as a Facebook fan page, Google+ page, blog, Twitter, Reverb Nation page, etc.
- **Fan Endorsements**: If you have rabid fans that do crazy things like paint themselves up with your logo, get tatoos of your likeness on their backs, or are just super enthusiastic, that could make for an interesting clip. Just make sure that the fans (three or four is all you need) are completely enthusiastic and really special or this element isn't worth pursuing.

***TIP**: If you use any endorsement from a fan, be sure to get written permission that it's okay to use it.*

It's a fact that the easier you make it for a writer or an editor, the more likely you'll get covered. Having these tools easily available will increase your chances of getting media coverage.

By the way, I don't believe in making this info available solely to writers. Make it available to everyone as it can lead to unforeseen viral opportunities. Just keep it up to date (I know how difficult that is, but you've got to try), and your press section will be good to go.

The Booking Info Section

If you're generating some buzz in your local scene, make sure that if an agent or promoter does check out your band that you have pertinent information available on your website for them. Create a "Bookings," "Book Me," or "Book My Band" section on your website, which can be similar to an online press kit, but instead includes specific additions like:

- **Statistics** about the number of newsletter subscribers, Facebook fans and Twitter followers you have. Remember that your social media presence is now taken into consideration by most bookers and promoters, as it's a vital part of their marketing too.
- **Average attendance** for your shows. Are you regularly selling out 50 ,100, or 500-seat venues? Make sure to include it.
- The **markets and venues** that you play in.
- A **photo gallery** with lots of quality live photos, including any that include crowds in packed venues.
- **Good quality live videos** meaning good video quality, good audio quality, packed rooms, and minimal audience talking. Audience sing-a-longs are always worth including as well.
- A stage plot of how your gear is normally set up.
- A typical **set list,** if you're a cover band.
- **Quotes from the media** that mention your live show.
- **Quotes from venue bookers**.
- **Quotes from fans** about your live shows.

Other than that, you should always blog and tweet about your live shows, which we'll discuss in Chapters 7 and 8. Post about the turnout, the crowd reaction, and post plenty of pics and live video whenever you can. All of this will help create the impression that you're a hard-working band that takes their live shows seriously.

The Social Media Connections

It's so easy to add links and buttons for Facebook, Twitter, YouTube and almost any other social network you can think of these days. You're missing a great opportunity for increased social interaction and an expanded audience if they're not included.

There are actually two types of icons; those that connect the visitor directly to your social media page, and sharing icons that make it easy for a reader to share the content with their own social media friends and followers.

One easy way to add social media buttons to your site is with something called niftybuttons.com. Just go the site, choose a set of icons, copy the URLs of each of your social pages, then paste it into the slots at niftybuttons. The HTML code is then generated for each of your buttons that you can copy and paste into your website code.

TIP: *Most social networks also have a way to generate the code for a number of different social icon versions as well.*

The Sitemap

Every website should have a sitemap, which is basically like an office building's directory in that it lists all the pages of your website in one place. Once again, it serves a dual purpose in that it's a last resort item for someone who can't find something on your website (hopefully the navigation is designed so this doesn't happen), and also the bots that the search engines send out love them, which can raise your search engine ranking.

Another advantage is that if your site has a lot of pages, chances are some of them are obscure and don't get much traffic. The sitemap will allow the search engines to index them, which suddenly makes them available to a search.

TIP*: Many website development programs will automatically generate a sitemap.*

Cross-Browser Compatibility

Even though you may love Firefox as your main web browser, there's still a big part of the world that uses Safari, Chrome and to a lesser degree these days, Internet Explorer, not to mention the iOS and Android operating systems for mobile. That's why it's important that your site is checked on every platform before it goes live to make sure that it appears as you expect it to.

One of the problems is that each browser displays a site slightly differently, so there will always be discrepancies. The trick is to make sure that they're not so major as the look and feel entirely breaks down on one browser while it looks fine on the others. Browser compatibility issues are just one of the many "pleasures" of website development that continue to vex designers everywhere.

Web Optimized Images

Site load time can be critical to the user experience, which is why so much attention is taken to optimize the images on any site. As an image file size gets larger, it becomes slower to load, which is why ideally most images are kept well below 100kB in size.

Optimization is a trade-off between image quality and a small file size. At some point, the image quality will suffer as the file size is decreased. Finding the ideal point is where the image detail remains sharp but the file size is sufficiently small. Here are some things to consider when optimizing the images for your site.

- **Make sure that the resolution of the graphic is set to 72 dpi.** 300 dpi is the standard for print (although it can go as low as 150), but that's overkill on a computer monitor. Newer monitors display at 96dpi, so you can consider using that resolution, but anything higher currently provides no advantage and just makes the file larger.

- **Save your graphics in a jpg, png or gif format.** Any other format may not display and natively will have a file size that's too large for a quick download.

- **Decrease the number of colors to 32**. Most color graphics won't lose all that much even when decreased from a million colors, yet it can make a big difference in file size.

- **Decrease the quality to an acceptable level.** Sometimes the difference between a jpeg quality level of three and ten is so small that you can hardly tell, yet it makes a big difference in the file size.

***TIP**: File sizes are cumulative to a page. Remember that seven 100kB images equals 700kB, which will load much slower than if they all were half that.*

Website Killers To Avoid

Here are a number of practices that are guaranteed to turn off your visitors. You know what they are yourself because you probably encounter them on other sites every day, but that doesn't mean you should emulate a bad practice. Not only do many of the following aggravate site visitors, but they're can mean site death when it comes to search engine optimization. If you want fans to find you, make sure these are avoided.

1. A "splash" page. A splash page is an opening page with a movie or flash animation and no information. The whole "Enter Here" thing is so Web 1.0. There's no info for a search engine to grab and your visitors hate them. Avoid at all costs.

2. Flash animation. It looks cool, but sometimes people just want some info and not cartoons. Search engines can't read any of the info in a Flash movie so they're a waste of time and money. iPhones and iPads can't display Flash, and most people hate it these days anyway.

3. Frames. Again, so Web 1.0. Sites with frames went out a long time ago. Get with the times and dump these babies.

4. Pop-ups. It doesn't matter where they come from or if they're selling something or not, everyone hates them.

5. Pull-down boxes for navigation. Designers love them, visitors hate them, search engines can't read them. If your site isn't that complex, stay away if you can.

6. Dead links. This is just poor website quality control. It happens to everyone at some point, but remember that both search engines and visitors hate them.

7. All graphics and not much text. Search engines love text. Visitors love text. Pictures are nice, but use them in moderation.

What Visitors Hate

Technology marches on, and as we know, the pace seems to get faster and faster all the time. The problem is, we all have to keep up in order to both stay relevant and keep our fans engaged. Now comes some research courtesy of getsharesquare.com (a site that helps mobilize your site) that's an eye opener in terms of what visitors really hated about artist's websites.

- 33% of the survey respondents said their most frequent complaint about an artist site was text that was so small that it required zooming.
- 31% stated their biggest complaint was video content that was broken or unavailable.
- 28% said they hated when buttons or links were too small to click.
- 20% hated when streaming music was broken or unavailable.
- 17% complained that recent news and upcoming event info was difficult to find.
- 29% said that they missed the ability to exchange an email address for free content.
- 25% said they really missed the ability to download an artist's song.
- 21% complained that they couldn't purchase tickets or merch directly from the website.

This is a fascinating report in that it indicates that a lot more commerce could be done if only artists would pay more attention to their websites. Many artists take their site for granted, but it should be the main point where all of your fan contact is directed, since it's the one portal online that you have total control of.

An Instant Band Page With Onesheet

For a new artist or band, not only is it important to get your music together, but your online presence is equally important as well. If you have the dough you can hire a company to integrate all of your social media on a new custom website, but that takes time. Most artists couldn't be bothered with programming their own site, and even if they could, that takes time as well; time which might be better spent creating great music.

Now comes Onesheet.com, a site that can get your artist page up and running in literally only a couple of minutes. The brainchild of Artistdata founder Brendan Mulligan, Onesheet sucks in all of your social media data from services such as Songkick, Twitter, FanBridge, SoundCloud, Sonicbids, Vimeo, YouTube, Facebook and more and displays it on tabs on the page. You can then upload a picture as a background, then easily tweak the layout and info box to give you an instant artist's page. The best part about Onesheet is that once you set it up, you don't need to update it because it's fed by your other social media sites. When you update them they update Onesheet to keep it up to date.

While it's fast and easy, there are a couple of downsides with the service that you have to consider. First of all, your URL is a subdomain of Onesheet. In other words, it's "onesheet.com/yourname" instead of your own custom "myname.com" URL. The other is that the page layout for every artist is the same except for the background image. Still, if you need something online right now, this is the one service that will do it quickly and extremely easily. It's free too, at least for now.

Website SEO Techniques

As stated before, SEO (search engine optimization) is the process of designing or fine-tuning your site so that it appears friendly to Google and the other search engines. There are a number of techniques for this, but let's begin with the basics.

Meta Tags

Hidden within the HTML coding of your site is information that search engines look at that we're normally not aware of. In other words, it's information about the information on the site, which is the definition of metadata. We call this kind of metadata "meta tags" and the most important of them are the title tag, description tag, and keywords tag, but there are also several other less important ones that we won't get into.

You don't have to be an HTML programmer to use these, as most of them will be easily available to you when designing a site, although each site development app displays them differently. What's important is that you use them correctly.

Placing Your Name In The Title Tag

The Title tag is the name of the web page. Your website has a title (using "theUnsigned" is our example), but each page on your site also has it's own title, and it's best to make sure it also has your name in it. For instance, if you have a contact page, a title that simply says "Contact" wouldn't be sufficient. The best would be "Contact The Unsigned" or "The Unsigned Contact Info." Likewise, if you have a press page, a title of simply "Press" doesn't cut it while "The Unsigned Press" does. Figure 4.2 shows how the title of my book page, "Bobby Owsinski's Books," shows up in the tab of the browser.

Figure 4.2: Site title in page URL and title

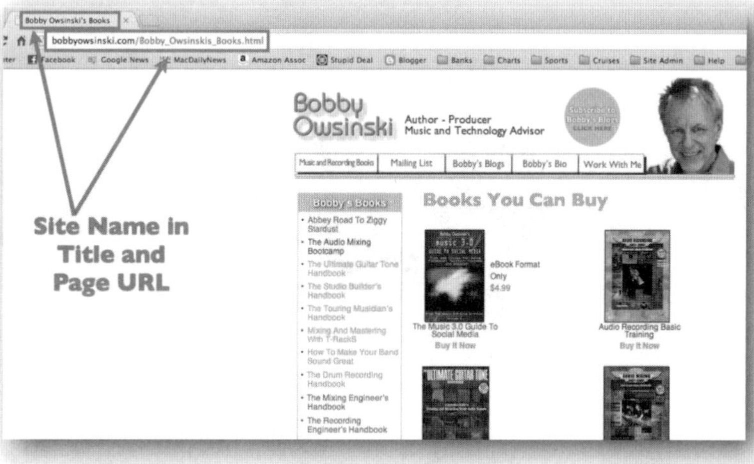

Placing Your Name In The Description

The Description is invisible text that tells the search engines what you're site is all about. When you do a Google search, this is the text that comes up describing your page. Just to show you how this works, if you look below in Figure 4.3 and 4.4, you'll see the description for a site on Google, yet when you look at the site itself, you don't see that same description anywhere on the page.

Figure 4.3: The Gibson site description as seen during a Google search

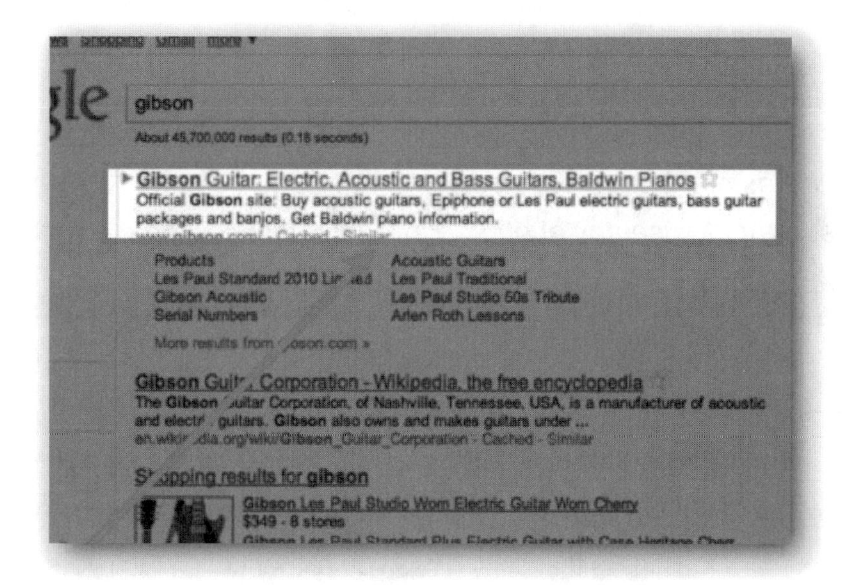

Figure 4.4: The description isn't seen on the Gibson site itself

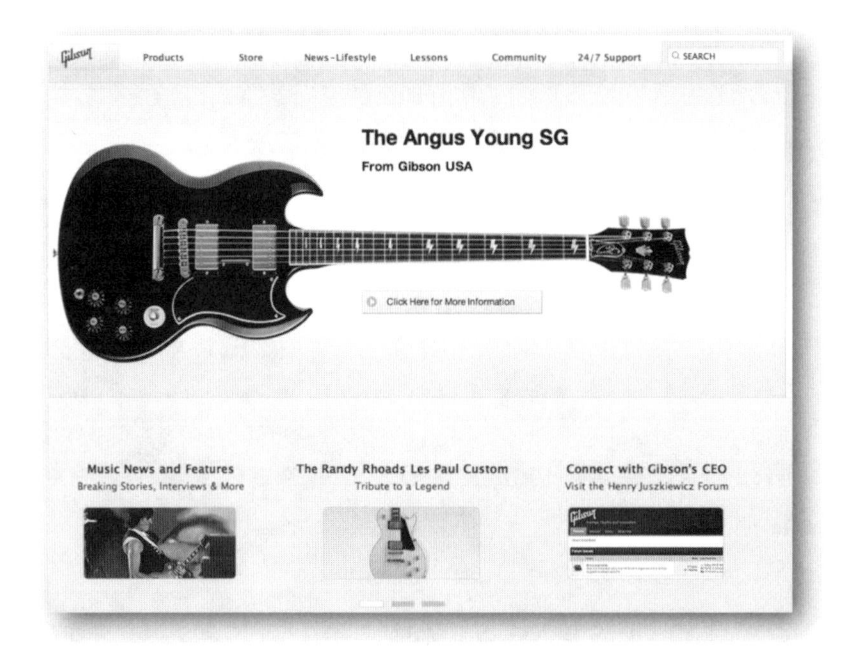

Both Google and Bing will fill the description in for you if you don't create one, but then you're at their mercy as to what they pick off the page. For that reason, you're better off creating one yourself.

The advantage of the description is that search engines use it to help with the search rankings. By making sure that your name is included (as in Figure 4.3 where it says "Official Gibson site"), it makes your search ranking stronger.

TIP: *One caution when creating a description, it must be less than 155 characters, but it's best to stay under 66 to be sure it's all displayed. Also be sure not to use any quotes (" "), since that will stop the description from appearing from the point where they appear onward.*

Placing Your Name In The Text Body

Pages that have between 200 to 600 words of text tend to rank better in a search than a page that has less copy and mostly graphics. One of the reasons is that copy gives you a chance to place your name in the text, which again is very strong from an SEO (search engine optimization) standpoint.

The key is to not have the name appear too much though. The ideal amount seems to change all the time, but it's generally acknowledged that two to three percent seems about right. That means that with 200 words of text, your name should only appear four to six times at most. Anything more and it might appear to the search engine as "keyword stuffing" and you'll actually be penalized.

TIP: *Make sure that your name appears in the very first paragraph of your copy for the strongest SEO.*

Keywords

One upon a time keywords were a big deal to search engines but they've become less of a factor in recent years. Just like with the description, the keywords are invisible to the reader of the site and are only read by the search engines. The problem is that only Bing now bothers with them at all and even then it's only to detect spam.

The best option these days is to not use them, but if you feel that you must, restrict them to only five at most, then make sure that they relate to what's on your page. In other words, if you think you sing like Chris Martin of Coldplay but your page has no mention of either Chris Martin or Coldplay, then don't use them as keywords. If you do, you can get penalized again for having keywords that don't relate to your page.

By the way, keywords don't necessarily mean a single word like "music," "guitar," etc. They refer to phrases as well, which are much stronger in that they better target an audience. For instance, "12 string guitar" is much stronger than just "guitar," and "Cleveland 12 string guitar" is better still, because it targets the audience even more.

The Importance Of Anchor Text

Many artists and bands (and even web designers who should know better) fail to realize the importance of *anchor text*. What is anchor text? It's the highlighted text that you use as a link to another site or page. The reason why it's important is that these words can determine your page ranking when someone does a search, since they carry more weight with Google than the other text on the page.

Here's an example of bad use of anchor text (forgive the gratuitous plug):

"To read my Big Picture Blog, click here."

"Click here" doesn't mean anything in terms of search. Do you think anyone will ever search for "click here?" Well, someone might (actually there are near 9 billion results on Google), but where do you think you'll rank? Even if you luck out and somehow wind up on page 50, you're still so far back in the search results that it won't do you any good.

A better use of the anchor text would be:

"Click here to read my Big Picture Blog."

“Big Picture Blog” makes much better anchor text and will take advantage of the way Google weights copy text. You can use your band name, a song title, or anything else that's relevant to get the best results, but a relevant keyword or keyword phrase is always the best. Just remember, anything is better than click here.

Site Speed

Google has over 200 criteria for site ranking, but one major factor that it considers is how fast your site loads. The reason? Users love fast sites, and fast sites have a higher engagement that slow sites. Google measures the speed in two different ways:

- How a page responds to the Googlebot that crawls the web
- The load time as measured by the Google Toolbar

The Value Of A Fast Page Load

We live in a very impatient world and that impatience could cost you fans, users or sales. A study created by the OnlineGraduateProgram.com found a number of startling facts about our desire for online speed:

- 1 in 4 people abandon a web page if it takes more than 4 seconds to load.
- 50% of mobile users abandon a page if it doesn't load in 10 seconds.
- 40% of mobile shoppers will abandon an e-commerce site that doesn't load in 3 seconds.
- Amazon estimates that it could lose up to $1.6 billion a year because of as little as a 1 second web page delay.

This means that you can't count on the ever expanding bandwidth of your visitors for your site to load quickly, you still must optimize it for speed, because tenths of a second count more than ever. This is one of the reasons to get a pro to build your website so you can be sure to get efficient, streamlined code. Page loading has become so much more than slimmed down graphics files these days.

***TIP**: Make sure all of your graphic files are small (30kB to 50kB is about right), and keep any video hosted through YouTube so it all loads fast. Google's too smart for even the smart SEO guys, so play by the rules and don't try to game the system.*

Content Relevance

All that being said, relevance is still the number one factor for site ranking. What is relevance? When the site name, metadata, and text copy of the site all match in relevancy to a search. For instance, if the site name is "JeffBeckTributeBand.com" but the site really tries to sell you insurance, there's not much relevancy there and it will be penalized as a result. Even if the JeffBeckTributeBand.com site is trying to sell tickets to Jeff Beck shows, it's still not about a Jeff Beck tribute band. As a result, even though it's more related, it's still not to relevant to someone who's searching for a Jeff Beck tribute band.

The point is to make sure that everything about the page relates to one another, in other words, the title, description, copy and keywords are all about the same thing.

Measuring Your Backlinks

Backlinks are links to your site on other websites. Backlinks are one of the best ways to improve your search engine ranking, so the more you have, the better. They're also a great way to find out exactly what people are saying about you as well. Here's a cool way for you to check those backlinks.

Go to the query window in Google and type "links:yoursite.com" (excluding the quotes) and you'll see all of the backlinks to your site. Here's an example for my main bobbyowsinski.com site below in Figure 4.5.

Figure 4.5: Using the links operator

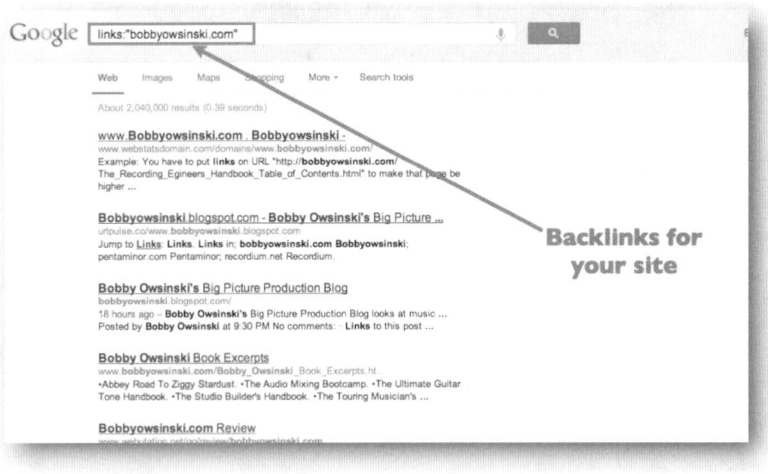

This method isn't perfect by any stretch of the imagination because, by Google's own admission, it doesn't show all the links to your site, doesn't give you the links in any kind of order, and isn't necessarily up to date. That said, it does give you an idea of who likes you enough to link to you.

***TIP**: Make sure there isn't a space between the links operator and your website name. In other words, it should be (using my own site as an example) links:bobbyowsinski.com*

The Importance Of Deep Links

Usually most bands and artists always provide a link to the home page of their site in any correspondence or social network post. Of course this is better than no link at all, but it might not be the best strategy. According to many SEO gurus, there's now some evidence that "deep linking" can bring you a higher Google ranking by also providing some value to the person following the link as well.

Deep linking is any link on your site that's not your home page *and* has the appropriate information. For example, if you have your picture taken with Katy Perry, it's better for both you and your visitors if you link them directly to the page that has the picture, rather than sending them to your homepage which does not, and forcing them to dig down through your links to find the correct page that displays you and Ms. Perry. Not only is this annoying, but you can get penalized by Google for providing a less than perfect user experience as well.

A better strategy might be to mention the picture and provide a direct link to a separate dedicated subpage with the picture, complete with the story behind the picture (don't skimp on the copy - 150 to 300 words is about right), the appropriate metadata (your name, Katy Perry, the place where the picture was taken, etc.), and the appropriate keyword phrases (your name, Katy Perry, the place where the picture was taken, etc.) baked into the copy at about a rate of about 2% (that's about six times or so for each keyword phrase for 300 words). If you use the keywords more frequently, Google may penalize you for "keyword stuffing", and your search ranking can suffer.

Seems like a lot of work, and it is. It's especially difficult to design copy around keywords. I'm a writer with a lot of words under my belt and I still find it hard, but it's worth it if it helps raise your visibility.

What you're aiming for is a lot of backlinks to your deep link, which will raise your ranking and visibility even more.

TIP: *Don't forget to submit this subpage to the various search engines and directories, but remember that the subpage has to be able to stand on its own or the entire exercise probably isn't worth it. If it takes the visitor only a few seconds to read the copy, then you don't have sufficient stickiness for it to be any benefit to you.*

The User Experience

Probably the biggest thing that any search engine looks for these days is the overall user experience of the website. That is, does the site contain the information that the user was looking for in the search. Was it easy to find once he got there? Was it relevant to the search and the SEO provided? Were there misspellings or dead links?

While you can fine-tune your site using all of the above techniques, if the experience is poor once the visitor hits your site, it's all for nothing as Google has algorithms that will actually measure that experience and penalize you when it's not a good one. That's why its best not to try anything underhanded in order to try to game the system when it comes to SEO. Google will find out in a flash and penalize you for it.

Website Measurement Techniques

What's the use of having all these great promotional tools unless you can measure how effective they are? As stated previously, in traditional advertising it's long been held that 50% of an advertising campaign works, you just don't know which 50%. That's no longer true online since so much can now be measured, in some cases much more granularly than ever before.

Four Free Website Audience Measurement Tools

There are all sorts of website audience measurement tools now available, but believe it or not, some of the free ones do a great job. While you can get traffic information from your website provider, here are four free measurement tools that can be used as a sort of second opinion when needed.

1. StatCounter: This is by far my favorite measurement tool. StatCounter provides a suite of measurements far more detailed than what you get from your ISP, like the visitor's entry and exit page, where the visitor recently came from, the keywords used to find the site, the time spent on the site, the number of return visits, and location information detailed enough that you can almost see into the visitor's house (see Figure 4.6). You just place a piece of invisible code on your website or blog and away you go. The free version of StatCounter only remembers the info for your last 500 visitors, and anything beyond that requires a monthly fee, but what you get for free version is still very useful.

Figure 4.6: A granular look at a StatCounter visitor map

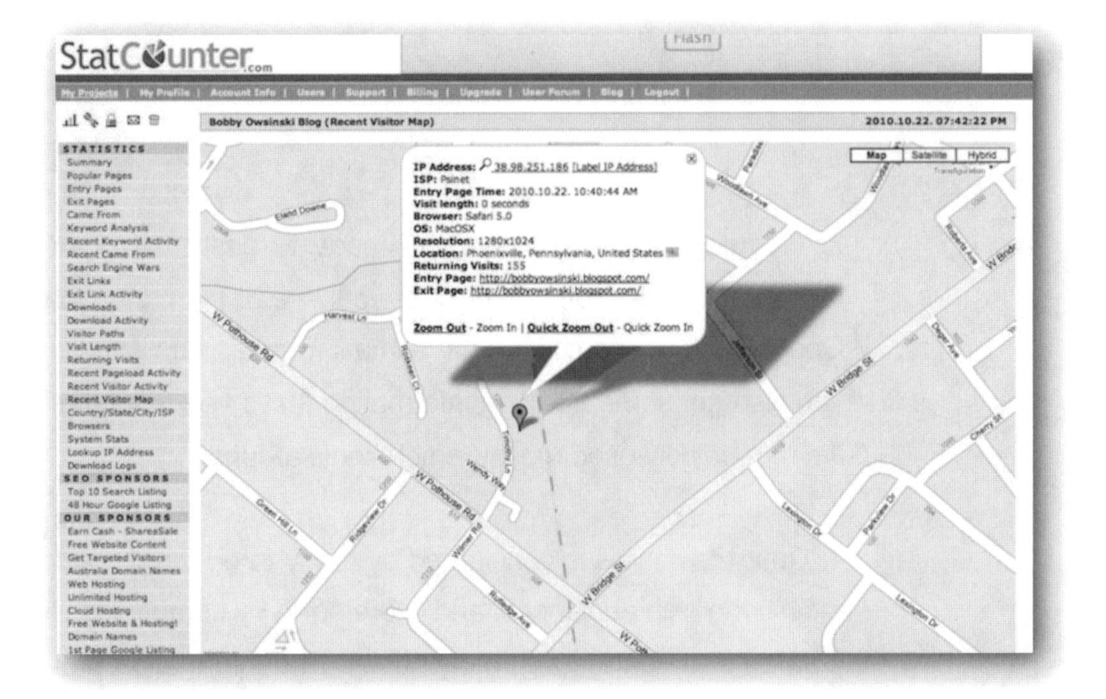

2. Tynt Tracer: Another tool that requires that you insert some invisible code, Tynt Tracer differs from just about anything else in that it measures how many copies of text or graphics were made from your site or blog (see Figure 4.7). In other words, if someone copies a piece of text from your site and inserts it on another site or blog, Tynt Tracer knows about it, and then can track how many visits came to your site from that copied piece. What's more, you can also program it to insert a Creative Commons license warning when someone copies and pastes your content. The analytics are difficult to decipher sometimes, but it's certainly a cool and useful tool.

Figure 4.7: A typical Tynt Tracer report

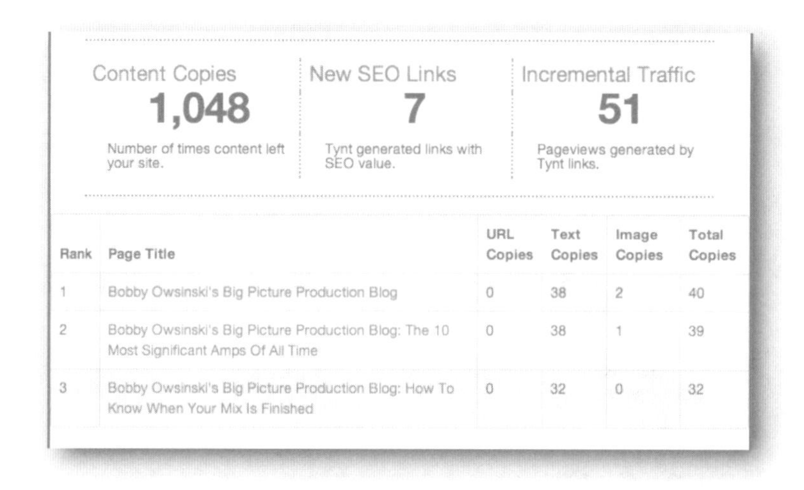

Content Copies
1,048
Number of times content left your site.

New SEO Links
7
Tynt generated links with SEO value.

Incremental Traffic
51
Pageviews generated by Tynt links.

Rank	Page Title	URL Copies	Text Copies	Image Copies	Total Copies
1	Bobby Owsinski's Big Picture Production Blog	0	38	2	40
2	Bobby Owsinski's Big Picture Production Blog: The 10 Most Significant Amps Of All Time	0	38	1	39
3	Bobby Owsinski's Big Picture Production Blog: How To Know When Your Mix Is Finished	0	32	0	32

3. Google Analytics: There's no code to paste into your website with Google Analytics. You just register your site or blog, then leave the rest to Google. You get somewhat the same information as with StatCounter, but you also get some trending information that's very useful. It's also one of the most widely used measurement tools around.

4. Quantcast: This is considered by many to be the de facto standard for measuring web audiences, and is preferred by companies like MTV, Time, Gawker and Fox among many others. The information provided includes traffic, demographics, geography, site affinity and categories of interest. Like some of the other services, it requires that you install some invisible code on your site for measurement.

There are a ton of paid measurement tools out there, but why spend any money until you really need to? These four will get you started and take care of most of your measurement needs for quite a while.

***TIP:** It's an interesting quirk that each measurement service will provide somewhat different data, which is okay if you expect it to happen up front. It's best to average the results and watch for trends in order to make the best use of what they offer.*

Website Performance Metrics

When it comes to measurement, one of the things that can happen is that it's easy to be almost overwhelmed by the data that a measurement tool can provide. Here's a way to interpret that data in order to understand just how successful your website really is. Thanks to Hubspot for the definitions.

1. Unique visitors: That's the total number of individual visitors to your site during a specific period of time, not counting repeat visits by the same individual. Obviously, if this number continues to increase, you're doing well.

2. New versus repeat visitors: This is a comparison of your unique visitors versus the number of visitors who came back more than once. Although it's great to have repeat visitors (and you really need them), a rate higher than 50% means that you're probably not growing your audience quickly enough.

3. Traffic sources: This is a breakdown of the specific sources of traffic to your website. There are two: *Organic traffic* comes from a link found on a search engine results page. *Referral traffic* comes from a link on another website. This tells you how well your search engine optimization is doing. A referral level of about 30% is what you're looking for.

4. Referring URLs: This measurement shows the specific, non-search engine URLs that send traffic directly to your site. They represent the inbound links that are crucial for boosting your site's search engine rankings, and tell you which sites or bloggers are linking to your site and what type of content they tend to like.

5. Most/least popular pages: This is a comparison of the pages on your site that receive the most and least traffic that tells you which kind of content your visitors prefer.

6. Conversion rate: This is the percentage of visitors to your site who take a desired action, such as purchasing a product or filling out a lead generation form. This tells you how well you're converting leads into fans or customers.

7. Bounce rate: This is the percentage of new visitors who leave your site almost immediately after arriving with no other interaction. A high bounce rate means that your visitors don't find your pages particularly compelling, or they may be looking for something other than what you're offering.

Interpreting the above metrics should give you some idea of just how well your site is performing. Hubspot has a bit more on all of these points, plus a few more, if you're interested.

Summing It Up

There's been a lot written in this chapter about how to create the best website possible, but it all can be broken down to just the essentials. Here it is:

- Have an easy to remember site name
- Use the same name in the URL, title, description and first paragraph
- Use 200 to 600 words of copy per page
- Have a mailing list signup section
- Have a press kit section
- Have a contact section
- Have social media connection buttons
- Back links are one of the keys to high search engine rankings
- Don't use more than five keywords maximum, but make sure that they relate to the content on the page
- Refresh your content as often as possible

TIP: *Remember that it's best if everything that's on your site is aimed at providing your visitor with the best experience possible. This will cause your site to rank high in a search, making it easier for people to find you.*

Creating Your Mailing List

Perhaps the second most powerful marketing tool you have after your website is your email list. The reason is that anyone who subscribed has not only given you permission to communicate directly with them, they're hoping that you do since they're interested in whatever you have to say and promote. Because of this conscious opt-in, the email newsletter is the most direct link to your fans and clients.

Mailing List Overview

Before we cover the details of getting a mailing list and newsletter up and running, let's take a quick overview of the world of email and how it influences our everyday lives.

Email Is Not Dead

It appears that reports of email's demise are untrue, according to a recent survey of 2,200 adults in the US and UK by Harris Interactive. Despite the rise of social networking, we're still addicted to it and we're not letting go. Here's what the survey found:

- 72% in the US and 68% in the UK check their email during their time off.
- 19% of Americans check email in bed (21% men and 16% women)
- 50% check their email while on vacation and during off-days
- 46% of American respondents check their email to ease their workload
- 37% are afraid that they'll miss something important
- 27% check work email at home because it's expected of them
- 26% check email on vacation because that's the only way they can handle the volume

While it may be popular to think that the use of email is declining in favor of social networks, the fact is that email is still a huge part of our everyday lives. The problem is that we get so much of it that an email newsletter may have a hard time rising above the rest of the email noise. That said, the data shows that people do check their mail and it's still important to them. It's up to you to send it.

Four Reasons Why Your Email List Is So Important

While the trend is to think that email is on the decline when it comes to communicating with friends, fans, clients and business associates as social networks like Facebook rise in popularity, it's a lot more important than you think when it comes to promotion. Here are four reasons why.

1. You control the message. Your email list is one of the most powerful tools you can have because you control the message, and if done well, it can feel a lot more personal than communicating via Facebook or Linkedin or any of the other popular networks. You control the information, the look, the marketing and the promotion in a way that's not possible in any social network, since each social network has its own look and feel as well as a terms-of-service agreement that can limit what you can say and do.

2. Your message is consistent. Although the ability to control the message is important, being able to control the *consistency* of that message is even more so. For most artists and musicians today, the problem becomes how to effectively communicate with all of your "friends" and contacts across various networks, because social networks are a closed environment by nature. That means that you have a set of friends on Facebook, another set on Twitter, and a different set on another network like Pinterest or Instagram. As a result, the look and feel will be inconsistent because of the nature of the various networks. If you're not consistent in your presentation, you're not controlling the message.

3. It's a memory prompt. One of the best things about a newsletter is that it reminds fans or former clients who you are. If a person hasn't been following you on a social network and therefore doesn't see any of your regular posts, that newsletter in their email box jogs their memory and reminds them you're around. It doesn't take long to drift from the public consciousness, and an email prevents that from happening.

4. You can measure its effectiveness. One thing that email can provide that social networks don't do nearly as well is sophisticated measurement. With email we know when a newletter was opened, if it was opened more than once (even if it's reopened again a year later), how long it was read, if any of the links were clicked, and if it was passed along to anyone else, among many other measurements. Obviously your personal email app on your computer can't do these things, and it can't easily reach out to thousands of people as well. That's why you need a service like Constant Contact, WhatCounts, or iContact, all of which also have the added convenience of constantly cleaning the list of bounces and outdated addresses.

Using A Mailing List Service

When I wanted to send one of my first email newsletters to a list of only about 1200 (which seemed large at the time but is really tiny in grand scheme of email lists), I was astounded to find that my Internet Service Provider (ISP) wouldn't allow me to send to more than 100 addresses simultaneously from my business account. That meant that I had to split my list up into 12 batches, which made the job take a lot longer than it should have. After a number of calls to my Internet service provider at the time, I discovered that just about every ISP limits the number of email addresses that can be attached to an email in an attempt to keep spam in check, yet I knew that there were companies that sent emails to millions of addresses at a time every day. How did they do it?

That's when I found out about email service providers or ESPs. ESPs have an agreement with the various Internet service providers to make sure that their customers aren't what we would consider spammers. While the odd few may push up against those boundaries, ESPs go to great lengths to make sure that you don't fall into that category by constant checking spam reports and large email address imports, then making you personally verify that your lists are opt-in and not purchased or just skimmed from a forum.

That said, the only limit to how many addresses you can send to hinges on how much money you want to spend, since almost all ESPs work on the same principle - the greater the number of email addresses, the more it costs.

ESPs are way more useful than just providing basic email delivery however, and are definitely worth the money. Among some of the other things they do are:

- clean your list for you, which means they automatically delete any old non-existent or invalid addresses (you have to do it manually if you use your personal email app, which is a big drag time-wise).
- provide a means to measure how well your email did in terms of open rate, click-throughs, pass-alongs, and a lot more.
- provide a means to easily subscribe and unsubscribe to the list (again, this is much more difficult to do manually).
- provide a host of pretty good looking HTML templates that you can use to easily design a professional looking email blast.
- give you a way to easily segment your list so you can target an email blast better.

Most email service providers offer many more services than the main ones mentioned here. In fact, each one offers slightly different features, so it's best to check out a few of them before you make a decision which one's right for you.

An Overview Of Mailing LIst Service Providers

Here's a list of email service providers to investigate. Each has their pros and cons, so it's best to check every one out thoroughly before you commit. Since most of them also have free 30 day trials, you can try before you buy to see if a particular service is what you're looking for.

TIP: *Some email list providers are free if you only have a few hundred addresses. Even with a volume that low, it's so much easier to use an ESP than your own email client. Try it. You'll wonder how you ever got along without one.*

As stated above, all of them have a nice selection of professional-looking email templates, but how they're customized is slightly different, so be sure to check that out. Of course, if you already have a web designer that can design a good looking HTML newsletter, the templates won't matter as much to you as the other features.

Mailchimp.com
Aweber.com
Campaigner.com
Campaignmonitor.com
Feedblitz
MyNewsletterBuilder.com
iContact
WhatCounts
Constant Contact
Get Response
Vertical Response
BenchmarkEmail
PinPointe
MyEmma

These are only just a sampling of the popular ESPs available, and you can also find a number of email list review sites that will give you a ranking and allow you to easily compare services.

TIP: *Even if you compare ESP features carefully, the best way to really find out which one will serve your needs is to use it for a bit first with the free trial they all offer.*

The Email Subscribe Form

After you've decided upon an ESP, the next step is to get your fans or clients email addresses into a list. There are a number of ways to do this, but first you have to create a list or lists.

Lists

All ESPs allow you to create multiple mailing lists so that you can target a list with a particular email when necessary (see Figure 5.1). For instance, if you're an artist, you may create a separate list for every city that you play in so you can email only those fans in a particular area, alerting them of your upcoming gig there. Perhaps you play in too many cities for that to be practical, so you might want to segment your lists by region instead. If you're an engineer or producer, you may want a list of past clients and another of potential clients. Maybe you want a separate list for engineering clients and another for production clients. You can have as many lists as you want, and you can choose to send an email to all of them or only one as is appropriate. Also, you can have the same contacts on more than one list, as most ESPs are smart enough to know to only send a single email in the event that you're sending to multiple lists.

***TIP**: One recommendation is to set up at least one list that's a "general" catch-all list as well as any other lists you might think you need in the future. Don't worry about naming it, you can always rename it or delete it later, and you can move email addresses freely between lists as well.*

Figure 5.1: A look at my lists on Constant Contact

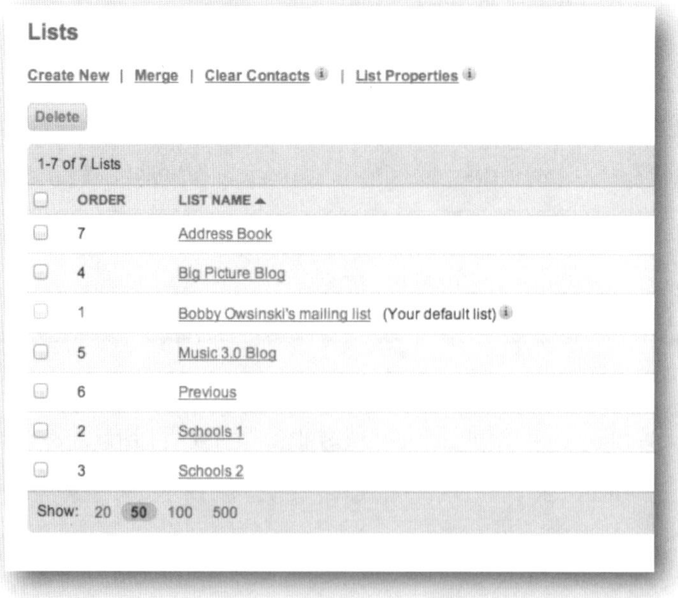

Lists

Create New | Merge | Clear Contacts | List Properties

Delete

1-7 of 7 Lists

ORDER	LIST NAME
7	Address Book
4	Big Picture Blog
1	Bobby Owsinski's mailing list (Your default list)
5	Music 3.0 Blog
6	Previous
2	Schools 1
3	Schools 2

Show: 20 50 100 500

Manual Entry

You've probably collected some email addresses already, and they will make up the bulk of your initial mailing list. All ESPs allow you to manually enter those addresses into any list that you choose in a number of ways. First you can copy and paste the addresses into the appropriate area, making sure there's a comma behind each (some ESPs want you to put each address on a separate line instead of a comma).

You can also enter in a large number of addresses by importing either an Excel file, a CSV file (comma separate value), or a text file. Some ESPs also allow you to import directly from your Gmail or Outlook address books (see Figure 5.2).

Figure 5.2: Manual entry of email addresses

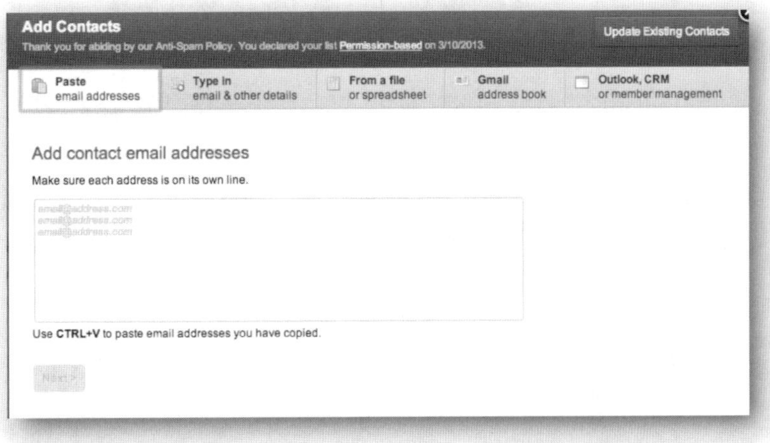

A word of caution about entering or importing a large group of addresses. No ESP wants to accommodate a spammer, since it can endanger their reputation and have them blocked by some ISPs. As a result, ESPs are very nervous if you suddenly show up with a list of 10,000 names, so they ask you to ensure that you haven't purchased the list or gotten it any other way than people personally opting in.

***TIP**: Make sure that you check out if an email service provider is blocked by any ISPs before you sign on to their service, as there may be a group of people that won't be able to receive your email if this is the case.*

If you're moving your list from one service to another, this won't be a problem, but if you're harvesting every email address that you've ever come in contact with, it might be. If after your first mailing there are a lot of bounces and spam reports, the ESP may terminate your service. That's why you have to be careful about using a list that you didn't grow organically. Everybody hates spam, so you have to be extra careful that whatever you send isn't perceived as such.

The Sign-up Form

It's all well and good to be able to manually import email addresses, but there's also a way for that to happen automatically when someone decides they want to be on your list. Every ESP has a way for you to generate the code for a sign-up form to put on your website, blog or social media page.

What you have to do is decide how much information that you need for the subscription to take place. Usually this means the email address for sure, but you also might want at least the person's first name so you can address the email personally to him or her (most ESPs will do that automatically for you), the city and the state they're in. You can also ask for a full address, phone number, school and anything else you think might be important, but remember that the more you ask for, the less likely you'll have someone sign up. It's a fact that people become more reluctant to reveal their personal info, and may just decide that the subscription is not worth the trouble.

Take the code that the ESP generates, paste it into the HTML code of your website (or have your webmaster do it), and you'll see something like in Figure 5.3 and Figure 5.4. The last thing you'll have to do is select which list this subscription will go to. That's why I suggest creating a "general" (you can call it whatever you want) list that only collects these emails, although it's also possible to have individual sign-up forms for your website, Facebook page, blog, etc. that each goes to a different list.

Figure 5.3: A typical newsletter subscribe form

Email*

Name

City

State

Country

Subscribe

Figure 5.4: A simple subscribe form

Subscribe To My Newsletter

Email: Join

Privacy by SafeSubscribe℠

The Welcome Email

When someone subscribes to your email, most ESPs allow you to automatically send a "welcome" email (sometimes called an "Autoresponder") to the new subscriber. This can outline when to expect to receive emails, what's in those emails, or even provide a link to something free in exchange for the email address.

Here's an example of the email that comes from subscribing to my newsletter.

Dear xxx (first name of the subscriber),
Welcome to the Bobby Owsinski Newsletter. I'm really happy to have you as a member of my community.

Privacy is just as important to me as it is to you, therefore, I promise not to sell, rent, or give your name or address to anyone.

At any point, you can select the link at the bottom of every email to unsubscribe, or to receive less or more information.

Thanks again for subscribing. If you have any questions or comments, feel free to contact me.

Sincerely,

Bobby Owsinski

email: newsletter@bobbyowsinski.com
phone: 818-588-xxxx
web: http://bobbyowsinski.com

The Double Opt-In

Some ESPs encourage something called a "double opt-in." An opt-in means that you've intentionally signed up to receive the email newsletter and weren't put on the list without your knowledge. A double opt-in means that instead of a welcome email, you receive a second chance to either opt-in or decline. That means that if you went to a website and signed-up your friend, your friend would get an email that basically says "Are you sure you're the one that opted-in, and do you still want to do this?"

ESPs especially love double opt-ins because it provides a higher level of security that your list won't be used for sending spam. The problem is that it also gives your subscriber another chance to change his mind in that if he doesn't take action to confirm his subscription, his original opt-in is no longer valid.

When People Subscribe

It's great when you do have someone sign-up to your list, but keep the following in mind:

- The highest unsubscription rate occurs among those who have been subscribers for less than 10 days.
- Unsubscribes tend to happen within the first few emails after someone subscribes.

On the other hand:

- The highest click-through-rate (CTR) is with those who have been subscribers for less than 10 days.

- Sending emails directly after a person subscribes is a very effective sales tool, since they're paying close attention.

That's why it's best to have a special email newsletter ready for new subscribers that tells all about your music and merch and where to get them. This is done using the "AutoResponder" part of your ESP. In fact, most ESPs allow you to program multiple autoresponder emails so the new subscriber can be contacted at regular intervals. This is the perfect strategy to keep them in the fold and strike while the iron is hot.

Crafting A Successful Email Newsletter

There's a lot of thought that goes into creating a newsletter. If your title doesn't attract attention, the email may not get opened. If the content is weak, the next one might not get opened, or worse yet, the person could unsubscribe. You could have a great offer that no one acts on because it's presented poorly or visually buried. Let's take a look at the elements of a great newsletter.

The Objective

Sending out a newsletter for the sake of sending one out isn't a good strategy. There has to be a good reason for you to communicate with your subscribers. Don't forget, they gave you permission to contact them in the first place. It's up to you not to soil that agreement. Before you decide to send any newsletter, ask yourself these three questions:

- **What is this email about?** Are you informing your subscribers about the latest news? Are you trying to promote something? Is this an announcement of some kind? Decide what your email is about, then keep that as your central focus.

- **Why do my subscribers care?** Is this something they would be sorry about missing? Is it something they want to participate in? What's in it for them?

- **What do they do about it?** Do you want them to pass something along? Buy something? Come to a show? Stay informed about your life? Whatever it is, be sure to ask them to do it.

The Subject Line

The subject line is extremely important because if done well, it entices the person that receives it to actually open it. Remember that we live in a world of spam, and people get so much email every day that if the title doesn't immediately register with them as important, it's in the trash.

It's important to keep your subject line to 55 characters or less. Most email clients that people use cut the subject line off after that many anyway, so keep your subject line short and to the point - five or six words max.

***TIP**: You might want to test multiple subject lines to see which one is the most effective. Have three or four sample lists with a limited number of subscribers (maybe 10 or 20) and see which one resonates best before you send the email out to your entire following.*

Above all, don't use something like "Hey" or "Yo" alone in the subject line. That has spam written all over it and chances are your open rate is going to be near zero. Put some thought into the subject line and you'll be rewarded with a high open rate.

Also remember that using a first name in subject line grabs attention. Something like this:

"Hey Jeremy! News From The Unsigned Band"

Most ESPs will allow this, as long as you've connected the first names in your sign-up form. Testing shows that the response rates go up 50 to 70% or more when a first name is included. Remember that "Come to my show" is too predictable and uninteresting. If it's boring, people won't open or read it, and they won't come to your show.

***TIP**: Always avoid 'scam' words in the subject line like "Free" and "Help." These will land your message in the junk box a great percentage of the time.*

The Salutation

As in the subject line, first names get attention, so try to use the first name of each person you send your newsletter to. That's why it's also better if you can at least collect the subscriber's first name on the sign-up form. If you have a large number of email addresses without a name, it's probably better to send a separate version of the email to them without a salutation at all, but avoid something that's too generic like "Dear subscriber," which degrades any personal impact that the newsletter might otherwise have. Something like "Greetings from beautiful downtown Burbank (or whatever town or city you want to use)" is a good catch-all that seems personal even if you don't have the subscribers name.

The Copy

The copy is the body of your email where most of the text resides. Here's what to be aware of when composing:

1. What's the news? Part of crafting a quality email is having a clear sense of what exactly the big news is. Your text should focus on the most newsworthy element of your announcement with supporting details (including multimedia links) that clearly lay out why this news is significant. Also, try to make it as timely as possible. There's no sense in focusing the email on something that happened months ago. Stay with the present or the near future.

2. Always give them the basics about the information you're conveying. Reporters call this the "who, what, why, when, where, how" model. If you have a show coming up, do your fans and yourself a favor by providing dates, times, locations, ticket links, a map and lineup of the show. Believe it or not, the majority of artists miss this when they send an email. If you want someone to respond and either come to a show or purchase something, give them all the information they need to do so.

3. Keep it short. Time is your enemy in a newsletter. The longer it takes to read, the less someone wants to read it. It's not that your fans don't care, it's just that either their time or attention span is short, since there's so much else going on at the same time. If you have a good story with good visuals, the newsletter can be quick, succinct, and to the point; all things that make everyone's job easier. The ideal amount of text is around 500 words. You can always add a link to a page on your site with more details.

4. Add some pictures. If your newsletter is all text, it won't be visually appealing. Once again, any hint of boredom and it won't be read entirely.

5. Don't concentrate on too many things. You may have a dozen things going on that you want to convey, but that will mean that the email will increase in length and there will be too many concepts for the reader to focus on. Try to keep it to the most important one or two items per email. You can either send people to a page on your site via a link for more info on the other items, or send another email focusing on a few of them in a week or two.

6. Keep important content above the fold. If your email is long enough that it requires the reader to scroll down to see it all, keep the most important information at the top before the reader has to scroll. This is known as "above the fold" and the concept comes from the newspaper days where the upper half of the page was where the top headline was located. The same idea still applies even in the digital world; keep the most important info at the top of the page.

7. Always be sure there's a link to a place with more info. The link could be to your website, a ReverbNation page, a blog, or anywhere else where the additional info is located. Always give the reader a way to find out more if he wants to.

8. Write without swearing. It may be part of your persona as an artist or band, but not all of your fans or clients like crude language. On top of that, ISPs like Yahoo mail, hotmail, AOL don't like it either, and your message can be directed into the junk box if you're not careful.

Your Call To Action

A "call to action" is when you ask the recipient to do something. Do you want him to come to your site? Come to a show? Buy something? No matter what it is, readers are more inclined to act if you ask them (surprise, surprise). Some typical call to action statements might be "Buy it here," "Order it now," "Click for more info," or even "Send me your comments" links in the email.

One of the things you should be aware of though, if the call to action has too much hype it comes across as selfish or gives the perception that all you want is the reader's money. If it's presented more as information that the reader might like instead of a sales pitch, you'll usually sell more and maintain your good will as well. Another thing to keep in mind is that you should always give before you get. Give the fans something special before you ask them to do something like vote for you in a contest.

Social Media Sharing

Even though you're communicating with an email, social media is still important. Each newsletter should also include links or icons to your social sites so people who aren't yet following you can do so easily, as well as embedded social sharing functions. This allows people to tweet or add your news to their Facebook status. Do this and you've just multiplied your audience.

Your Signature

Make sure to include all of your info in your signature. If people want to contact you, they shouldn't have to go through a game of hide-and-seek to find out how. The very minimum that you should include is your website, your email address, your Facebook page and Twitter address. Don't forget to include your YouTube channel address either.

Legal Requirements

While it may seem that it's entirely up to you about what's contained in your email, be aware that every mass email blast that you send now requires several things by law. These are:

- **Easy opt-out:** You have to provide an easy way for subscribers to unsubscribe if they want. Once a subscriber opts out, you then have 10 days to stop sending them messages (although most expect it to happen immediately), and the unsubscribe option needs to be available for at least 30 days after the e-mail is sent. Most ESPs will automatically remove the address to a "do not send" list if the subscriber chooses to unsubscribe.

- **Identify your topic:** The subject line of your e-mails has to clearly and accurately identify the content of the e-mail. Any misleading or bogus subject lines are construed as spam.

- **Return address:** You have to include a legitimate return email address, as well as a valid postal address. Some ESPs even make you include a phone number. If you don't want people to know your home info (I don't want to broadcast it myself), open up a PO box, and get a Google Voice number if a phone number is required.

- **No email address harvesting:** You can't collect addresses from chat rooms, discussion forums, or blog comments. Once again, people must opt-in and give you permission to send something to them.

- **You can't offer a reward for forwarding:** You can invite subscribers to "forward this newsletter to a friend," but you can't entice them to do so with offers of money, coupons, discounts, awards, or additional entries in a giveaway.

Remember that spam is a serious business. It's not only bad form, but you could be held legally liable as well.

The Best Times To Email

You've finally finished creating your newsletter email and it's time to hit the send button. But is it really? It turns out that the exact day and time that's optimum to send your email has been extensively studied, and thanks to the built-in scheduler now offered by ESPs, you can be sure to have your email sent at the time when it's most likely to be opened.

The Best Day Of The Week For Email Marketing

What's the best day of the week to send your email newsletter? This is a critical decision because if you send it on the wrong day, you'll have fewer of your fans open it. Why? Usually because the timing is bad and their attention is on something else. That's why you want to be sure to pick the right day.

Here's some info from an article on gather.com that analyzes every day of the week as a potential email day. The article drew no conclusions and was able to provide a compelling argument for almost every day except the weekend.

MONDAY: After a long weekend, many email users make it a priority to organize their inboxes. This means there's a good chance that they'll run across your message and open it. The problem is that many consumers don't have the time because Monday is such a busy day as most people have to deal with the work backup from the weekend. If you choose to send an email on Monday, *it's best to do it late in the morning, preferably just before lunch*, as this is when they're more likely to have the time to check their inbox.

TUESDAY: By Tuesday, many consumers have organized their work week and have a little extra time to devote to checking their inbox. Like record releases, I've always felt that Tuesday is the best day to release or send anything. It's usually a slower news day, everyone is over the rush and pent up obligations that Monday brings, and you're not caught up in the business craziness that grows ever more intense as the week progresses.

WEDNESDAY AND THURSDAY: By mid-week people are preparing for the weekend and how they'll spend their personal time. On these two days, they often have a little extra time to spend in their inbox. The problem is that there's still business that needs to be handled and only two days left to get it done. Depending on the recipient, they may hold your message off until next week, or forget about it altogether. If you choose, mid-week to send your email, *keep your marketing message friendlier and less aggressive* as subscribers plan their time off.

FRIDAY: People tend to receive less email on Friday, which in turn, increases the visibility of your message. The problem is that by the time Friday rolls around, some consumers are in such a rush that they may automatically ignore any email that doesn't pertain to their job. If you do choose Friday, *send your message early in the day* so the recipient has more time to read it and take action.

SATURDAY AND SUNDAY: Believe it or not, people do check their inboxes on the weekend, and open rates are 45% higher and click rates 10% higher than the rest of the week. The problem is that by sending emails on Saturday or Sunday, you run the risk of coming off as too intrusive and annoy your subscribers, which is a good reason to avoid the weekend. If you do choose the weekend, limit your mailings to subscribers who are the most responsive on these particular days, especially targeted fans that you want to remind about a gig.

Selecting The Time To Send Your Email

Just like there's a best day to send your newsletter, there's also a definite science behind the time of day to send your emails. It's been studied extensively, most notably by Dan Zarrella and Pure360. Remember that all times are *Eastern Standard Time.*

- **Most opens occur between 5AM and 7AM.** Most people check their email first thing in the morning even before they leave for work. Remember that open rates are as much as 53% higher in the mornings.

- **7AM to 10AM is the next best time for opens.** The second most prevalent email opening time is at the beginning of the working day.

- **10PM to 6AM is an email dead zone.** Most emails sent during this period are ineffective.

Remember that these are trends and might not apply to your particular audience. The best way to proceed is to use these timings as a starting point, then experiment to see if another time works better. It's easy enough to schedule emails to do so, just make sure that you have enough of a sample size before you make any ironclad decisions on exactly what's working.

To sum things up, don't send those promotional emails out without first thinking about the timing. It could mean the difference between your fans reading it or not.

Frequency Of Emails

Now that you've gotten your email lists together and that first email out of the way, the next question always is, "How often should I email?" This basically depends upon how much news you have and what your subscribers expect.

You're probably currently on some sales lists like Buy.com or Ebay Deals where you receive an email every day. As you know, you only glance at it at most, stopping only when something catches your eye or if you're specifically looking for an item, which probably isn't all that frequently.

That's not the fate you want for your email though, as you'd prefer that your readers devour every word.

Here are some rules of thumb on email frequency:

- If you dislike the process of creating an email or just don't have anything to say at the moment, send an email every quarter (three months) just to keep your name in the mind of your fans and clients.

- If you have a fair amount of news that's occurring on a regular basis, an email every month or two can be very effective.

- If you're starting to break out in a big way, you may have enough content for once a week. This is rare for most artists though, and it's hard to constantly come up with enough information that your fans will find interesting.

- It's okay to send an email more frequently or out of sequence if something unexpected happens, like you're nominated for an award, your album is reviewed in a major magazine, or some major event happens. Fans want to hear this, so don't be afraid to send something to alert them.

***TIP**: For most artists, bands, engineers, producers and music business folks, an email every month or two is about the right frequency, as it's just long enough that your fans don't feel like they're being spammed and not too long before they forget you.*

Gig Reminders

Gig reminder emails fall into a different category in that they can be a lot shorter and a lot more frequent. While the email sequence below may seem like a lot of emails, remember that for true fans, you're doing them a favor by keeping them informed, and you're marketing yourself for other things at the same time. A potential reminder strategy is:

- **The day a show is announced or tickets go on sale.** As soon as you know that you're playing at a venue, send out an email. This could be to the entire list if it's announcing a tour, if it's the monthly schedule for a cover band, or if you believe that people will travel to see the show.

- **A week before the show.** Send out a reminder but concentrate more on the band, regarding a new part of the show, new songs, a music video, or something that you want to the fan to see.

- **3 days before the show.** Send out a reminder and include more information about the club and who else is playing.

- **1 day before the show.** Once again, remind the fan about a a different feature of the show or the music that's unique and won't be seen or heard any other way than attending. You can change the headline to "You don't want to miss this," or "See our new show tomorrow night."

- **The day of the show.** Send out a short reminder in the late morning to just the portion of your list in the general area of the club. Use a headline like, "Can you make it tonite?", or "Last chance to buy tickets!"

- **The day after the show**. Send an email with backstage pictures, pictures of meet and greets with fans or just fans in the audience, as well as links to videos. This is a nice shout-out to those that were there, and a prod for those that weren't not to miss you next time you're in town.

Of course, if you're lucking enough to have sold out your show, you won't need to send as many reminders. That said, you might send one headlined "Sold Out!" that either announces another gig or another way for the fan to hear your music or buy your merch. A contest for two last minute tickets (put them on your guest list) also works well.

***TIP**: In every reminder be sure to include all the pertinent gig information, including the name of the venue, the full address, the phone number, the time you're going on, and other acts on the bill. Consider including a map or a link to one as well.*

Artists and bands are sometimes timid about sending out so many gig announcements, but fans that ordinarily would attend really do forget. Remember, you're doing them a favor by reminding them.

***TIP**: When sending out multiple emails in a short space of time, be sure to continually change the headline and the email contents.*

Building Your Mailing List

Just like with your social media follows and Likes, building your mailing list takes some work. In general it comes down to the following:

- **Trust in your site.** If your site or social page makes people uncomfortable in any way, chances are they won't give you their email address.

- **An incentive of some kind.** Generally speaking, people don't want to give their address out unless they're get something in return. Don't think about the fact that you're getting their email address, think of what's in it for the fan. He only may care about regular communication, but usually access to something free (a song, ticket, ebook, article) gets better results.

- **Make it easy by not asking for too much information.** The more info you ask from a potential subscriber, the greater the chance that he'll give up while subscribing. Asking for just an email address gets the greatest response, but adding a first name allows you to include a personal greeting.

- **Cross-promote across social media, business cards, banners, and anywhere else you can think of**. Anywhere you get a chance to mention your email list, do so.

- **Reminders in your content.** Mention your mailing list in any podcasts, blogs, or videos, because sometimes even if it's right in front of them, a reminder is still needed.

Your email list is extremely powerful for communicating, interacting, and promoting to your fans. Put sufficient time and effort into it and you'll be richly rewarded.

6

Using Facebook For Marketing

Facebook launched in February of 2004 and quickly grew into the powerhouse that we know as today. While many see it for its flaws, the mere size of the network (over a billion users) makes it a social source that can't be overlooked. In this chapter we'll look closer at how to use Facebook not only for promotion, but for increasing your fan base as well.

Facebook By The Numbers

Here's an interesting set of statistics from Facebook itself. A couple of figures jump out, like the 2 billion Likes per day, and the fact that the network has zero penetration into China and only 60% into India and the US. Presumably that still leaves some room for growth. Check out these facts:

- It's the second most popular visited site on the Internet after Google.
- 50 percent of active users log on in any given day.
- About 70% of Facebook users are outside the United States.
- An average user spends 700 minutes per month on Facebook.
- More than 30 billion pieces of content are shared on Facebook each month.
- Each day, Facebook Pages have created 5.3 billion fans.
- Each day, 55 million status updates are made on Facebook.
- More than 150 million active users currently access Facebook through their mobile device.

The numbers don't lie, and any one of the above points is enough to make the case to use Facebook. Put them all together and it means that being a part of it is almost mandatory when it comes to social promotion.

Facebook Basics

Before we look at using Facebook for marketing, let's take a look at some of the basics, since there may be a bit of confusion about a few of its features. This is especially the case when it comes to personal versus fan pages, but as you'll see, there are good reasons to have both.

The Difference Between A Personal And Fan Page

There are two kinds of pages that you can have on Facebook; a personal page and a fan page. They're not interchangeable and each has its own advantages and disadvantages.

The Personal Page

First of all, you can't administrate a fan page unless you have a personal page, so there's no getting around having one unless someone else is administering your fan page for you. The next thing is that the personal page is the best place to stay in touch with family and friends. You can still have fans follow you, but you can segment them using a feature called "Lists." This will allow you to communicate just with the people you wish so you can keep things private if necessary.

To do this, scroll down to the Group or Friends section on your home page. Click on Create List, name the list and add the appropriate friends, then hit create.

Perhaps the two biggest reasons why a personal page is no substitute for a fan page is the fact that a personal page can have a maximum of 5000 friends, plus you can't access any of the analytics (called Facebook Insights) available.

Your Facebook Fan Page

The fan page differs from a personal page in that you can have an unlimited number of Likes and access to Facebook analytics, but it also has a number of additional advantages beyond that. These are the things other than the privacy aspect that make a fan page attractive.

- **Pinning posts on the Timeline.** If there's a particular post that you'd like to appear at the top of your timeline, the administrator (hopefully you) can pin it there (see Figure 6.1). This will keep the post at the top of the page for seven days, after which it will return to the date when it was posted. This ensures that everyone will see that particular post for a week, at which time it's probably old news anyway. To pin a post, click on the edit button on the top right of a post.

Figure 6.1: Pinning a post to the Timeline

- **Highlighting a post.** This is a variation on pinning, the difference being that instead of appearing at the top of the page, highlighting makes it stretch out the width of the page so it's more noticeable (see Figure 6.2). It still stays in the same place, but it visually sticks out of the page. To highlight a post, click on the edit icon at the top right of the post and select highlight next to the star.

Figure 6.2: Highlighting a post

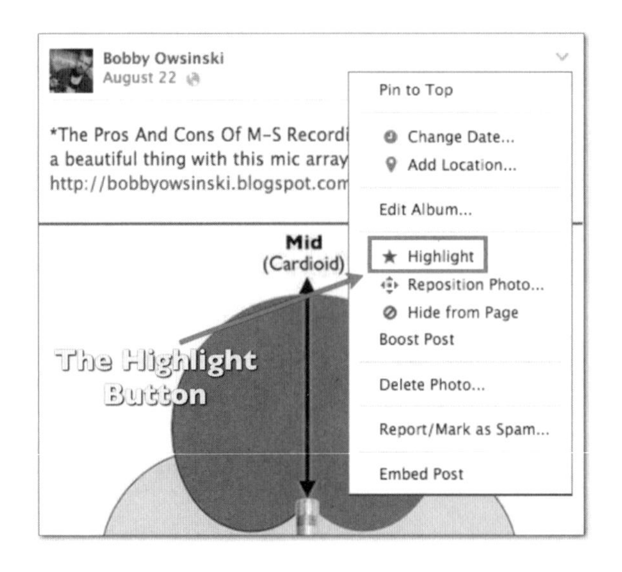

- **A unique experience.** The beauty of a fan page is that each fan gets a different experience. If someone visits your fan page, they also see what their friends are posting about you, even though it's not posted directly on your fan page.

The Cover Graphic

One of the things that you should take the time to do is to upload a "cover" photo or graphic. This allows you to brand your page beyond your profile picture. Although you can upload any photo and it will expand or contract to fill the space, it's best if you can create one that's 851 x 315 pixels with a file size of less than 100kB. That way it will load quickly and contribute to a better looking user experience.

***TIP:** Make sure that you use a photo of you for your profile picture, not one of your baby pictures, not an avatar, and not one of a celebrity that's not you. People won't trust either your personal or fan page if they can't trust your profile picture as well.*

When To Start A Fan Page

If you're an artist or band starting out, I don't believe that it's a good idea to jump right in with a fan page until you've established a personal page first. After all, it doesn't do much for your brand if you only have a couple of Likes and no traffic. I didn't create a fan page until I had almost 1900 friends on my personal page, but that was way too long to wait. I recommend that you start your fan site when you have a good healthy following on your personal site of at least three or four hundred. On top of that, make sure that at least half of those are fans and not friends or family. That way, when you start your fan site, it will be easier for the fans to transfer there and you'll have a modest following right from the start.

Facebook Promotion Overview

Using Facebook for promotion is a completely different animal than for casual personal use. Everything you post should have some thought put into it to get the best interaction. Let's look at how that's done.

What Should I Say?

A major concern that artists have is not only what's appropriate to post, but also being afraid they don't have enough to say. Believe it or not, if you're popular enough to have fans, then you also have plenty to say that they'll be interested in. Things that you might consider mundane are anxiously scarfed up by super fans who crave every tiny tidbit. Here are some ideas to start with.

- **A behind the scenes story.** Fans love details, so don't be afraid to tell them where you're recording (don't give the exact name if you don't want to be disturbed) and why you chose the studio, location or rehearsal space. Other information that super fans want are things like how long it took to record or mix a song, when it was or will be released, and how the players, director, producer or engineer was hired.

- **Where the idea came from.** Every song came from somewhere and fans love to know when, where and how it was created. If you didn't write the song, you can still tell them what you did to bring the song to fruition during rehearsals, preproduction or recording. The same goes for the concept for a video.

- **The people involved, especially fans.** Who's the director, producer, engineer, musicians, cameraman, etc.? Was a fan involved in the selection or have anything to do with the project, gig, or tour?

TIP: *Giving a shout-out to fans always takes precedence over anything else. It's the ultimate feel-good promotional tool.*

- **Interviews with others on the project.** If you can't think of anything to say about the project, gig or tour, ask some of the others connected with it. Surely somebody has some unique insight that you just can't see.

- **Trivia about the project, no matter how small.** Real fans crave trivia. Things that you consider mundane and not worth mentioning could be a goldmine for a super fan. For instance, something as small as the fact that you keep breaking the G string on a certain guitar, which made you switch to a different heavier brand, seems like nothing to you, but some fan will find the fact totally fascinating. The same with the mic you used on the guitar amp or vocal when recording. How about the mic positioning? How about the kind of tea you drink before a gig to protect your voice?

Keep in mind that if you only have ten fans, there might only be one that finds the minutia compelling, but the super fans are the ones ultimately paying the bills and those are the ones to cater to.

TIP*: Generally speaking, the things that people want to know are the things you take for granted.*

Crafting A Promotional Post That Works

As stated a few times above, using Facebook for promotion dictates the way in which you post. That's because you have to craft each post in such a way that provides you with brand building, promotion and information. Let's look at some post examples.

"Having breakfast after the gig. Just had bacon, eggs and potatoes. The bacon was greasy and the potatoes were burnt. The coffee was good though."

This is a bad post and here's why. First of all it's way too personal. Who cares about your breakfast? Even if Beyonce or Adam Levine posted this it would still be boring. Second of all, it's too long. As you'll see, shorter posts tend to work better. About the only thing that's okay here is the fact that he mentioned it was after a gig, which provides a slight hint of something a fan might want to know, but where was the info about the gig?

Let's look at an improved example:

"Great gig at the Capitol tonite. You people ROK! 2 girls jumped on stage and Joey boogied with them."

This one's better because it gives us some information. The gig was at the Capitol (which we assume is a club), then there's the shout-out to the fans that attended, which is always a good idea. Unfortunately, there's still something lacking. How about this one:

"Great gig at the Capitol tonite. You people ROK! 2 girls jumped on stage and Joey boogied with them. Pictures and video at http://theunsigned.com/pix."

This one's great because it gives us the same information, plus it gives us a link to actually see Joey boogying with the audience. The link is to the fictitious band (at least for this example) called "The Unsigned." Attach a picture to this and you have the best of all worlds.

Let's look at another example.

"Back in the studio today. Feeling tired after a long weekend of partying. Catching a cold."

Who cares that you're tired? And why should I feel sorry for you because you partied too hard? And your cold concerns us how?

This one's a bit better:

"In the studio today with Johnny Rox for some hi-energy rockabilly."

This post gives us some interesting info. We find out who he's in the studio with and the kind of music they'll be doing. It can still be improved though.

"Back in AIR studios today with Johnny Rox for some hi-energy rockabilly. Excellent rhythm section of Jack X and Ronaldo. Pictures at http://theunsigned.com/airpix."

This one almost has it all. It tells us where (AIR studios), with who (Johnny Rox) and even some of the details (the rhythm section of Jack X and Ronaldo). Then it tops it off with a link to some pictures. What would make this even better is if a picture were attached to the post.

Post Creation Rules

After seeing the comparisons between posts, you can see that we're observing a number of rules. They are:

1. Keep it short. Facebook suggests that somewhere between 100 and 250 characters (which equals a line or two of text) gets 60% more likes, comments and shares, while other studies have shown that posts of 80 characters or less get 23 percent more interaction. That said, don't restrict yourself if you can't tell the story or get the point across in a limited amount of characters.

2. Keep it professional. Just like when you're writing a press release, an article, or almost anything else, you want to keep to the basics of who, what, when, why and how. You don't have to get them all in there, but these are the things that make a post interesting. Keep your personal feelings out of it as much as possible until you get a lot of experience posting, and even then have it only creep into the conversation occasionally.

***TIP**: When you post something personal it shows that you're human, which people like. Just keep it to the occasional post.*

---

3. Include a link. Always include a link to additional information, pictures, video, mailing list, or your website. If you have someone's attention enough for them to read your post, it's likely they'll take action even further if given the chance.

That's said, the type of link that you include does make a difference. Using a long URL can get you three times the engagement on Facebook, mostly because people trust it more than one that's been shortened. What's the difference? Take a look:

Long URL:
http://bobbyowsinski.blogspot.com

Shortened URL:
bit.ly/vjgIUQ or ow.ly/eMLi2

Shortened URLs work great for Twitter when the number of available characters is limited, but always use the longer one for Facebook.

4. Include a photo. Posts with photos receive 39 percent more interaction than ones without. That said, posts with videos receive fewer likes and views, mostly because people don't want to commit the time it takes to watch an entire video. That's not to say that you should stay completely away from posting videos, just remember that in this case, less is more.

5. Engage your fans. Ask them questions, ask their opinions, ask them anything, but get them talking to you and to your other fans. In social media, their participation really matters as it keeps the fan base healthy, and gives you feedback as to how you're doing and what they want from you. Posts with questions have 92% more comments, but be sure to place them at the end of the post.

6. Call to actions work. When fans are asked to like a post, they do so at three times the rate than when they're not asked, as well as comment at a rate more than three times times the norm. When asked to share a post, they're seven times more likely to do so.

***TIP:** Be careful when using a call-to-action that asks for a Like, comment or share. This can violate Facebook's terms of service agreement and get you banned if you offer to trade something for it! There are ways to do this with a third party application (which we'll cover in a bit).*

---

7. Bonus: Experiment with emoticons. In some cases, emoticons can provide as much as 52% higher interaction, while in other cases, the interaction can be lower than average. :D and :P have the highest interaction rates.

The Best Time To Post

While you might be writing the best, most engaging posts, they do you no good if there's no one reading. The question then becomes, "When is the best time of day to post on Facebook?"

The Studies

There have been many studies on the subject, but most of them have found pretty much the same thing:

- Facebook usage is highest at 11AM, 3PM, and 8PM ET.
- The biggest spike occurs at 3PM ET on weekdays.
- Wednesday at 3PM is the busiest Facebook period of the week.

- Fans are the least active on Sunday.

- Posts that occur in the morning tend to perform almost 40 percent better in terms of user engagement than those in the afternoon.

- The top of the hour (:00 to :15 minutes) sees more interaction than other parts of the hour.

- In what seems to be a contradiction, 65 percent of users only access Facebook when they're not at work or at school, which means in the evening.

- The highest clickthroughs come at 3PM ET on Wednesday, with links posted from 1PM to 4PM getting the highest average clickthroughs.

- Links after 8PM and before 8AM struggle for attention.

- Posts with questions have a 15 percent higher engagement rate. A question starting with the word "would" gets the most engagement, followed by "where," "when," and "should." "Why" gets the least engagement.

Like with many of the stats that we see online, you have to take some of these items with a grain of salt and see what works best for your specific application. The only thing that they all have in common is that posting at the top of the hour (i.e. 8AM) is a lot more effective than anything else.

In Practice

I have found that 8AM, 3PM and 8PM ET do indeed get the most traction, but 11AM can sometimes work as well. One of the things that I don't like about evening posts at 8PM ET is the fact that Facebook viewing begins to drastically drop off afterwards, meaning that the shelf life of the post is a lot shorter. That's why I personally try to make my final post of the day at 3PM at the latest.

TIP: *Release major stories in the early morning. If you post between 11AM to 4PM ET, you risk your content getting pushed down by news feeds and other traffic.*

When it comes to the weekends, I've found that traffic definitely decreases. Since my Facebook posts are generally about my blog posts, I usually post a "week in review" post of only the blog post titles on Saturday and Sunday. I've found that anytime in the morning generally works well, although I've settled on 9 or 11AM ET most of the time.

I've also found that posts that contain a photo or graphic also do much better than those that don't have one. With so many posts being text only, one with any sort of graphic sticks out from the crowd. If the picture or graphic is in any way interesting or entertaining, all the better.

Scheduling Posts

After reading the last topic about timing your posts, you're probably thinking, "I just don't have the time to wait until exactly 3PM to post, and I'll be in a rehearsal at 8PM. How am I going to do this?" That's the beauty of the scheduling function within Facebook (see Figure 6.3). If you take notice there's a clock icon on the bottom left of the status update box where you post. You can schedule the post by clicking on the year, month, day and time.

Figure 6.3: Facebook scheduling

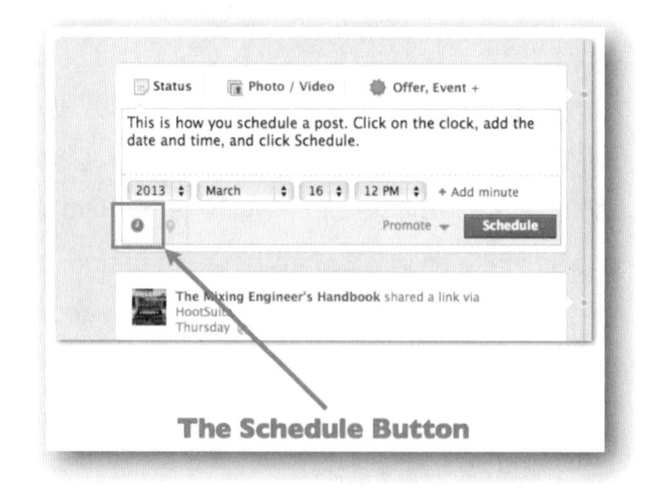

There's another way that may be a bit more streamlined, especially if you have more than one Facebook fan site and also post to other social sites like Twitter and Google+. A number of services are available that not only help with scheduling, but with viewing posts and analytics as well. Although I happen to use Hootsuite (seen in Figure 6.4), there are a number of others that do basically the same thing. Here's a partial list, although new ones come available all the time.

Tweetdeck
Blurster
Hubspot
Buffer
SproutSocial
TodayLaunch
Spreadfast
SocialFlow

Figure 6.4: Scheduling posts with Hootsuite

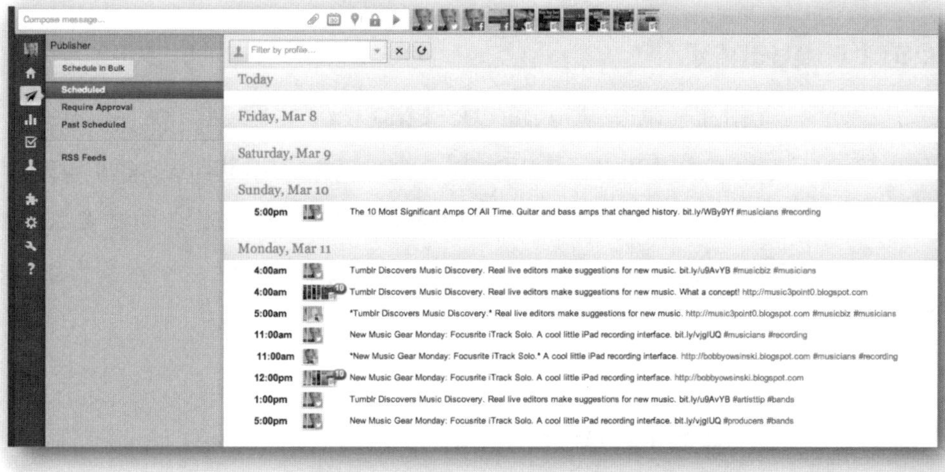

All of these services allow you to schedule your posts to at least Facebook and Twitter (some post to other networks as well). Many have a free option that's somewhat limited, and others will charge depending upon the features and analytics that you require.

One of the best parts about these services is that they also allow you to view all of your posts from the various networks and pages in one place, rather than continuously flipping through different social sites (see Figure 6.5). That allows you to view what's happening at a moments glance, a valuable time-saver when you have a lot of networks to tend to.

Figure 6.5: Hootsuite showing newsfeeds from all accounts

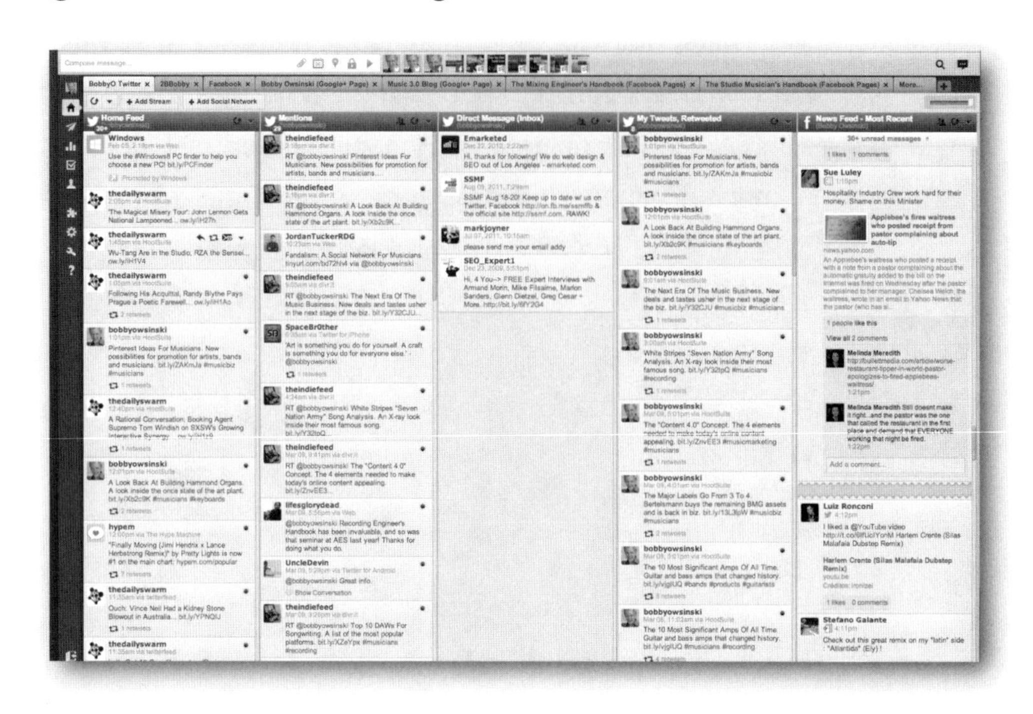

Post Frequency

Yes, it's true, you can post too much. Facebook suggests that one or two posts a day get the most response, and there's evidence that posting any more begins to become counterproductive. In fact, brands that post more see 19% less interaction. Once again, less is more. It's better to have one great post than a number of mediocre ones.

Understanding Edgerank

Let's face it, you have a Facebook fan page for one reason - to connect with your fans. While I don't believe that there's a one-size-fits-all formula for how this is done, there are some suggestions on how to get not only the best fan engagement, but also to improve your "Edgerank."

Facebook uses an algorithm called Edgerank that determines which items are the most relevant to populate your news feed. The more popular the story, the more likely it will show up on people's news feed. What that means is you have to optimize your content in order to make sure that it will have a high relevancy, and as a result be seen by more people. It's sort of like organic SEO, but just for Facebook.

What Edgerank does is personalize Facebook for each reader, so it's possible that many of your friends may not see every post that you make unless you follow the guidelines to keep things interesting. Just like with blogging, email newsletters, or any promotion online, you really have to work it to not only keep the audience that you have, but to grow it as well.

The way Edgerank works is that it assigns a value to every post based on affinity (the relationship between the friend and the user), weight, and time. Weight is determined by the type of story, if it contains rich media, and any comments it might have. Time is when any action (like a comment or like) might have been taken.

In order to improve your Edgerank, you must always be aware of the following (some of these we've covered already):

- **Post content that's relevant, engaging, and timely**.

- **Use photos and graphics where possible.** Photos are the most valuable and powerful content that you can post, followed by videos and then links.

- Use time-based words like "today," and "limited-time only."

- **Put your fans in charge occasionally.** Ask your fans questions. Let them decide which song will be the next single, or which video they like best, or the album cover artwork. They like to be involved and the news feed algorithm likes it as well.

- **Target your status updates.** If you have fans all over the world, most don't need to know about a local or regional gig or release. Target the appropriate posts as tightly as you can to the area necessary to get the word out (check out the post targeting example in Figure 6.6).

Figure 6.6: Facebook post targeting.

- **Diversify your content.** A combination of how-to's, artist or band trivia, breaking news, polls, fill-in-the-blanks, photos and videos, or third party content keeps it interesting.

The Facebook Like

One measure of how well you're doing on Facebook is the number of Likes that you receive either for your page or any particular post. The Like button allows a user to express his support or enjoyment for certain content. On Facebook, when a user clicks the Like Button, the content then appears on his or her news feed, so the content is then shared with his or her friends. The total number of Likes is also displayed.

Understanding The Like Button

It's important that you don't get too hung up on how many Likes you receive. People click the button because you've moved them enough that they want to endorse you or your post. That said, be careful how you assess a post that gets more Likes that you expect, since it may be that your fans are responding to a link, a photo, or even an emotion that was evoked, rather than to your cleverness.

Also remember that perhaps only ten percent of your fans will see any given Facebook post, and only about one percent will Like it. For example, at the time this book was written, the Black Keys had about

800,000 fans and get around 800 Likes per post. The one time they exceeded that number was when they when they posted "Lotsa Grammys" and received over 7,000 Likes.

Justin Bieber has 22 million fans and gets between 25,000 and 50,000 Likes per post, and Mumford and Sons has 1.3 million fans, but pulled an impressive 17,000 Likes on one post that simply said, "TOUR!!!"

When you read this, those numbers will undoubtedly be higher, but the totals don't really matter. The point is that most posts receive far fewer than one percent Likes, and only the most popular ones come in at one percent or slightly above.

The reason why an artist should continue to post without worrying about getting Likes is the same reason why advertising works - *it's all about the impressions*. The more impressions, or views, the more likely the viewer will take some action at some point in time, like download some music, go to a show, or buy a T-shirt.

That said, if you have 1000 Facebook fans, this is what you can expect on an given post:

1000 fans
Average post seen by 100 fans (10% of 1000 fans)
Average number of Likes = less than 10 (1% of 1000 fans)
Total impressions = 100 (the number of fans that see your post)

As long as the information you post is valuable to the reader in some way, it's worth doing because you're communicating and engaging. In other words, it's nice to be "Liked," but it's not necessarily a sign of a successful post.

***TIP**: Be careful not to be lulled into thinking that if someone doesn't register a Like, they're not actually reading the post. We all know that's not the case, because in fact many of us see and react to posts every day without actually registering a Like.*

The Secrets To Getting Liked

The Like button is becoming more and more important in social networking, so it's worth incorporating into anywhere that you have an online presence, if possible. This can be done with the aid of any number of helper sites like AddThis.

Facebook reports that Like buttons get three to five times more clicks if:

- The post shows thumbnails of friends.
- The post allows people to add comments.
- The Like button appears at both the top and bottom of an article or post.
- The post appears near visual content like videos or graphics.

Facebook also noted that video site Metacafe placed a Like button above its videos, in addition to one below, as the arrows point to in this screenshot in Figure 6.7:

Figure 6.7: Using top and bottom Like buttons

After doing this, both the use of the Like button and traffic from Facebook increased. In this case it was discovered that:

- The number of daily Likes more than tripled, going from an average of 2,000 likes per day to over 7,000 likes.

- Daily referral traffic from Facebook to Metacafe doubled, going from about 60,000 to 120,000.

- Total Facebook actions (Likes, shares, comments) rose to 20,000 per day.

TIP: *The words that lead to the most shares on Facebook are "best," "most," and those that explain, such as "why," and "how."*

Like-Gating

Likes can be used for other things than a simple endorsement, and can be used as a gateway to original content, to a download, or as a redirect to another page as well. This is what's known as Like-gating. Even though it's against the Facebook terms of services agreement to offer any of these things, using a third party app works without incurring the service's wrath because the apps strictly tailor their service to Facebook's requirements.

The key to using the Like as either a gateway or redirect is by incorporating a service like Woobox, which can also be used for contests, coupons, sweepstakes, polls and rewards as well. Like most third party apps, there are free parts to their service, but most of their features will cost you. It's still not too expensive at $29.95 a month for the entirety of what they offer.

A download gate can be set up with a company called InboundNow. All you do is go to the site, fill in your Facebook URL and your download link, then your email address. The code for your download Like gate is then generated and you can embed it on your website, blog, email, or anything else you can think of.

The Land Of Fake Likes

It never takes long for someone to come up with a way to game an online measurement that the music industry finds useful. Once upon a time, the major labels used MySpace followers as a measure of a band's popularity. That was until it was discovered that there were multiple ways to fake those numbers. Of course, the number of website hits were once used as a measurement too until every unknown band seemed to have a million.

Now it's possible to purchase Likes as well, and the price goes anywhere from $.01 to $1.07 for each one, depending upon the quantity purchased. The problem is that while having 10,000 Likes may look impressive, it's a foundation built on quicksand, since it gives you no indication of how well your real social media strategy is working. And as you can see from the Figure 6.8 below, it's pretty easy to spot if someone wants to take the time. Buying them really doesn't do anything except cost you money, so it's best to stay away.

Figure 6.8: Fake Likes that all originate in Mexico City

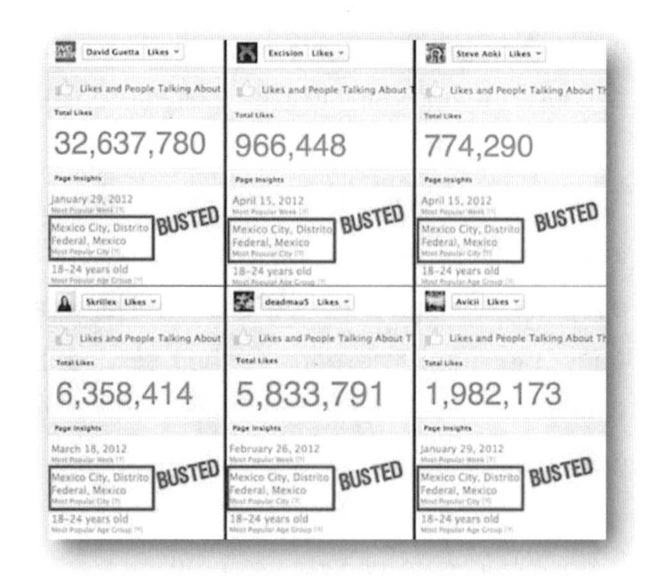

Facebook Guidelines To Observe

Those that use Facebook a lot don't often think about it, but there are a number of guidelines that you agreed to when you first created either your personal or fan page. These are worth being aware of since a violation is enough to get you banned from the service, which is something that you definitely don't want.

Want some examples? Facebook has a number of guidelines for your cover photo like:

- It can't have price or purchase information in the photo (like "50% off").
- It can't include a call to action to Like, comment or share with your friends.
- It can't include contact info like web, email or mailing address (there are better places to put this rather than on the cover photo as well).

Facebook is also very sensitive to how contests are run and wants you to closely abide by their rules. Here's what you should know:

- Contests asking for submissions or votes via comments or liking are prohibited.
- All contests or giveaways must be administered within apps on Facebook.com.
- You can't notify contest winners through Facebook solely through wall posts, messages, or chat. You must reach out to them at least through a direct message or email.

Kind of puts a damper on things, right? Fear not, there are a number of third party providers that can help you run a Facebook promotion, like Wildfire and Offerpop, but they do cost money. That said, before you decide on any contest, read the Facebook promotion guidelines first.

TIP: *One of the biggest violations of Facebook's terms of service agreement is that you can't promise to give someone something if they Like, comment or share your post unless you use a third party app.*

Seven Ways To Increase Your Facebook Fan Engagement

Fan engagement is the best way to increase your Facebook fan base. Here are six ways for that to happen that you should always keep in mind.

1. Engage, but don't advertise. The soft sell always works best. The key to Facebook is all about engagement and the best way for that to happen is to get rid of the "Buy My New Album" thinking. Instead, try asking a question like:

"Hey everyone, we just released our new album. We're trying to decide on the next single. Please have a listen and leave a comment about your favorite tracks. [link to your album on your store site]"

2. Ask questions, or ask for your fan's support. This is one of the best ways to engage them without hard selling them. Remember that when fans leave a comment or review, it will appear on their friend's news feeds, and other people are much more likely to buy after online recommendations from friends.

3. Give a virtual high-five. It's important to respond to any comment that's left. At the very least, "Like" their comment. This is the online equivalent of a high-five from the stage. A Like, a response, a thank you, or a shout out is a subtle way to reward your fans. When they see a status update from you, they'll be thrilled, and they may even share it again.

4. Reward fans, then ask them to reward their friends. Free tracks are a great way to reward your fans, and they aren't really "free" if you capture the fan's information, or get them to share it with their friends, which increases your reach by hitting their friend's Ticker or All Friends feed. Once you capture the fan's info, you can then build the relationship. Many times, they'll later reciprocate with a purchase or by attending a live show. As an example, in a recent Nimbit promotion, Suzanne Vega teased her fans with a free download, and later found that 61% who received that free download also made a purchase.

5. Advertise yourself to fans of similar artists. Facebook makes it incredibly easy and affordable to create an ad that's perfectly targeted to your demographic (see the section on Facebook ads later).

6. Make everything an event. This is one of the secrets of multiple single song releases rather than full albums. Every release becomes an event. You can expand upon that idea in just about any direction, from gigs or giveaways on your birthday to your best fan's birthdays, to making every gig a special occasion.

These ideas are something that you should consider, since Facebook is one of the most powerful social media tools at your disposal.

7. Always be ready to sell. The best time to make the sale is when the fan is excited, and that's when they discover your music. Your chances of making that sale are greater if they can purchase directly on Facebook instead of somewhere else.

Promoting Posts

Another thing that Facebook allows you to do is to pay to promote individual posts. Regular unpromoted posts are typically only seen by only 12 to16 percent of your friends, but choosing to promote a post will include a larger portion of your friends and make the post appear higher in the Newsfeed.

You can choose to promote a post on your personal page by clicking on the *Promote* button located at the bottom between the *Comment* and *Share* buttons of a post. You'll now be taken to a pay screen where you'll be asked to enter your credit card number or select Paypal. The cost is $7, and the post will now be marked "Sponsored." You can check to see how many more people saw it as a result of the paid promotion.

Promoting a post on a fan page is somewhat different. First of all, the *Promote* button is located by itself on the bottom right-hand corner of the post (see Figure 6.9). Secondly, you're actually charged depending upon how large an audience you want to reach (see Figure 6.12), but the number is limited by your existing audience. You'll be given a number of selections to choose from, each with a different fee.

Is promoting a post worth it? Record labels and marketers alike claim that it can be very effective if your target audience is selected carefully. The best thing is to dive in and give it a try a few times while keeping your allocated money on the low side. If you have a post that you feel strongly about, has a call to action and a link to where you want the audience to go, it's worth a shot.

Figure 6.9: Promoting a post on a fan page.

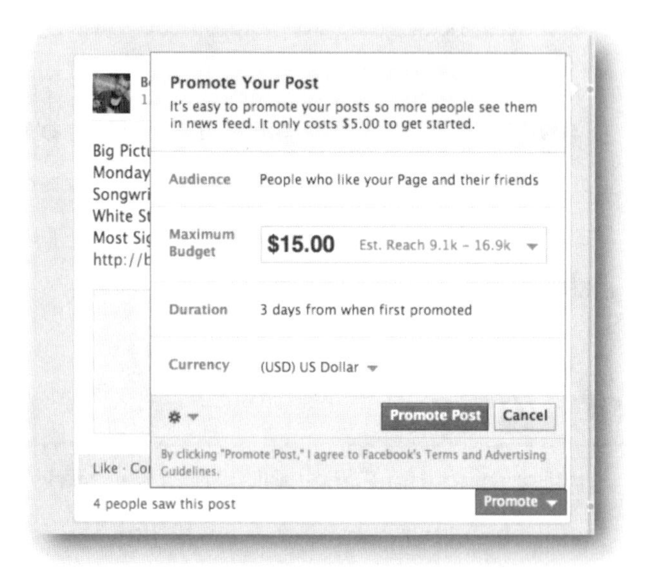

***TIP**: Only choose to promote a post if you think that the post will still be relevant for at least three days after the promotion begins.*

Using Facebook Ads

One way to get more fans, clients, Likes and followers is by using Facebook ads. The idea of buying ads can be scary, but as you'll see, this is a great way to get the word out in a targeted way without breaking the bank.

Before you begin, be sure to clearly define your objectives and goals. Do you want more Likes? Do you want to expose more people to your music? Do you want to sell more merch? Do you want more website traffic? Make sure you understand what your priorities are before launching into an ad campaign, since the more uncertain you are, the less likely your campaign will succeed. After you've figured that out, go to the "Create An Ad" link on the right side of your Facebook page and you're off.

Designing Your Ad

Designing your ad is pretty simple, thanks to the advert layout page.

1. Select your destination. The first thing you'll do is select either a Facebook or external URL destination that you want your ad centered on (see Figure 6.10). This means that you can promote a Facebook page or post, but you can also promote something external to Facebook as well, like your website or blog. The option that you choose depends upon the goal of the campaign, which you'll select next.

Figure 6.10: Selecting the destination

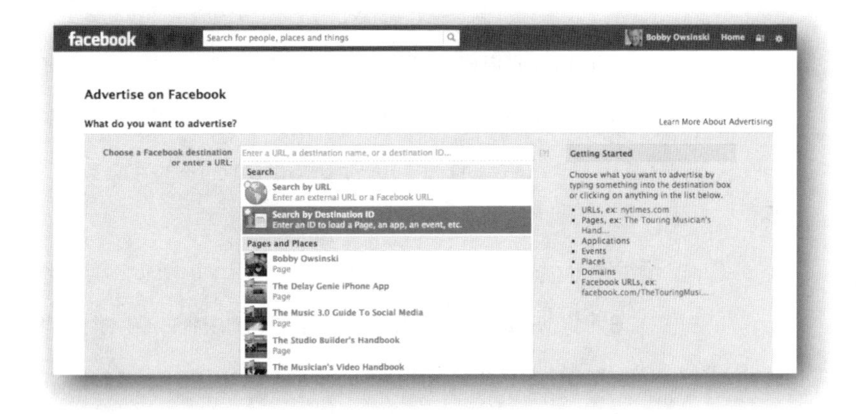

2. Select your goal. In the next area you have three goal choices, starting with "Get more page Likes" and "Promote your page posts" (see Figure 6.11). If you choose either of these, the amount you'll pay for the ad will be based on the number of people that see your ad (called the CPM, or cost per thousand). A third "Advanced" option allows you to pay only for people who click through to your site. One of the problems with this is that you may pay for clicks that don't turn into actions, which can eat up your budget fast. That's why it's best to only choose this option after you've had some experience using the CPM model first.

Figure 6.11: Selecting the promotion goal

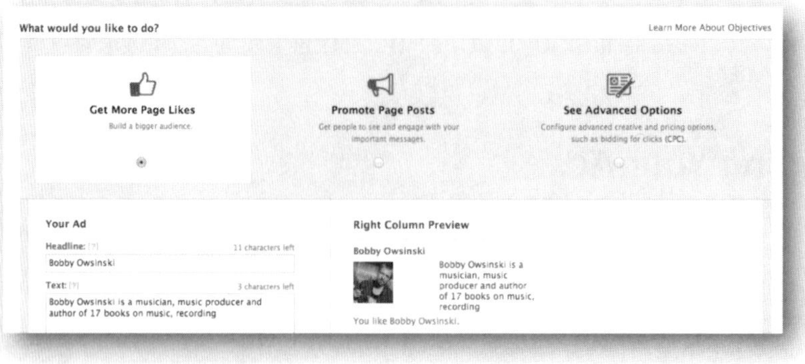

3. Design your ad. The next section is where you design your ad. If you just want Likes, you get to choose your headline and the text. Keep in mind that you only have a total of 25 characters for the headline and 90 for the text, so everything has to be to the point. You can also use either your existing profile image, one from your library, or upload a new photo. You then see a preview of what it will look like on the right side of the page.

If you want to promote a page post instead, you can either choose a post that has already been posted (and have it refresh as long as the campaign goes on), create a brand new post, or even choose a URL.

One of the other things that you can do in this section is to make sure that if anyone Likes you page post, comments, or shares, your post will show up on their status as well. This now comes at an extra cost.

4. Target your audience. One of the best things about Facebook ads is that you're able to precisely target your audience (see Figure 6.12). You can target the location either on a country, state, city or zip code level, as well as age, gender, interests, relationship status and even friends of connections.

***TIP**: To reach the right people, type in names of similar artists in the "Precise Interests" field. That will target your ad to people who entered that artist as music they listen to. Also, pick a geographic region that makes sense. If you're a touring artist or band, only select the areas where you'll be performing.*

Figure 6.12: The target market section

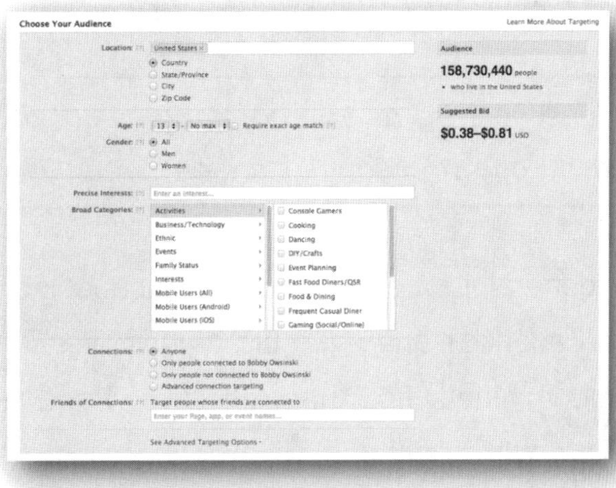

5. **Name, price and schedule.** Now comes the area where you name your campaign, select the amount of money you want to spend, and schedule it (see Figure 6.13). The beauty of Facebook ads are that you get to choose the price you want to pay, and how often you want to pay. If you only have $3 to spend a week, you can schedule the ad to run continuously until that amount is reached, schedule that amount per day, or even choose to run on a day in the future. Finally you can choose whether you want to pay for impressions or clicks, or if you want Facebook to optimize your campaign for increased engagement.

***TIP**: Set your daily budget low at first, "Select Pay for Clicks" (not Impressions), and set your "Bid" below what's suggested. This way you'll pick up ads on off hours, or when other campaigns end.*

Figure 6.13: Selecting the price

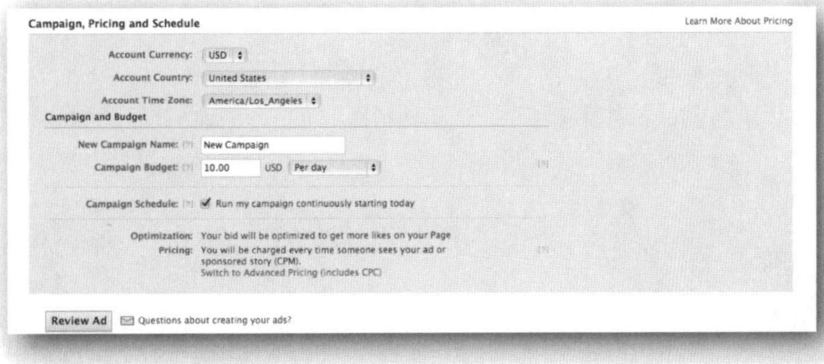

6. Review your ad. Finally you get to review your ad before you confirm you want to run it.

***TIP**: Fine tune your ad as you go along. Set it up, check back to see how it's doing, then change your settings to see if you can increase your reach*

In general, it's been found that Facebook ads definitely do drive behavior on Facebook and even big brands like Ford, Subway, Dr. Pepper, Tide, among others find them effective. Page ads are a great way to build Likes, while post ads drive engagement and build your audience. Plus, you don't have to spend a lot of money to do it. It's a great option without having to worry about breaking the bank.

7

Marketing With Twitter

Twitter is great for building your brand and an amazing way to reach a lot of people that you probably couldn't reach any other way. That's said, after seven years and over 500 million active users, many musicians are still confused by Twitter. Many seem baffled as to why anyone would want to use a service providing short 140 character messages, or why they should be bothered using it as a promotional tool. Top that off with the many horror stories of PR disasters started by the errant tweet from celebrities and professional athletes, and they're skittish about even getting involved in this highly successful social network.

The flaw in that thinking is that Twitter works and works well for promotion and marketing, if you know how to do it. That's what this chapter is all about.

Twitter Basics

Twitter is a social platform that allows you to communicate with others in short, 140 character (or fewer if you want) messages called "tweets." You can think of it as a broadcast service, where your tweet is available for the world to see, but the ones that directly see it are your "followers," (sometimes called "tweeps," which is short for Twitter + peeps) which are people who've decided they like what you have to say. Whenever you tweet, your followers will be see your tweet in a timeline on their Twitter page. You can also tweet directly to a person who is following you, which is called a Direct Message or DM. If you like a tweet that you see, you can spread the word to your followers by Retweeting, or RT.

Twitter allows you to "favorite" a tweet, which is sort of like a bookmark. If there's something that you like or find useful, by favoriting a tweet you create a list that everyone can see on your profile.

When you sign up for a Twitter account (it's free) you get to select your screen name. This usually comes after the @ sign, so as an example my Twitter name is @bobbyowsinski. When you see a tweet that starts with someone's screen name, that means there's a public conversation going on with that person.

***TIP**: Give plenty of thought to your screen name. Be sure that it's as short as possible yet stays consistent with your website, Facebook and other social sites.*

Following And Followers

When you like what someone's tweeting and want to view all of their tweets, you follow them. Like Facebook, you can organize the people that you're following into lists so that it's easier to keep track of the information you want. These lists can be public or private. If you decide you don't like what someone is tweeting, or the volume of tweets is too heavy, you can simply unfollow them.

***TIP**: When you first sign up, Twitter will help you go through your address book to see if anyone you know is a Twitter user already. You then have the option to invite them to follow you.*

When people follow you, it's an unwritten rule that you should follow them back, although I don't believe that's absolutely necessary, especially for a brand. One way that many people are taught to get a lot of followers quickly is to follow everyone that they can find, hoping that they'll reciprocate. That works, but it's an empty gesture, as you want real followers that are truly interested in what you have to say. If you want to use that approach, try to stay at least within your genre of music and with people that have common interests.

That said, if you follow some of my upcoming advice, you'll get plenty of followers organically, but only if you're really are worth following in the first place.

Twitter Etiquette

This is a fairly simple medium, but there are certain unwritten rules that attempt to keep people from annoying one another. Despite this group etiquette, you'll still no doubt run into situations that may make you want to scream, but keep in mind that it's probably bugging others as well. Rest assured that sooner or later the offender gets the message and either mends his ways or leaves. Let's take a look at what you should know.

- **Don't use all caps.** One of the things that netizens universally hate is someone COMMUNICATING IN ALL CAPS. This is considered the equivalent of shouting, is more difficult to read, and just plain impolite.

- **Don't be rude.** What's rude in real life is rude on Twitter as well. The problem is that people are more easily offended online because they can't see any facial expressions or body language, and as a result, what you consider to be a rather harmless tweet can kick up a firestorm. The way around this is to think through every tweet before you send it and stay away from any provocative language.

- **Don't use an affiliate link in a tweet.** Links in a tweet are a good thing, but it's bad form to include one that's blatantly trying to sell something or make money.

- **Don't ask someone for a favor publicly.** Just like doing it in a crowded room, it's uncool. Better to ask in a private conversation. Use DM instead.

- **Don't auto-DM.** It's possible to set up an automatic direct message welcoming someone when they follow you. Save your time and money as this is considered bad form. If it's not personal, an auto-DM can do more harm than good.

- **Issue a high volume warning.** If you're going to be tweeting more than normal (like from a show, conference or event), tell your followers in advance. No one likes their Twitter feed to be controlled by one person.

- **Don't be negative.** Nothing turns off followers faster than negative commentary. If you can't say something nice and be positive, don't say it at all.

- **Don't provide too much information.** Twitter isn't a place for details. There's not enough room in the limited number of characters that you have, which means that you have to resort to more tweets, which puts you into the realm of over-tweeting. As with most things online, less is more.

- **Pause between tweets.** Another thing that makes people crazy is a big volley of tweets one after the other. Take a break before your next tweet. Give other people a chance to get their tweets seen as well.

Following these online etiquette rules will not only help you keep your followers, but will keep you in good Twitter standing. It's just a little bit of courtesy, but well worth it.

Your Twitter Profile

Many artists, bands, brands and companies sign up for a Twitter account but don't take the time to properly create a profile. This is important because you'd be surprised at the number of times that people who are interested in you want more details about who you are. They get that info first from your profile, which can be linked to your website or Facebook page. Here's how to get the most from your profile.

- **Upload a photo.** Just like Facebook, a profile picture is important because it gives people confidence in you, your band or your product. Instead of a picture, this could be a logo as well. Resist the temptation to post a baby picture or avatar, or worse yet, nothing. What will happen is that an empty egg shape will appear in the picture slot, which is known as an "egghead" (see Figure 7.1). This is something that you don't want to happen as it signifies your indifference to the platform.

Figure 7.1: A Twitter egghead

- **Your bio.** You get all of 160 characters to provide your story. This allows you to get right to the essence of what it is that you do. You can also place a link here, although there's a place for a link to your website that's not part of the 160 characters.

- **The header.** It's now possible to upload a photo or graphic for the background of your bio, called the header. It's recommended that this graphic be 1256 x 626 pixels, but anything close to that size with a 2 to 1 length to width ratio will work. You can also resize the picture, and select the color of your bio text (white or black) so you can choose the one that contrasts best against the color of the header.

- **The design.** You can't do too much to the design of your page, but you can customize it enough to make it feel consistent with your website and other social networks. You can do this three ways. The easy way is to pick one of the premade themes, but that won't say a lot about you other than you won't take the time to customize your site. You're able to change the background of the page by uploading your own color or picture (see Figure 7.2). If you want to do that, download one of the many templates available (they're all about 1600 x 1200, with the left column around 200 to 235 pixels) and design it from there. The only stipulation is that it must be under 2MB in size. Lastly you can select the background color and color of all your links.

Figure 7.2: Custom Twitter background to SNEW

That's all it takes for creating a profile that looks consistent with your online look, and provides the right look and information when someone clicks on it.

Using Twitter For Promotion

As with Facebook, just being on Twitter isn't enough; you have to use it properly for it to be successful as a marketing tool. That means it's not just the fact that you tweet, but how and why you do it. Let's take a look.

What Should I Say?

Once again we come to the dilemma of what's worthy of posting, or in this case, tweeting. Here's a quick list:

- announcements
- events
- upcoming gigs
- post-gig comments
- backstage comments
- blog posts
- new song or video releases
- contests
- questions
- fan shout-outs

- current industry news or your views on it
- artist or band trivia

These are just a few ideas about what to tweet about. One of the reasons why tweeting from events works well is because Twitter is all about the latest news, and tweeting from an event is about has fresh as you can get. You also receive the added byproduct of being perceived as an expert as well.

Crafting A Promotional Tweet That Works

As with Facebook, it's how you say it as much as what you say that makes a difference. Let's look at a typical post from the band we're following in this book - The Unsigned.

Rehearsal soon. Need to go to the store to get something to drink. Bottled water is so expensive these days so I'll take Gatorade.

This is only 130 characters long, but just like some of our previous Facebook post examples, it doesn't tell us much that we care about hearing. It's an endorsement for Gatorade perhaps, but that doesn't help your marketing very much. How about this one instead:

At rehearsal in The Cave. Working on two new songs for the next Unsigned record. Producer Joey M with us. bit.ly/U3bbYA

Here we have a nice concise 119 characters that tell us a lot. We find out that the band (The Unsigned) is rehearsing at a place calledThe Cave (the fans my already know what and where that is), that they're working on new songs for an upcoming recording, and that their producer is in attendance. Plus, they've included a link so that you can either see some photos or a video. It's the perfect who, what, when, and why post, complete with a link for more information.

Personally, I always tweet the title of my latest blog post along with a short description and a link like this:

Making Money From YouTube. A new strategy for using YouTube views as a revenue source. bit.ly/u9AvYB #musicmarketing #musicians

This works because of the information that it provides, which is the promise to more info if you follow the link. We have the name of the post, a short description, the link, and then a couple of words preceded by a #, called a "hashtag." That's what we'll cover next.

***TIP**: Even though each tweet has a maximum of 140 characters, studies have found that tweets are more effective if they're less than 120.*

The Hashtag: The Secret Behind Successful Tweets

Hashtags are simply keywords with the pound sign (#) in front of them. It's an unofficial feature of Twitter that's now widely accepted and supported, and is an easy way for people to search for and find a particular topic. It's also the best way to build your Twitter following.

Here's how it works, using one of my own tweets.

The Secret To The Merch Table. Want to sell more merch at gigs? Here's how. bit.ly/7GFjDq #merch #bands

This is a simple tweet regarding a post from my Music 3.0 blog a while back, complete with a shortened URL link. At the end are the hashtags #merch and #bands. That means that anyone who does a Twitter search for those keywords will see my post and follow me if they're so inclined.

Here's another way I could've used the hashtags in this tweet.

The Secret To The #Merch Table. Want to sell more merch at #gigs? Here's how. bit.ly/7GFjDq

In this case I embedded the hashtag directly into the tweet text. This works too but I find it too difficult to read, which can quickly turn into a negative for less sophisticated users that think they're looking at some sort of code they don't understand. Leaving some room at the end for the tags works a lot better.

Here's another example.

Mix Comparison: From Rehearsal To Master. A mix at various stages of production. bit.ly/vjgIUQ #musicians #recording

In this case there are three hashtags at the end, which really isn't a good practice. It's been found that more than two hashtags can actually be counterproductive.

Selecting Hashtags

Now that you know what a hashtag is, you're probably wondering how to select them. Here's how to do it.

Looking back to the first tweet above where both "merch" and "bands" appear in the tweet:

1. I researched the potential keywords first to see what kind of activity each word had by going to search.twitter.com.

2. On the site I did a search for "#merch" and determined that there was a sizable enough result that it was worth using (see Figure 7.3). If the search had brought up less than ten results, I would have tried a different word instead. Since it brought up a few pages of results, I knew that the hashtag was something that was searched for often, reached my target audience, and was therefore a good candidate to use in the tweet.

Figure 7.3: Search for #merch on search.twitter.com

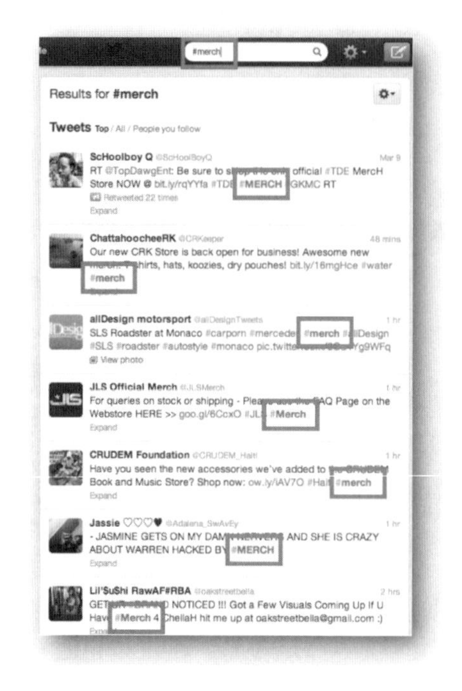

3. One of the other things that comes from a hashtag search is ideas for other hashtags. In this case a number of candidates came up when I tried an alternate - "#merchandise," which brought up alternatives like #bandshirt, #apparel, #tshirts #clothing and #fashion.

***TIP**: Keep a list of potential hashtag candidates. You'll always find a place where some will be more appropriate than others.*

I did the same thing to find the hashtags for the second tweet. I did a quick search and discovered that #highpass had a lot more searches than #high-pass, and #mixing more than #mixer (there was also some confusion with a food processor as well), so those are the ones I chose.

Hashtag Sites

There are a number of sites where you can do twitter searches to come up with the appropriate hashtags.

- search.twitter.com is an all-purpose Twitter search site. If you're looking for any keywords related to hashtags, be sure to place one in front of your search term (like #keyword). If you select "advanced search" you can make your search even more granular.

- hashtags.org has gone through a number of changes over the years. It gave you straight up hashtag info at first, then disappeared for a while, and now provides trending information that gets more granular for a price. It's still worth checking out since you can get a larger picture of how a particular hashtag is being used.

- cloud.li provides a word cloud of keyword alternatives that you can choose from.

- tagcrowd is another word cloud site, but it works either on the text that you input or a website. It then does an analysis and determines a word cloud. You can use the keywords it provides in another search to see how viable they are as a Twitter hashtag.

Remember that a quick look at both the searches and trends before you select a keyword can make a difference in your Twitter traffic, which ultimately attracts new followers.

Other Uses For Hashtags

While you're probably mostly concerned about building your brand by tweeting using hashtags, they do have other uses that are more widely used. Here are a few:

- **Breaking News.** Because Twitter is mostly a broadcast medium, it's excellent for breaking news. As an example, if you can't drive down the street because of a traffic jam, a quick look on Twitter will probably tell you the reason long before you'll hear it on the news. In fact, one of the reasons that the Arab Spring was so successful was because of quick information exchanges through Twitter using hashtags like #LibyaFeb17, #arabspring and #SyrianRevoltion.

Want to know what's happening in a town you're going to? Do a search for #Cleveland (or whatever town) and you'll know in a flash. Want to know the most up to date news on an event, just do a hashtag search for the event and you'll know more than most journalists covering the story. Twitter means instant news, and you can use that to your benefit.

- **Branding**. Movies and television shows now use hashtags as a way of promoting the show and as a gateway to second screen activity. Generally you'll see the # with the name of the movie or show behind it. Of course, this can be used for artists and bands as well. In the case of our fictitious band The Unsigned it might be #Unsigned or #TheUnsigned.

- **Complaints**. Hashtags have become a major way for Twitter users to express their displeasure with something, be it a product or service. This is sometimes known as a "bashtag." An example of this is when McDonalds customers shared their discontent by using the hashtag #McDhorrorStories, which was latter shortened to just #McDstories.

Sometimes a person can show anger at a situation with something like #HateBadService or #AnnoyingWaiters, but these do nothing more than let off some steam unless they begin to be widely used.

- **Comments**. The opposite of a bashtag is a positive comment like #BeautifulDay or #GreatMusic. Once again, these serve no purpose other than to make a point, since they generally don't focus on a specific situation or event.

***TIP**: Stay away from bashtags or anything negative as this can grow out of proportion quickly to the point where you won't be able to control the story. Negative usually begets negative.*

Remember that using hashtags is a great way to help people find you, but *don't forget to include a link* in your tweet to take them to your blog or website as well, since that's the real goal.

Sharing Photos, Songs and Video On Twitter

As with other social networks, rich media such as audio, video and photos usually get much higher engagement than text-only tweets. Here are a number of ways to use rich media in tweets.

Twitter Photo Sharing

Sharing a photo on Twitter is easy. When you compose a new tweet, an icon of a camera will pop up right below the text insertion point. Just click on it to take a photo either with your computer, upload a picture from your computer, or take a picture with your phone. If you have an iPhone, the share button will allow you to post the picture straight to Twitter or Facebook if you have the apps installed. Also, if you're an Instagram member, you can post directly from there as well.

If you have an older iPhone or a different smartphone, you might need to use one of the helper programs like twitpic or Yfrog to post to your account. Regardless which way you do it, posting a picture is definitely worth it as your engagement will increase.

Twitter Song Sharing

It's also possible to share songs as well as photos. There are several apps that can help you do that, but a couple of goods ones are song.ly and blip.fm. With song.ly, you type in a song title that you want to tweet or the link to an MP3, and your followers receive a link to a page that they can listen to the song without downloading it. With blip.fm you choose a song, enter in any information (be careful because you can enter more than Twitter's standard 140 characters), then a blip (a song tweet) shows up in your stream. Of course, you can always just post a link to a streaming site like Soundcloud as well.

Twitter Video Sharing

Twitter recently launched their answer to video, called Vine, and it lets users share video clips of up to six seconds on social networks like Twitter, Facebook and the Vine platform itself.

While six seconds doesn't seem like much, professional broadcasters will tell you that it can be a lifetime, especially where every tenth-of-a-second increment counts. That's why Vine may be the next big social thing, since it makes videos easy to both create and consume, and just like Twitter, is perfect for our short attention span world.

Want a quick look at some vines? You can start off by going to Vinepeek, an unmoderated real-time stream of Vines from all over the world, but if you want to get started posting vines yourself, go to the Apple App Store (it's an iOS app) and download the Vine app.

When you first open Vine, you will be asked to log in either with your Twitter account or email address, then you'll be asked if you want to receive push notifications and to let Vine access your location info. After you've signed in, you'll be taken to a landing page where you'll be served up an editor's choice of Vine feeds until you start following the people that you choose.

To create a Vine, press the camera icon on the top right of the home page, which will take you to a new page that features a camera view, a status bar and and X to exit (see Figure 7.4). To record, hold your finger on the screen, where you'll see the green status bar indicate how much you've recorded. Remove your finger and Vine will stop recording.

Figure 7.4: The Vine camera view.

***TIP**: You don't have to record all six seconds at once. You can record for a few seconds, stop, set up for a new shot, then record again for sort of a stop-motion movie.*

After you've finished recording you can preview what you've shot and choose to keep or delete it. You're then able to share it on Vine, Twitter or Facebook. Remember that if you choose to share on Twitter or Facebook, you also have to share it on Vine as well. If you don't choose to share it, you can save it anyway as a "camera roll," otherwise, all Vines are public. You can also choose to add a caption.

Not to be outdone, Facebook's Instagram has answered with up to 15 seconds of video, which can be also be directly shared on Twitter.

These short videos can be a lot longer than you think, but still short enough that people are much more likely to watch than a regular movie.

Tweet Frequency

Tweets don't live very long. Although the lifetime of a tweet is two hours at most, 92 percent of all retweets and 97 percent of all replies happen within that critical first hour. After that, they're as good as gone. That's why you may want to repost a tweet a second time if it's an important announcement. You'll probably have a completely different audience in the morning than later in day, so this is a strategy that can work without disturbing your followers too much.

What I usually do is post a tweet in the morning and repeat it later in the day, only with a different set of hashtags. That way, a tweet can have twice the potential reach to new followers. I also make sure that there's at least four hours between repeated tweets.

The Best Time To Tweet

If you're using social media for promotion, then you already know that the timing of when you post is critical to your success. Do it when most people are busy and not paying attention and you'll never get your message in front of them.

Chapter 6 illustrated that the ideal times for Facebook posts were at 11AM, 3PM and 8PM Eastern time. Studies also show that later in the day is the best time to tweet as well.

According to Dan Zarrella, a researcher at Hubspot who looked at millions of tweets and showed their results in a webinar entitled "The Science of Timing," the later you tweet in the day, the better. The reason is that from 2PM to 5PM ET your followers are more likely to see your tweet because there are fewer things demanding their attention. In fact, 4PM was deemed to be the best time of the day. Zarrella also found that weekends are great for tweet attention as people are more relaxed and aren't conflicted by work.

Finally, Zarrella has also put together a nice page called TweetWhen that will analyze your last 100 tweets and tell you when the best times for you to tweet are. Here are some other stats about tweet timing:

- The most click-throughs come between 1 to 3PM EST Monday through Thursday.

- Not much happens after 8PM weeknights.
- Peak traffic time is from 9AM to 3PM EST Monday through Thursday. That doesn't necessarily mean that you'll get more responses though, since there's already a lot more competition for attention.

I have personally found that the best times for me to tweet are 7AM, 11AM, 2PM, 4PM and 8PM ET on weekdays. I've also found that 1PM and 5PM can be effective on the weekends, although Sunday is better for engagement than Saturday.

That said, Twitter is a dynamic medium that should be used that way. If there's something exciting happening, it might not always be possible or wise to wait for the so-called best times to tweet. There are certain announcements, like for a gig or a song release, that work best if they're scheduled for the best time of the day, and these are the ones that you time to make sure you get the most people viewing.

Scheduling Tweets

Since there are posts that work best if they're scheduled for the best times of the day, it's important to find a way to do that without disrupting your life. That's where a scheduler comes in. As with Facebook, posting your tweets at the right time is an crucial component in how many people you reach. And like Facebook, it's probably not feasible that you'll be available at exactly 4PM to send that tweet out. That's why it's vital that you schedule your promotional tweets, and once again there are many ways to do that.

One of the most popular platforms for this is Tweetdeck (see Figure 7.5), which is available both from your browser and as a stand-alone app. I like the browser version better as the app seems to take up a fair amount of computer horsepower, but you'll find it's features are similar to Hootsuite or any of the other social media schedulers. Yet another one that works great is Socialoomph, and like the others, they have both a free and a paid version.

Figure 7.5: Tweetdeck timelines

While a scheduler makes it possible to send the exact same message to Twitter and Facebook, that can cost you followers either on Twitter or Facebook as no one wants to see the same post repeated on different social networks. It is okay if you slightly change the post though, as that will get you double exposure without it feeling too overbearing.

***TIP**: If you post a tweet on Facebook, make sure that you don't use a shortened URL or include the hashtags.*

Twitter Measurement

As with everything online, it's possible to measure how well you're doing on Twitter, although the measurement details can sometimes raise some eyebrows because of the differences between measurement tools. That's why it's best to look at the trends more than any actual scores that the following services provide. If you see a metric suddenly jump up or down, you want to know why. Likewise, if you see something trending up or down month over month, then it's time for some real analysis. Here are a few measurement services to check out.

- **Klout**: Klout gives you a score based upon the total action from your Twitter, Facebook, Google+, Foursquare, Instagram and Linkedin accounts. You're able to see the approximate number of mentions, retweets, followers and lists you receive, as well as a 90 day history.

- **Topsy**: Topsy is another measurement tool that has some free elements, but for anything granular it will cost you. It's great for searching trends, hashtags, and just about any other social detail, and the Pro version can give you exact counts of mentions, sentiments, impact and trends.

- **Trackur**: Trackur is another tool that provides social influence and sentiment analysis for a price. It looks at all social platforms, not just Twitter.

- **Kred**: Kred is pretty cool in that it looks at your entire social community and scores you on your influence. It gives you a 30 day follower count, shows influence and outreach, and shows your top locations and communities, among other things. You can also look at the Kred scores of others globally, check out the scores for books, movies and TV shows, and see what your friends are scoring. It's free for now.

- **Tweetstats** analyzes your tweets over time and is a good way to look at your personal stats in a nice graph.

Useful Twitter Tools

Here are a few helpful Twitter tools that can help you get a handle on social media management. These tools are free and easy to use.

- Trim the fat with TwitBlock. TwitBlock scans your followers and looks for signs of spam, assigning the most suspicious ones a number rating based on a set of predefined criteria. The higher the rating, the more likely the follower is a spammer, and you can choose to block or unfollow them.

- With Tweriod, timing Is everything. Just like with all your other social tools, when used for promotion, you want to send tweets at a time when they'll reach the most people. Tweriod analyses the tweeting habits of your followers, then suggests the best time for you to tweet.

- Twellow is a Twitter yellow pages directory. It's interesting in that if you search for a keyword, you'll see users that use that keyword in their profile based on who has the most tweets.

Social media can be time consuming so anything that helps relieve that burden a bit is welcome to most of us. Try these tools out to make your Twitter promotional experience a little more efficient and easier.

Twitter Commerce With Chirpify

For many artists, Twitter is a great tool for promotion, but the problem until now was that you couldn't easily use it for commerce. Now a platform called Chirpify provides that ability.

The way it works is that the artist uploads the content listing to a Chirpify dashboard, then click's to tweet using a hashtag that the company calls an "actiontag." If the fan sees the tweet and wants to respond with an instant purchase, she simply replies to the tweet with the actiontag attached. Chirpify recognizes the response, then sends a secure download link via a direct message or an email to download digital content, or places the order for merch or even a ticket.

As soon as the can connects her Twitter account and PayPal or credit card accounts via Chirpify, the sale happens. If the fan is already registered, there's no need to register again.

Chirpify takes a reasonable 5% commission plus a transaction fee of $.30 along with any PayPal fees, although the company has flat monthly pricing for labels or major users. It's currently begin used by artists as diverse as Green Day, Snoop, and Tim McGraw.

One of the big early users has been Amanda Palmer (there's that name again), who recently sold about $19,000 worth of T-shirts in 10 hours using the service. If you're a big Twitter user, take a look at Chirpify. It just might be another revenue source.

Using Contests To Increase Your Followers

Photographer Scott Bourne uses an old idea to increase his Twitter followers by frequently holding a contest to win a high-end Canon camera. All you have to do is follow him on Twitter, and send out only a single tweet regarding the contest.

Scott asks his contest entrants to tweet only once in order to observe Twitter etiquette and avoid spam, and is very careful to spell that out on his entry page. He's also careful to spell out any possible problems that might occur either because of the entrants location or ethics.

The contest is a very clever use of social media, but it's clearly only part of Scott's strategy. He wants to raise his follower numbers, then be able to market to those followers later. He might not even want to directly market to them, instead just informing them and keeping them close as fans and market to them through his web site or blog. Either way, the contest is a winner.

Twitter Tips And Tricks

Now that you've read about all the ins and outs of Twitter, let's summarize with 20 tips and tricks:

1. Set up your profile. Your bio should include who you are and what you tweet about.

2. Be sure to use a photo of you, not a baby picture, celebrity or avatar.

3. Include your website or blog link in your profile.

4. Use fewer than 120 characters in any tweet for greater response.

5. Place a link in every tweet.

6. Don't use more than two hashtags per tweet.

7. Stay away from bashtags or anything negative.

8. Use link shorteners like Bit.ly, Tinyurl, or Ow.ly to make more room for text and links.

9. Use a Twitter client like Hootsuite or Tweetdeck to see all your Twitter feeds in one place and obtain Twitter analytics.

10. Don't worry about your number of followers. If your content is good, they will come.

11. Find your favorite brands/bands/artists/companies on Twitter and follow them. Tweet them your feedback.

12. Find people talking about your band, music or brand and follow them.

13. If someone mentions your brand/company/you, be sure to respond.

14. Set up Google Alerts for topics of interest to tweet.

15. Tweet live from events. Tweeting from events keeps your followers and positions you as an expert.

16. Balance tweets, replies and retweets. Too much of a good thing is too much.

17. Tweet photos. A picture is worth a thousand words.

18. Don't feed the trolls. You'll always find a person who wants to pick a fight. Don't get in the ring.

19. Whenever someone mentions you, add them to a "Fans" list. Follow them closely and tweet them separately about gigs, videos and song releases.

20. If you use Hootsuite, create a search stream for any mentions of your band, song or video, including any misspellings.

***TIP**: Make sure that you add a "Follow Me" Icon to all your online pages to give people outside of Twitter a chance to follow you.*

8

Setting Up A Blog

A blog is one of the best ways to keep a consistent dialog with your existing fans while building a larger audience, and it's even possible to make some money at it as well. Blogging is an especially useful venture if you have strong opinions, are an expert at something, or have significant experience in an area. That said, building a successful blog does take time, and, like most other ventures online, depends upon how and when you do it.

Blogging Overview

A blog is an in-depth text broadcast. Think of it as talk radio, only with text. You broadcast your idea (a post on your blog), then if it catches the attention of enough readers, people respond and comment. Just like radio and television has Arbitron ratings to show how many people are tuning in, the number of page views each post gets is your ratings system.

Depending upon how serious you are about it, blogging can be a part of your online strategy in many ways. If you're a prolific writer who has a lot of expertise in a particular area (musicians have lots of expertise in music, travel and recording), you can share what you know. It can also be used as a way to keep fresh material on your website, or as a place for more extensive communication with your fans.

A blog is an excellent way to say a lot more than what's possible in any kind of social media. You have way more than the 140 characters Twitter makes available to you, way more than is appropriate for Facebook, and is much more accessible than a YouTube video, since most people would rather graze through text then wait for a video to end.

Blogs provide a greater ability than social networks to add graphics and photo galleries, the ability to have multiple pages of background material, and a way to easily access archives to your posts. Simply put, a blog doesn't replace another social media platform, but a social media platform can't replace a blog either.

Blogging Platforms Overview

Right now there are four major blogging platforms; Wordpress, Blogger, Typepad and Tumblr. While various website software packages have their own blogger tools that you can also use, the big 4 are specifically designed for blogging, and as a result they have more tools and provide far greater control than some blog add-ons that come with a website package. That's not to say that much of what we'll talk about won't apply if you're using a blog add-on to your website, since the essence of this chapter works on any platform, it's just that a dedicated blogging platform has a variety of advantages that are worth using when you're starting out.

Blogger

Blogger is owned by Google, is dead easy to set up and use, and is free. The service is hosted on Google's servers, has a number of attractive templates to choose from, and is easy to post and update. You can use the blogger URL (i.e. bobbyowsinski.blogspot.com) or have your own URL mapped over it (i.e. yoursite.com) for a $10 per year fee. There's also hundreds of widgets available that allow you to insert anything on your blog from the current local weather to eBay listings to the joke of the day in order to keep a steady stream of fresh content available.

Blogger is my personal blog of choice and the host for both my Big Picture production blog and Music 3.0 music industry blog for five years and nearly 2000 posts (see Figure 8.1). The reason why I chose Blogger is that when I first started blogging, the platform felt the easiest of the the Big 3 blogging services (Tumblr wasn't available then). I'm not so sure that's the case today, but in the name of continuity and consistency (both of which are important blog qualities as you'll see), I continue to use it even though some of the others may offer more.

Figure 8.1: The Blogger post entry page

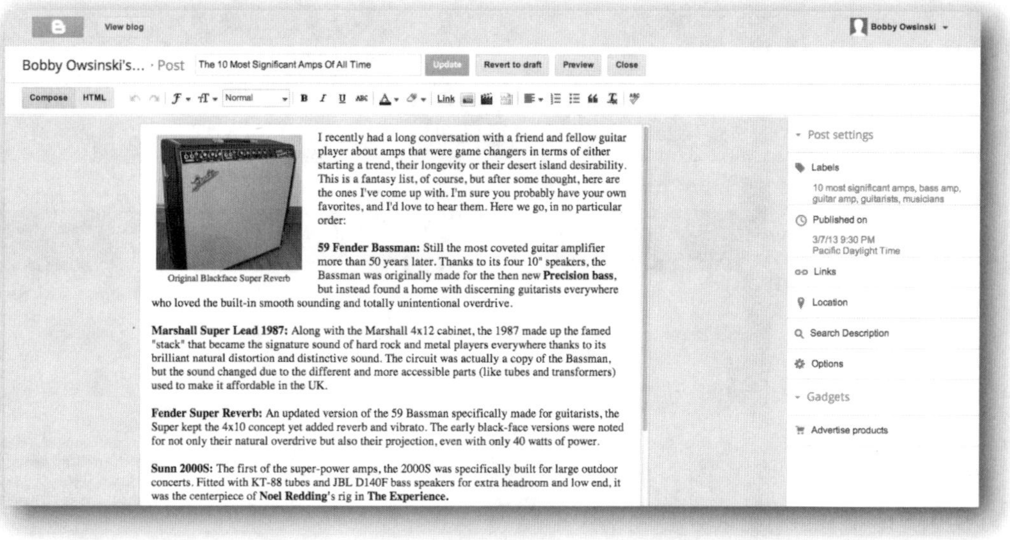

Wordpress

Wordpress is the most popular blogging platform in the world with over 66 million users, and continues to gather users thanks to the constant improvement of its many features. It has a bigger infrastructure of features, templates and widgets than the other blog platforms, and it's also possible to host it directly on your server instead of using the Wordpress host service (see Figure 8.2). The way this works is that anything that's "consumer" oriented is hosted at Wordpress.com and has a wordpress.com extension (i.e "yourname.wordpress.com"), while the software with the pro features and support is available at Wordpress.org. From that site you can download the software so that Wordpress can be installed on your web host (many web hosting platforms already have it installed), which will give your blog your personal URL (i.e. "yourname.com").

Figure 8.2: The Wordpress post entry page

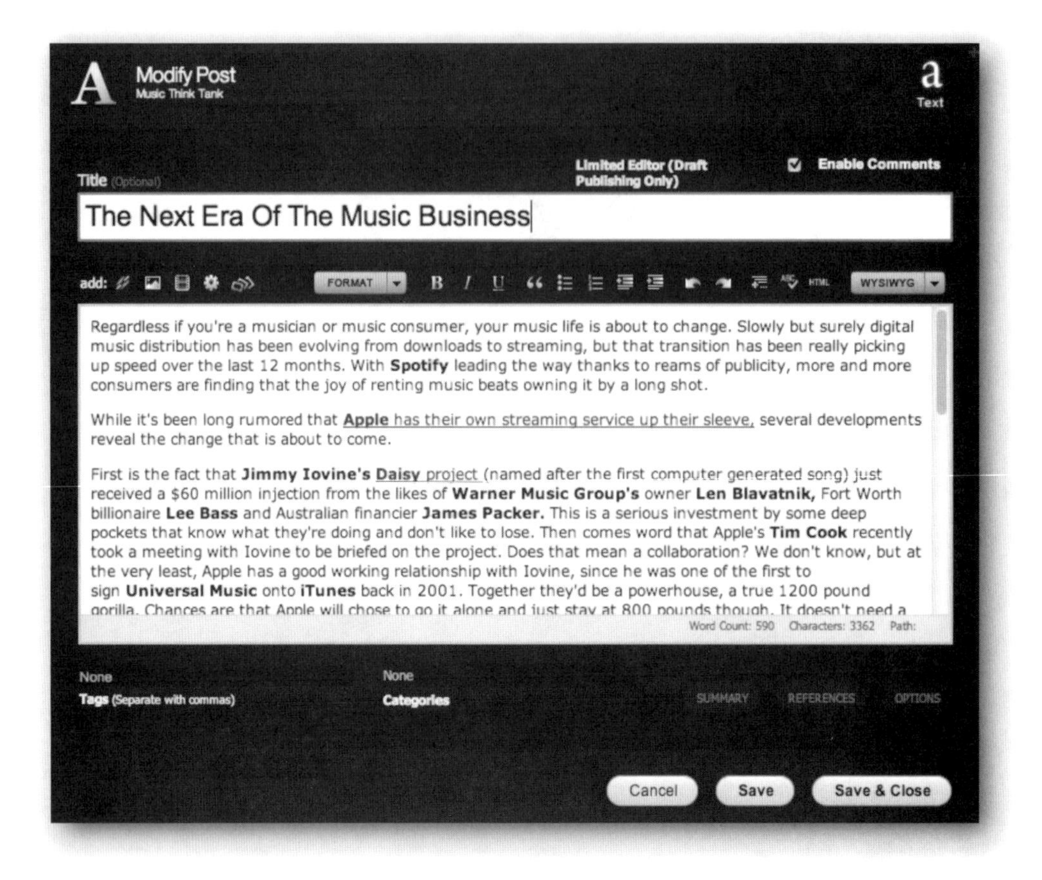

One reason that many pros choose Wordpress is that even though Blogger is owned by Google, Wordpress blogs seem to consistently rank higher in Google search rankings.

While using the services of Wordpress.com's blog hosting is about as easy as using Blogger, setting one up from scratch using the hosted Wordpress software can be tricky. Although there are plenty of templates that you can buy that seem like they're an out-of-the-box solution, that's usually not the case, so be prepared to spend some time learning how to make things look and perform the way you want. There are plenty of good tutorials that can be found on YouTube and the web, but I've found the ones on Lynda.com to be particularly good. You can go to lynda.com/trial/bowsinski for a free seven day trial.

***TIP**: Be careful when buying a Wordpress template since the features you may want may be available only in the "Pro" version of the package, which can cost considerably more than you expect to spend.*

Regardless of which version of Wordpress that you use, the price is right, as in free. That's not to say that it's cost-free however, since getting the exact look and features you want will cost you either in time, the cost of a template, or hiring the help you need to make it work.

Typepad

Typepad (see Figure 8.3) is more of a business platform in that it's very easy to add monetization modules, it has a great user interface, and its look can be programmed from the ground up. The down side is that it will cost you anywhere from $8.95 to $29.95 per month for the privilege of using the platform, as well as having to pay for the services of someone to program it for you if needed. That said, Typepad has amazing support from real live people, while the other platforms basically rely on forums to answer your questions.

Figure 8.3: Typepad post entry page

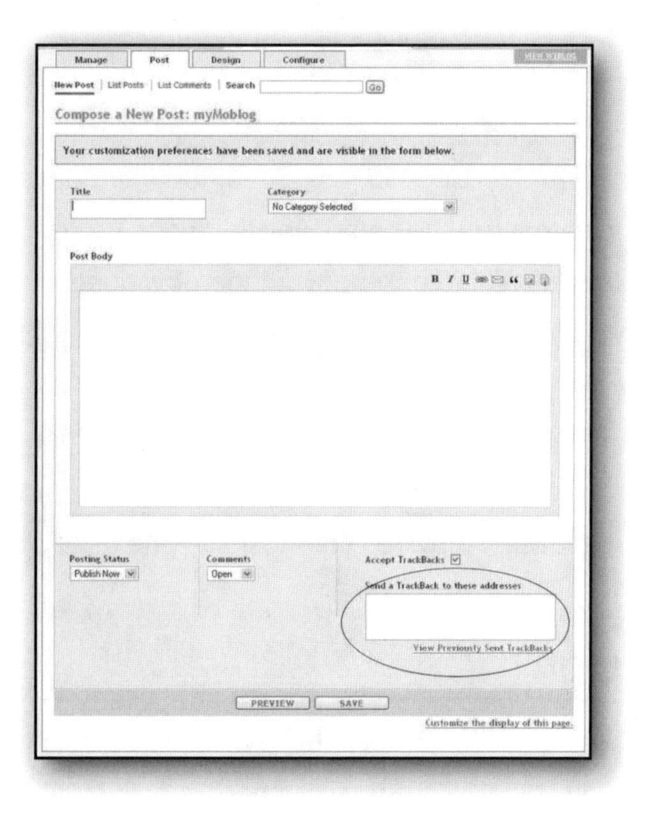

If you're new to blogging, you're much better off starting with either Blogger or Wordpress to get your feet wet before transitioning to Typepad. This is for pros only.

Tumblr

Although the newest in the game, Tumblr has rapidly risen to become the blog platform of choice of millennials. That's because it's the fastest and easiest to set up, but that's at the expense of looks and features. Actually, Tumblr is more accurately defined as a microblogging site that straddles a social media site. That means that the posts are shorter and actively encourage personal communication with the reader.

While Tumblr is widely used, it has far fewer features than any of the other platforms, plus you're not allowed to monetize it, which is a non-starter for a business. What Tumblr really is good at is that it's very personal and intimate, and if you want a younger audience, this is a good way to get it since they've embraced the platform with vigor. That can also be a downside as well, but it all depends upon the demographic of the fans you're trying to reach.

All Tumblr blogs look and feel the same, even though you can skin them differently in the same way that your Twitter page can be customized. You also don't have the advantage of widgets or Google Adsense advertising to make money, but what you do have is quick and instant communication.

What's interesting is that many pro bloggers host their professional blog on one of the other platforms, yet keep a personal one on Tumblr because it provides the most intimate of all blog engagement.

Blog Design

While continuity between your website and social media is important, your blog is one place where the content is truly king. As a result, it's better to get started blogging immediately using a plain vanilla template than to wait until you create the perfect design. Because of the way blog platforms are implemented, your custom design can be inserted at just about any time. That said, you still do want to brand it so it's consistent with the rest of your online presence.

Even with their most basic templates, most blog platforms give you a wide variety of looks and functionality to choose from. Among the things you can modify are the appearance of:

- The blog header
- The navigation bar
- The layout of the page
- The color of the text on the header, sidebar or posts
- How many posts appear on the page
- If the entire post will be viewed or only a portion
- The background color of both the header, the page, and behind the text
- Insertion of widgets (limited function apps within the page)
- A blog roll (links to suggested blog)
- Your blog archives
- Your other websites or those that you recommend

These are just the tip of the iceberg, as you'll find a host of different features that you can customize with each template (see Figure 8.4).

Figure 8.4: The Blogger layout page

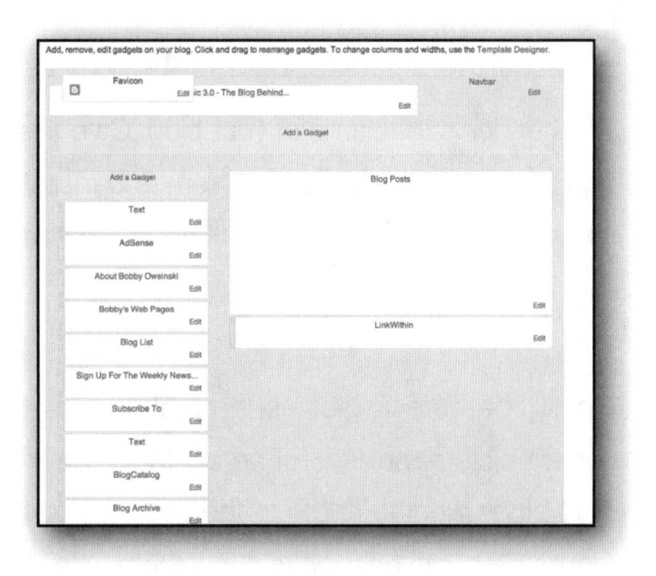

The design of your blog isn't critical for it to be a success, but it does help your branding if the design is consistent with your website and social media presence. That said, it's better to have a blog presence immediately than to wait until you get the design just right. It's easy enough to tweak the design later as you go along. Let's look at the major elements that go into designing your blog.

The Template

After you register for the platform, the first thing you'll have to do when setting up your blog is to choose a template. This can take a lot longer than you think, as most platforms have dozens to choose from, as well as many variations on each. Plus, each can be modified in terms of style, color and placement of the elements. Most likely you won't find exactly what you're looking for, but choose something that's close and modify it as needed.

Those modifications can be quick and easy or can be down to the html and CSS level if you have the chops. In order to get started, just get something that puts you in the ballpark first.

Layout

The layout consists of the elements that you'll be using and where they're placed on the page. On some platforms, this is easier than on others, but once again, trying to get it in the ballpark just so you can get started.

Header

The header is the name of your blog. Give this some thought as it may stay with you for a long time. Also remember that it's best if your name or the name of your band is involved, if not in the header name, than in a subtitle.

Profile

Finally, be sure to set up a profile page. Make sure you have a real current picture, not one of an avatar or when you were a kid. People that read blogs want to relate to the author, and they can't do that if you don't feel comfortable enough to show them who you are.

Your RSS Feed

RSS stands for Really Simple Syndication and allows people to easily stay informed by retrieving the latest content from the sites they're interested in. These posts are read through what's known as an RSS reader, which can be either a stand-alone app or built into your browser. This saves time by not needing to visit each site individually or joining each site's email newsletter, and allows someone to review a large amount of information in a short amount of time. For a publisher (you, the blog owner), feeds permit instant distribution of content with the ability to make it "subscribable." RSS feeds use a universal icon as seen in Figure 8.5.

Figure 8.5: The universal RSS feed icon

Most modern web browsers handle RSS feeds, but in a limited manner. They use an RSS feed as a dynamic bookmark folder with automatic bookmarks to all the news in the feed. Unlike news aggregators, browsers will not save the news if you don't check on it every day.

Even though RSS has been the standard for web feeds for a considerable time, it's often confusing and uses non-standard conventions due to its scattered development over time. As a result, a newer syndication standard called ATOM was created in response to the design flaws of RSS. Essentially both RSS and ATOM do the same thing, but ATOM does it better and is designed to be somewhat future-proof. If you have a choice of which standard to use, choose ATOM, but don't lose any sleep over it if that choice is not available.

RSS feed URLs look something like this:

Atom: http://blogname.blogspot.com/feeds/posts/default
RSS: http://blogname.blogspot.com/feeds/posts/default?alt=rss

In this case, we're looking at feeds from the Blogger platform, but substitute "wordpress" for "blogspot" and it looks the same for that platform (see Figure 8.6).

Figure 8.6: The RSS feed from Blogger

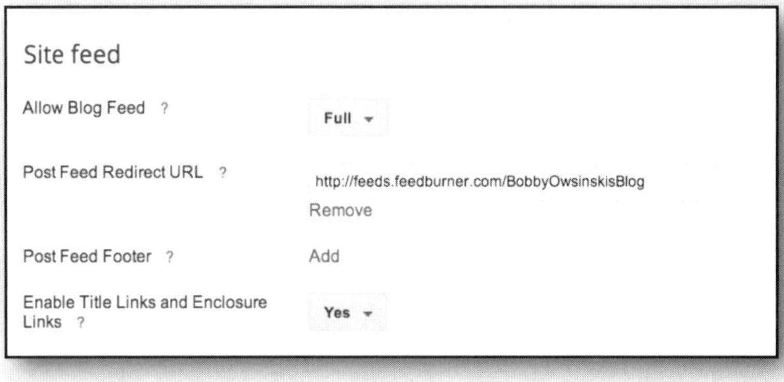

FeedBurner

Google Feedburner is a feed management service that makes your blog feed easy to subscribe to. Once you sign in from your Google account, you claim your feed by simply typing in your blog address. In most cases, Feedburner automatically extracts the feed address from your blog (see Figure 8.7).

Figure 8.7: The Feedburner feed extraction or "burn" page

You can then add buttons to your site, like a subscriber button, a generic RSS button, or choose from dozens of others such as ones for Google Reader, Netvibes, Bloglines, etc. Just pick the button you want, your blogging platform, and Feedburner provides the HTML code. It's been found that readers are more likely to subscribe if you offer a button for the newsreader they're already using and familiar with, so it helps to give your readers a few options here.

Since Feedburner is a feed management system, it allows you to consolidate multiple feeds into one. This can make it easier for your readers to consume multiple blogs (if you have them) and for you to measure what they're reading. Speaking of which, Feedburner also has a range of analytics available that looks at your subscribers and what they consume and react to.

Feedblitz

Not everyone understands RSS and Atom feeds, and only a fraction of Internet users know what these are and how use them. If you don't provide an alternative mechanism for users to subscribe to your content, you're missing out on reaching over 80% of your potential audience.

A very convenient service that aggregates your posts and sends them to your followers in an email is Feedblitz. Since many people don't want the hassle or complexity of dealing with a feed subscription, receiving these posts by email works perfectly well for them, and that's what Feedblitz does. It puts a subscription box on your blog where people can sign up to get an email with all your posts from the previous day or week.

Feedblitz handles the post summaries for nearly 100,000 blogs and allows for a pretty good level of interactivity and analytics. It watches over your email list the same as the email services described in Chapter 5, allows you to set when the email is sent and what's in it, and handles multiple sites (see Figure 8.8). While all this used to be free, now the prices are similar to other email services in that they're based on the number of active subscribers on the list.

Figure 8.8: The Feedblitz dashboard

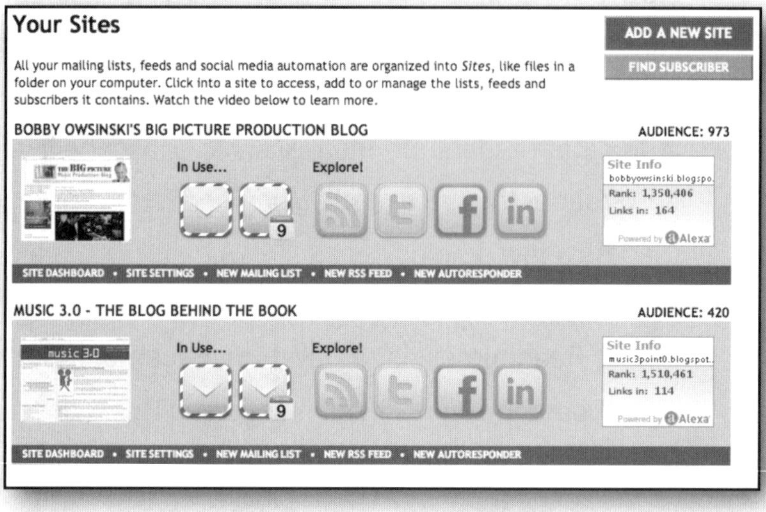

The fact is, if you already have a mailing list provider, you can probably arrange for it to do the same thing as Feedblitz. Just check that it will work with an RSS feed and you're good to go. If not, give Feedblitz a try at feedbiltz.com.

What To Write About

Just creating a blog for the sake of having a blog probably isn't a good idea. You want to be doing it because you have more to say than can be properly handled by your social media platforms. If you're an expert in a subject, that should be pretty easy because you probably have a lot of ideas regarding the current state of your business, it's future, and the topics of the day. If you're a musician, you probably have plenty to blog about as well. Typical topics might be about:

- **Life on the road.** A look at the various towns, venues and the people you meet while traveling from town to town.

- **Life in the studio**. Behind the scenes in the studio, the personnel you're working with (the studio manager, the engineer, assistant, etc.), how a song was written and developed, what kind of instruments or mics you used, how long it took to record and mix, and a million other things that so many people find interesting.

- **Life in the business.** The music business continues to evolve and you probably have lots of thoughts on piracy, streaming, ticketing, 360 deals, record labels, management and everything else that goes on behind the scenes.

- **Life outside the business.** Maybe you're a runner, a vegan, a skydiver or a baseball fan, and you want to discuss these issues as well.

- **Topics of the day.** Maybe you're politically charged. If so, follow a site like Politico (or Fox News on television) and give your take on some of their articles or commentaries. If something like GreenTech is your thing, then set up a Google Alert for every time that's mentioned in the news in order to keep your readers up on the latest advances (see the next section for more details).

As I mentioned previously, I write two blogs five days a week and that means I always have to have something to say, even when I think I have nothing. Here are some tricks I use:

- **Post a video.** Go to YouTube and find a video that you think your readers might like. Embed it into your blog (click *Share* below the video, then *Embed*, copy the code and paste it into the html of your blog), then write a brief take on what you liked or didn't like, or about some of the special things to notice when watching.

- **Follow some newsmakers on Twitter or Facebook.** Perhaps there's a site you really like that constantly has posts and articles that might be relevant to your blog. Follow them on social media (or just read them every day), then either use their topics for ideas to write about, or quote a portion of an article in your post.

***TIP**: Don't directly copy an article and use it as your own. It's misleading, dishonest and a form of piracy. If you do copy something or use a portion, be sure to provide a link back to the original post and give profuse attribution to both the site and the author.*

- **Keep a list of topics handy.** Whenever I see something that I think might be useful to my readers, I immediately copy the link and create a quick draft post that isn't published, but I can come back to at a later time. That way, I always have about ten topics that I can refer to if one day I come up dry, or I know I'll be traveling or in the studio and won't have time to create something new.

- **Create a Google Alert.** A Google Alert is a short post that Google will send you whenever a certain topic is posted. For instance, I have one for all of my books, so if someone posts about *Music 3.0*, I get an alert with a link to where it was posted. That way I can follow the link and read the post or article for myself. You can do the same thing with any topic. If your passion is Tibet, you can create a Google Alert for any articles on Tibet. If that's too broad, you can narrow it to "horse racing in Tibet" (be sure to use the quotes to tell Google to use the entire phrase) and just receive alerts whenever something on that topic is posted. Go to google.com/alerts to create and keep track of alerts.

- **Once a month, do a search.** Take a period of time every month (I take about 30 minutes) and do a search about a particular topic. Believe me, you'll have so many links to choose from with so many points of view that you can't but help get ideas for a few posts.

- **Make a list.** People love lists because they're fast and easy to read. Top ten lists are always good (it could be either your top 10 or someone else's), checklists are fun, and "xx (pick a number) best tips" are always good. It doesn't matter how many items are on the list, just that you've made one.

- **Interview someone.** Even if you've run out of things to say, chances are you know someone who has plenty to contribute. Simply interview a friend or colleague for new post material. I used to have a weekly post I called "6 Questions," where I asked the same six questions to a different person every week. The trick here is to have enough questions that you still have something interesting if someone doesn't write too well or feel like writing at all, but not so many as to make it seem like work. Of course, you can always do a live audio or video interview, or do a Google+ Hangout On Air, then post the result on your blog (we'll go over how to do that soon in the Chapter 10 on Google +). The point is, don't limit your posts to just you.

- **Guest Posts.** Speaking of having another voice, you can always open up your blog for a guest post either from a friend, band member, or even an avid reader who posts a lot of comments.

- **Post an excerpt.** I'm an author so it's easy for me to post a short excerpt from a chapter in one of my books, but if you want to write your first book, here's where to start. Begin by posting bits and pieces of your upcoming chapters. If you've written some magazine articles or reviews, you can repost a part or all of them (make sure you get permission if you don't own them yourself).

- **Repost a favorite.** After you've been blogging for a while, hopefully you'll find that your audience is increasing. That means that your new readers probably haven't seen any of your previous posts unless they've gone back and read all your archives (which most probably haven't done). It's okay to post something that you've previously posted, as long as there's been enough time since it was last posted. I like to let at least a year go by. Make sure that you identify it as a previous post.

That's just a few ideas for posting if you go dry. Remember, there's always something to write about if you look around hard enough.

Post Length

Some people get into long, rambling posts that go on for several thousand words. Keep in mind that most readers probably won't stand for that on a regular basis. They don't have that kind of time to spend, and if you've done that amount of work without the help of an editor, chances are you probably could have said the same thing with more impact in about half as many words.

That's why it's best if you keep each post to between 200 to 600 words, especially if you post frequently. These are very digestible bites, and even if a reader doesn't necessarily like the particular post, they don't feel like they've wasted much time after reading it. If you only post monthly or even quarterly (not a good idea, as you'll see), then you can get away with a much longer post, since each one is almost like its own event.

My Writing Method

When I write my books (including this one) I use what I call "The Three Pass Method." That means that in the case of a book, each chapter gets at least three writing passes. I've found this to be so successful that I use the same method for writing everything, as well as for other types of creation as well. Here's how it works.

Pass 1: Stream of consciousness. The first pass is totally stream of consciousness where I don't worry about spelling, punctuation, grammar or anything else. All I want to do is get the ideas on the paper (figuratively speaking, since I'm using a computer) before I forget them. You are not looking for, nor care about, perfection.

Pass 2: Refinement. The second pass is refinement, where I go through and fix all the things that I let slide during the first pass. This is where I pound sentences into understandable paragraphs, insert the correct punctuation, and fix all the spelling errors.

Pass 3: Polishing. The third pass is polishing, and this is where I go through the entire chapter after everything's been fixed and do any final tweaks that the text might need. Usually at this point you can notice if a sentence doesn't make as much sense as you originally intended, or if you're failing to get your point across in a paragraph.

Sometimes I may go through a fourth or fifth time as well, but never more than five, because by that time, I'm just making things different and not necessarily better. I make sure that each of these passes are on a different day to make sure that I have time to get away from the project and clear my head to get a fresher perspective on things.

Applying The Method To A Blog

I use a condensed version of this method for writing my blogs, since I don't have the time to wait three days for three different passes. It's not as effective as my book-oriented three day method, as some errors still slip through, but it's surprisingly efficient.

What I do is write my first pass in a stream of conscious manner to just get the ideas down, then I immediately do a second pass to tighten things up. I always try to post a photo with every blog, so the time I spend looking for something appropriate is enough time for me to get away from the blog to look at it somewhat fresh when I come back to insert the photo in the post. At this time, I do one last pass to make sure everything looks okay and tweak wherever it's needed. I may make a fourth pass later in the day if I feel that I didn't get something right or some new information presents itself, but that doesn't happen often.

All told, each post takes me from 15 minutes to an hour to create, depending upon the complexity (really complex ones like my song analysis posts can take longer). That said, the time is about half of what it was when I first started blogging, and the same will happen to you as well. Experience will make you faster.

Photos In Posts

Just like on Facebook or Twitter, a photo inserted into a blog post can result in an increased number of views. This doesn't have to be a recent photo or even one that you took yourself, it just has to relate to the post. Of course, a graphic designed in Photoshop or another graphic design program can have the same effect as a photo.

If you're tempted to do a Google graphic search and use a photo off the web, keep in mind that if you use a picture without permission, somewhere down the road you may be asked to either pay a fee or delete it from your site.

There are a number of sites that provide royalty-free images with no or low-restrictions, like FreeRangeStock, Pixabay, Unsplash, Photodropper, and 500px.

LinkWithin

A very cool blog widget that shows and links related stories under each post is called LinkWithin. The widget retrieves and indexes all stories from your blog archive, not just recent stories, making them accessible to new or casual readers of your blog who would not otherwise encounter them. The widget links to stories that are relevant and interesting to readers of a particular post, keeping them engaged with your blog, and increasing your traffic (see Figure 8.9).

Figure 8.9: LinkWithin recommendations

The best part is the widget is free and also ad-free. It's available for Blogger, Wordpress (self-hosted) and Typepad, but a version can also be installed on other blog platforms as well. The LinkWithin site makes it easy to install into your blog, and provides instructions to make it appear right below your blog post. It takes about the same amount of time to install it as it took you to read about about it. This widget is well-worth installing since it provides valuable backlinks to your past material.

The Secrets To A Successful Blog

I've been blogging for about five years now, going from a grand total of five views the first week on my Big Picture production blog, to well over 120,000 a month as I write this (the *Music 3.0 blog* is at about 60,000). I blog every weekday (five days a week) every week with no breaks for holidays or vacations. Every night at 9:30 you'll see my latest post, which as you'll see, is one of the secrets to a successful blog. Let's have a look at all of the secrets:

1. Post on a consistent basis. This is the number one most important rule of blogging. Once you decide you're going to blog, your next decision is when and how often you're going to do it. Once that's decided, it's best if you stick with that forever! If you decide that you're going to blog every Tuesday at noon, then you better be sure that next Tuesday at noon a new mussing will be posted no matter what. This is actually pretty easy in that all blog platforms now have a built-in scheduler so you can write your post whenever you're inspired, then have it post at your designated time. In fact, as I write this I'm sitting on the promenade deck of a cruise ship anchored off an island in the Bahamas. I knew I'd have a spotty, expensive Internet connection this week, so I wrote an entire week of blog posts in advance that will post at exactly 9:30PM every night while I'm away.

You may ask why I chose 9:30PM as the my time to post and I'll tell you that when I first started blogging, that was the time when I generally finished writing them. Since I had inadvertently chosen a blogging time, I knew I had to stick with it, so I've been posting at 9:30PM ever since, even though I generally write each post early in the morning.

Why do you need to be consistent? Studies have shown that by losing your consistency, you begin to suffer viewer attrition. If people can't be sure when you'll post, they generally don't check in as often. Think of your favorite television program. If you know that it will be shown every Friday night at 8PM, you set your schedule around that (forgetting for a minute that you can also might be able to watch it on YouTube afterwards). If the network begins to change the time of broadcast (or even worse, the day), then you don't know when to tune in and find something else to watch at that time instead. Same with your blog.

2. The more frequently you post, the better. The way to get regular viewers is to have frequent posts. More posts give you more of a chance to get more readers. I'm not suggesting that you should post every day like I do (that's a hard schedule, believe me), but once a month isn't enough to get any traction either. That said, you have to have something to write about as well, so be sure you have plenty of material to fill up those posts. Once or twice a week is plenty in most cases.

3. Content is king. When it's all said and done, a blog is successful because the content was useful to the reader. It doesn't matter where it came from, if the reader feels that his time was well-spent on your blog, then you'll be successful. That doesn't mean that every post has to be a home run, but you have to have a high batting average, and you will if you take blogging seriously.

Why Blogs Fail

There are five main reasons why blogs never get any traction or can't keep readers after they get them. They are:

1. Inconsistent posting. Assuming that you have something to say, a knack for saying it, and people who want to hear it, the biggest reason why a blog fails is because it's not updated on a consistent enough basis. The more you post, the more likely your blog will find followers. The more consistently you post, the more regularly they'll read.

2. Non-relevant posts. All good blogs have a theme. It can be narrow (my *Big Picture blog* is about music production while my *Music 3.0 blog* is about the music industry) or it could be wide (your daily life, like my friend Quinn Cummings' ever entertaining QC Report), but the fact is that the readers come to your blog expecting a consistent theme. If your posts are suddenly off-topic (say local politics on a hi-fi blog), that's when you see the most reader attrition occur. For a wide themed-blog, that could mean getting too specific too much of the time (post after post about dogs, for example). Find your theme, then stay on-topic as much as you can.

3. Posts that say nothing. Many bloggers get into trouble by posting what amounts to a bunch of words with no point, or posts that add no new information for the reader. Every reader is short on time, and if he feels robbed of that time from reading a post that adds nothing to his life, he may soon become an ex-reader. Have a take, be provocative, or provide a different perception or point of view; anything to make the reader feel that the minutes it took to read your blog were well-spent.

4. Posts that are too negative. Unless your blog is based on something negative (like "the end of the world is coming"), blog posts that are consistently negative turn readers off. It's okay to go negative sometimes, and it's even good for a blog to have some controversy, but post after negative post will usually lose far more readers than it adds.

5. Posts that fan the flame wars. Flame wars are running battles with commenters. Someone will make a comment that takes issue with something you posted, and you take issue back, which leads to the commenter taking issue with your taking issue, and you taking issue back yet again. This goes back and forth and usually changes the subject several times (getting more personal as it goes along) as it descends into something that most readers don't want to follow. Where you really can get into trouble is posting about a negative comment, as that just stokes the war even more. After a few rounds of this, sane viewers run away.

Blog SEO

Search Engine Optimization applies to blog posts the same way that it applies to your website. While a good user experience and great content are still the key to SEO, being aware of a few things can make a difference if someone is searching for you on Google or any of the other search engines (there are well over 100 believe it or not) at some point.

- **The post title:** Ideally you want a title that's short and easy to spell with a keyword in it. Preferably the keyword would be the first word, if possible. That may make for a title that reads badly, but I wouldn't obsess over it, just be aware. The best keyword is one that's both relative to, and can be found in the post.

- **The post body:** Once again, the strongest SEO is when one of the keywords appears in the first paragraph, then between two and three percent of the text. That means that if your keyword phrase is "recording studio" for example, it should appear two or three times per hundred words. If it doesn't, don't worry as your ranking won't drop a huge amount just because of that, but if helps a bit if you remember the rule.

- **The post graphics:** Every picture or graphic should have an "alt" title, which is an alternate title that appears if a browser can't interpret your page and just shows text (see Figure 8.10). As it turns out, search engines love these tags, so make sure that you fill them in.

Figure 8.10: An Alt title

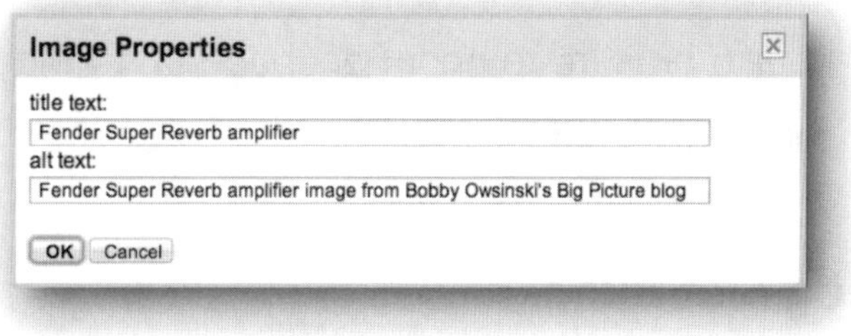

Image Properties

title text:

Fender Super Reverb amplifier

alt text:

Fender Super Reverb amplifier image from Bobby Owsinski's Big Picture blog

OK Cancel

- **The meta tags:** Meta tags are keywords that describe your post. All blogging platforms have the ability to insert these with a post. Not only are they helpful for SEO purposes, but they're useful when doing a search of your archives as well.

***TIP**: Google is taking keywords and meta tags less and less seriously as time goes by, so don't obsess over them.*

Promoting Your Blog

The beauty of a blog is that it works in synergy with all your other social media because there's an element of cross-promotion involved. That means that you can promote your blog via your social media (as well as your website), and promote your social media via your blog.

One of the things that I do is post to both Twitter and Facebook about what I post on my blog. I'll post or tweet the title of the blog post as well as a short description of what the post is about. That way more people are aware of the blog post in general, and the topic in particular if it interests them. Here's an example:

The Band Pre-Production Checklist. Tips to make your band record-ready. bit.ly/vjgIUQ #recording #musicians

Take notice there's a link to the blog, as well as the appropriate hashtags for Twitter. Since the lifespan of a tweet is so short, I usually just insert the blog link instead the individual post link where it shows up on its own page. If I ever repost something from the archive, then I'll use the individual post link.

I'll also be sure to post Facebook and Twitter links on the blog so people can follow me if they like.

Popular Blog List Sites

One way to get your blog noticed is to submit it to some of the popular blog list sites. These are also a great way to find blogs to follow as well. Here's a brief list of the top sites:

- Alltop: Perhaps the grandfather of all blog discovery sites, Alltop is known for its tight topic-based groupings.

- Technorati: One of the biggest blog directories on the web, it has a great keyword search function to help find specific blogs, posts and experts.

- BlogCatalog: A good looking site that regularly features niche blogs that are frequently overlooked on other blog directories.

- Guzzle.it: This is directory that allows you to look for topics that you're interested in. You're also able to display blogs visually, texturally or both.

- Yourversion: Once again, this is a topic-based directory, but it has the distinct advantage of having a nice suite of mobile apps for iOS and Android.

- Paper.li: This site looks at social posts about blogs and allows you to construct what amounts to your own personal online newspaper from the results.

- PostPost: More of a social-oriented site, PostPost delivers all the interesting blog posts and other content that your friends have liked on Twitter.

All of these sites have a submission area where you can submit your blog to be listed in their directory. It doesn't take long (although it may take a few days before the listing becomes active) and can be well worth it when it comes to gaining followers.

Tying Your Blog To Your Website

Regardless if it's your website, blog, Facebook page or YouTube channel, people come back more regularly if there's new material posted. Because it takes longer to redesign a website than almost anything else online, people usually do it a lot less often than they should, but the one way to keep your site refreshed with new material is to tie your blog to it.

This can be done a couple of ways. For instance, you can use the blog's RSS feed to link to a section of your site (see Figure 8.11). The problem with this is that even though your visitors will notice, Google might not, which negates some of the effect of the refreshed content.

Figure 8.11: Using the RSS feed to display a blog on a website (at the bottom)

The other way is have the blog be a part of the home page of your site, with links to the rest of your site. In this case, the blog would have the same domain name as your site (in my case, bobbyowsinski.com). Of course, if Wordpress has already been installed on your hosting site, this can be a little easier to implement. Either way, your site will be refreshed with new material, which will keep viewers returning.

Using A Blogging Platform As A Website

Many web designers have learned that a blogging platform (especially Wordpress) can make a wonderful platform for a website. Blogs originally featured a single page with posts, but through the years they've developed the ability to have multiple pages complete with links from a main page. Now many platforms and templates have become so sophisticated that most of the features of web design software like Adobe Dreamweaver are actually built directly into the blogging platform. These include drop-down menus, rotating banners, tabbed and toggled content, SEO control, and much more.

While using a blogging platform like Wordpress can provide a very quick modern looking website, the reason why many designers like it is because it's also fairly easy for an end user to update when they're ready. The downside is that while a web design app basically gives you a "what you see is what you get" picture of your site before it's published, using a blog platform for a website basically means that you're designing off-line in the abstract, and you only see how it really looks when you publish it (see Figure 8.12). This can take a fair amount of time for a beginner to get the hang of, as it takes some experience to get a feel for what will happen before you actually tell it to do so. A quick way to learn how to program Wordpress to act as a website is through one of the Lynda.com Wordpress courses. Go to lynda.com/trial/bowsinski for a free trial.

Figure 8.12: The control panel for the Elegant Themes Wordpress theme

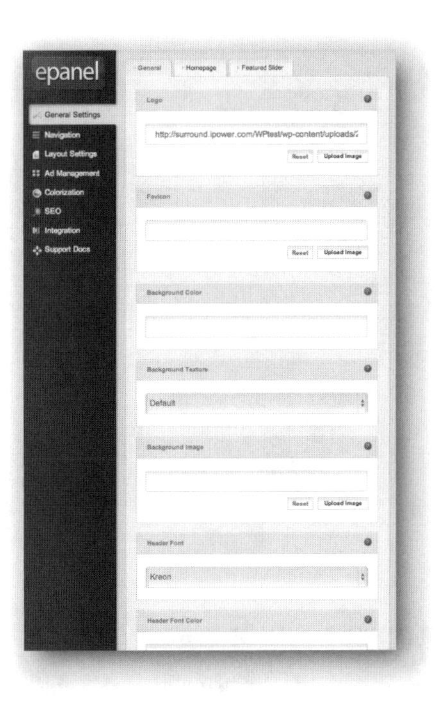

Making Money With Your Blog

Yes, it is possible to actually make money from your blog if you have sufficient readership. To do this, you must decide that it's okay to go commercial and it won't be a hinderance to your audience's enjoyment, since it will require the addition of some ads onto the page. Here are the two main ways that revenue is generated from a blog.

Google Adsense

Google AdSense is a program that allows blog and website owners to host automatic media adverts that are targeted to the site content and audience. These adverts are administered, sorted, and maintained by Google, and they generate revenue on either a per-click or per-impression basis.

You actually have quite a bit of control over Adsense adverts in that you can control the number of ads per page, how large they are, and where they're located (see Figure 8.13). Although Google figures out the general audience that would work best for your content after a few days, you always maintain the ability to block or filter certain ads, advertisers, or certain categories of ads.

Figure 8.13: Google ads in the sidebar and below the post on the Music 3.0 blog

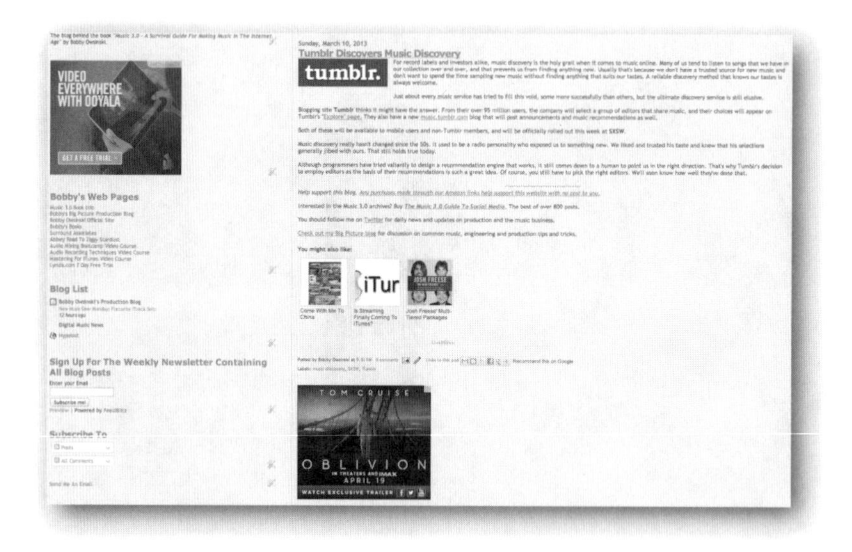

Most bloggers are apprehensive of inserting ads after they've built their following, but it generally has little effect on readership if done in moderation, since most visitors are already used to seeing ads on other web and blog pages. I've found that an ad on the sidebar and another after every second post works well without seeming intrusive.

To sign up for Adsense, go to google.com/adsense. You'll need an existing Google account (which most likely you already have if you have a Gmail account), but you can also use a new Google account as well. After you've registered, you select the sites or blogs that you'd like to monetize, then provide either banking information so Google can directly deposit into your checking or savings account, or a snail mail address so they can send you a check. Google Adsense also provides a nice set of analytics that show how much you make daily and from what source.

Another benefit from Adsense is that you can also set it to insert ads in your RSS feeds and on your YouTube videos (more on that in Chapter 9 about YouTube).

Affiliate Programs

Another way to make money is to be a part of an affiliate program from Amazon, Linkshare, or others. With an affiliate program, a link is placed in the text that takes the reader directly to the product page for more information or a purchase. If a product is purchased, you receive a royalty payment. The more purchases that are made through your site in a month, the more your royalty rate increases.

The best part of affiliate links is that a person doesn't have to purchase only the item that was linked in your blog. Once the reader arrives on the seller's site, any purchase from that point on is credited to you.

I always put affiliate links in a blog post if it's pertinent, especially when one of my books is mentioned. The interesting thing is that each month my books are only between one-third to one-half of the purchases that I receive a royalty on. Considering that both of my blogs pertain to music, I've received royalties on baby carriages, women's apparel, tools, and a host of other decidedly non-music purchases.

Amazon is pretty much a can't miss affiliate in that it sells such a wide variety of items (see Figure 8.14). To register, go to affiliate-program.amazon.com. The registration procedure is similar to Google Adsense. For Linkshare (which is the largest affiliate program other than Amazon), go to linkshare.com. The good thing about Linkshare is that they represent a wide range of businesses, from Macy's to Wine USA to Tiger Direct to Hotels.com and hundreds more. It's also the easiest way to become an iTunes affiliate.

Figure 8.14: The Amazon Affiliate window

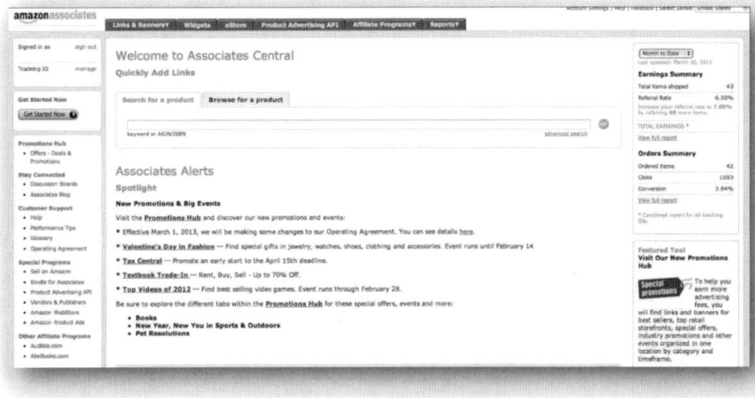

Blogging can not only be one of the most rewarding and fulfilling activities that you can do online, but it can also be a powerful item in your promotional toolbox as well. It's virtually free and easy to set up, and can truly provide a host of benefits if you're willing to follow the recommendations outlined in this chapter.

✦

9

Marketing With YouTube

If a picture is worth a thousand words, then a video is definitely worth a heck of a lot more. That's why YouTube is one of the most powerful networks available for marketing an artist, band, or brand.

YouTube has the ability to visually reach so many people in such a short amount of time that you can almost consider it as a social "force multiplier" (to use a military term) that grows in power every day. As an example, it wasn't that long ago (2009) that singer Susan Boyle had a huge viral hit with what we thought at the time was enormous number of views at 100 million. Fast forward to 2012 and K-Pop singer Psy had the most widely viewed YouTube hit ever with more than 1.4 billion (yes with a B) in less than six months! Chances are good that you'll never hit that number of views, but there's a very good chance that someone might discover your music on YouTube. After all, it's the #1 place after radio where people discover new music.

That's why YouTube is essential to an artist's social strategy, but there's a lot more to it than posting a video and hoping that it will go viral. Indeed, having that happen is like winning the lottery, but in reality, a video doesn't have to have a million views to be effective. Let's look at the various tips and tricks used to make YouTube an outstanding promotional tool.

YouTube By The Numbers

YouTube is a huge behemoth of a network that's grown far beyond anyone's expectations. The following numbers come from YouTube itself and are quite staggering:

- 60 hours of video are uploaded every minute, or one hour of video is uploaded to YouTube every second.
- Over 4 billion videos are viewed a day.

- Over 3 billion hours of video are watched each month on YouTube.
- More video is uploaded to YouTube in one month than the three major US networks created in 60 years.
- 70% of YouTube traffic comes from outside the US.
- YouTube is monetizing over 3 billion video views per week globally.
- YouTube mobile gets over 600 million views a day.
- Over 700 YouTube videos are shared on Twitter each minute.
- 100 million people take a social action on YouTube (*likes, shares, comments, etc*) every week.

Music Discovery On YouTube

According to Accustream iMedia Research, 38.4 percent of YouTube's 1 trillion views were music videos, while streaming services like Pandora reported 8.2 billion hours of radio, Spotify 37 billion, Rhapsody around 7 billion, and Grooveshark at 2 billion.

That means the number of YouTube music views are larger than all other services combined. That's the best reason to place your songs on YouTube, because that's where people look first to find new music, at least currently. What's more, it doesn't have to be an expensive music video and it doesn't have to even be professionally made (although that helps a lot) to be effective.

***TIP**: A video with just the lyrics and the name of the artist as the song plays sometimes works just as well as a full-blown production. When it comes to music videos, the music still comes first.*

Creating A YouTube Channel

Your YouTube presence is composed of both your YouTube channel and your individual videos. Having one without the other is an incomplete strategy that will cost you both brand identification and views. Therefore, if you haven't yet created a YouTube channel, or want to create a different one for your band, now is the time to create it.

To create a channel, you have the option of doing so using a Google identity or creating a new account with a different username. If you have any kind of Google account, whether it be for Maps, Gmail or Google+, that's your Google identity. You'll use the same password that you normally use when signing into one of those products.

Let's say you want to create a new channel for your band that's different from your personal channel. Here's what to do:

1. Click on the icon near your name.
2. Select "Switch Account."
3. Either select another Google account or "Add Account."
4. Create a new channel.
5. Name your channel (hopefully after your band).
6. Select the type of channel (product or brand, arts, entertainment).
7. Select the audience that it's appropriate for.
8. Verify your account.

After your account is verified, sign in with your user name and password and you're ready to begin uploading.

Don't sweat the channel type selection (step 6). It's confusing whether you belong in the product or brand, arts or entertainment categories, as music and your brand cover all three. There's also no evidence that choosing one over the others gets better results, so any choice will do.

***TIP**: Be sure to make a note of the URL so that you can send people to the channel later.*

Optimizing Your YouTube Channel

Just like your Facebook and Twitter profile pages, a YouTube channel page is another opportunity to reinforce your musical branding. There's less flexibility in how you can brand that channel than there used to be, but there are still places where you can get creative.

Branding And Design

There are a number of areas that are available on your channel that enables you to emphasize your own design or brand. Let's look at them:

- **The Channel Art**: The channel art is the banner at the top of the page where you can display a customized graphic. YouTube suggests this graphic be 2560 x1440 pixels so that it works on all types of televisions, tablets, smartphones and computers, but what YouTube will show on most computer browsers is 1546 x 423. This is known as the "safe area" and is where you should place any critical graphics information since anything outside that area might not show up on a device with a smaller screen. The graphic can be up to 2MB and in either a JPG or PNG format. The Channel Art upload section is accessed by clicking on the pen icon on the top right of graphics box, as shown in Figure 9.1. You can access a template for the channel art, as well as a design tutorial, by clicking on "How to create channel art" at the bottom of the upload pop up box.

Figure 9.1: Accessing the Channel Art.

***TIP**: Your channel art should be attractive and consistent with your brand, but don't be afraid to also feature any of the personalities, characters or content of the channel.*

- **The Channel Description:** You access your channel description from the *About* tab underneath your channel name. After the *About* box pops up, select the pen icon on the upper right to edit. From here you can enter or edit the description. Be sure to include all the information about your channel in the description, such as what to expect from the video content as well as who's involved (like the members of a band).

- **Website and Social Media Links**: The website and social medial links are accessed in the same manner as above; through the pen icon on the top right of the box. Here you can add links to websites, blogs and social networks (see Figure 9.2). The first weblink you entered will appear on the lower right side above your channel art, as will the social network icons. The others will appear in the *About* box.

Figure 9.2: The website and social media links editor.

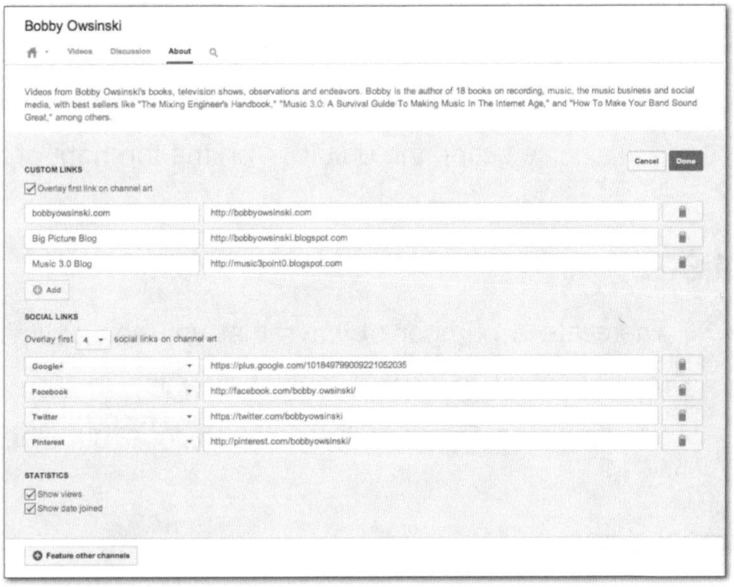

- **Channel Icon or Avatar:** The avatar is either a picture of you, your band, or product that appears on the upper left of your channel page. The avatar can be up to 800 x 800 (you're able to crop it) and 1MB in size, although the smaller the file size the better, since it will load faster. The picture is stored with your Google+ account, and you can also access any pictures stored there to use as your avatar.

- **Featured Video/Trailer:** Another thing that you can do is feature a particular video or trailer at the top of the page when someone who is unsubscribed visits your channel. Simply select the pen icon on the top right of the box, select a video, then hit save. You can see what both subscribers and non-subscribers see by toggling *Unsubscribed trailer* and *Subscriber view* next to the edit icon.

- **Playlists**: YouTube allows you to create multiple playlists, which can have a great influence in how your fans consume your content. If you have a fair number of videos, you might want to create different playlists for different parts of your fan base, since each may have a different desire of what to watch. While your superfans will want to see everything you upload, your casual fans may be more selective. You can select the order and layout of these playlists, or create a new one, by selecting the edit icon on the top right of the playlist box.

Channel SEO

There are a number of ways that you can optimize your channel so it's more friendly to search engines, which in turn will make it easier for people to find. Some of these are obvious, but others are not.

Your Channel Name

The way that most people, artists, bands and brands point viewers to their YouTube channels is by providing a simple URL that looks like this:

http://youtube.com/yournamehere

In my case, my YouTube channel is called polymedia (it's a long story why I don't use bobbyowsinski) so my URL looks like this:

http://youtube.com/polymedia

The problem with this is that both YouTube and Google searches actually look at it like this:

"http://youtube.com/user/yournamehere",
or my my case, "http://youtube.com/user/polymedia"

It seems like such a small thing, but if you add the "user" into the URL yourself, Google ranks your channel higher than if you don't use it. Thus for me:

"http://youtube.com/user/polymedia"
will rank higher than
"http://youtube.com/polymedia"

Reports are that people who have added the "user" to their URL's have jumped in rankings from in the 20's to the top 3. It doesn't look as nice, but if Google likes it better and will rank you higher, that's the way to go.

Keywords

Your channel's keywords can be found in the *Advanced* tab under *Channel Settings* in the Video Manager (see Figure 9.3). Enter 5 or so keywords or keyword phrases that describe your channel, and separate them with quotes. While you're there, select "Allow my channel to appear in other channel's recommendations" so other channels can recommend you as well.

Figure 9.3: Channel keywords found in the *Advanced* section.

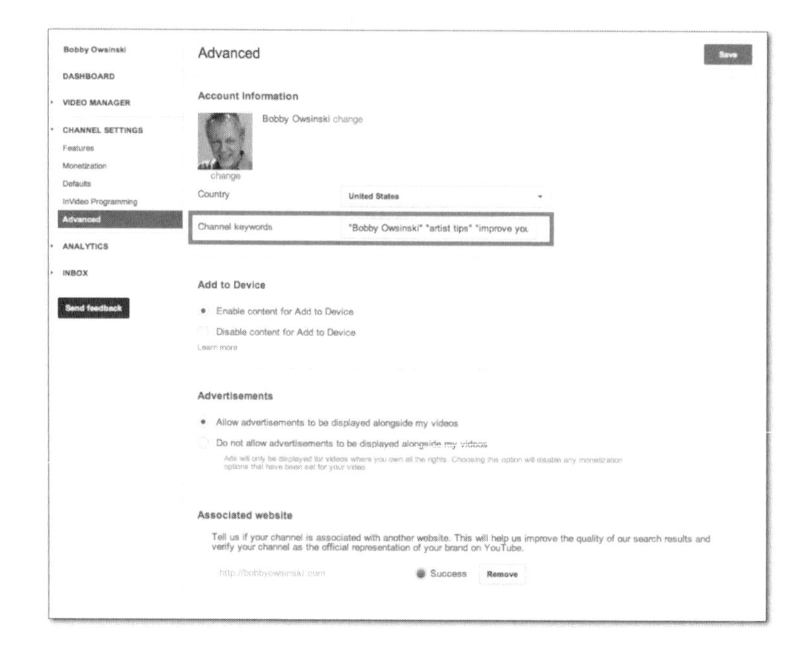

***TIP**: Don't forget to include your band name in the keywords.*

Feature Other Channels

Select "Feature Other Channels" in the *About* box in order to feature related channels on your channel. This is a great way to cross-promote with other similar artists to extend your reach and give your content some fresh ideas. Remember that the channels listed there are also listed as suggested channels when a user subscribes to your channel.

Optimizing Your Videos

There are a variety of ways to optimize your videos so they're easily found either by a Google search or YouTube search (which are basically the same thing since YouTube is owned by Google). While there's an entire science built around this, here are some easy basics that will get you most of the way there.

Video SEO Basics

The title, keywords and description are the basics for good video SEO, yet it's surprising how often their importance is overlooked. Here's what you need to know:

1. Name Your Video Something Descriptive. The title is the most important part of your video SEO. It has to be something that's short, easy to remember, and descriptive all at the same time, which isn't always easy to do. Let's look at a couple of *bad* examples first:

Bad Example: RrkSvle334.mov

Many video editing apps provide default names to movies that might make sense to a machine, but won't help anyone to find the video or know anything about it. The example above is one of those incomprehensible titles that violates the easy to remember and descriptive traits that we're looking for. Here's another bad example:

Bad Example: "The Unsigned Music Video"

Staying with our fake band The Unsigned, we can see that at least we know this video has something to do with the band, but we really don't have any idea about anything else. Here's a better title:

Better Example: "Tomorrow Today - The Unsigned"

This is much better because we now have the title of the song and the artist all in the movie title. This works pretty well for a music video, but what if the band was in the studio and shot a behind-the-scenes video? A mediocre title would be:

Bad Example: "The Unsigned In The Studio"

This is mediocre because it doesn't give us enough information. What was the band doing in the studio? What's the name of the studio? Here's a better way to title it:

Better Example : "The Unsigned Recording At La Grange Studios"

That gives the potential viewer a lot better idea of what the video is about. Sometimes even adding a date to the end can be helpful, although that also places an age on the video, which can be undesirable. That's not all we can do with the title though.

***TIP**: Don't make the title too generic (like "Music Video"), since it won't rank highly as a result. Do make it easy to spell, since it takes Google longer to learn it if it gets typed incorrectly during a search.*

---

2. Choose Your Keywords Based On Your Title. One of the best things about the last title is that there are a lot of keywords in it that we can use as meta tags to make it easier to find. "The Unsigned," "Recording," and "La Grange Studios" are all keywords that we can use as tags, but we can improve the title a bit more with a few more descriptive keywords like:

"The Unsigned Recording Basic Tracks At La Grange Studios"

or

"Recording Basic Tracks At La Grange Studios - The Unsigned"

This is gives us a few more keywords that can be used as meta tags for SEO. Now every word except "At" is a keyword, which makes the title strong not only for the search engines, but for your fans to determine if this is something that they want to watch or not.

***TIP**: Put your most important keyword first in the title if possible.*

---

3. The longer the description the better. One of the most overlooked portions of a video is the description (see Figure 9.4). Not only can this be loaded with pertinent information for the viewer to read, but search engines love it. Each description should contain a full "who, what, when, where and how" that completely explains the video and includes links to the website and social media. Anything from about 75 to 200 words works, although more is better, so don't be afraid to expand on the explanation and include the artist or band member's names, song title, album title, date recorded, date released, record label, and what happens during the video. Also don't be afraid to sprinkle in keywords where appropriate.

***TIP**: The correct ratio of keywords in your copy is around two to three percent, or two or three times every hundred words. A higher ratio may be considered "keyword stuffing" by the search engine and get you penalized with a lessor search ranking.*

---

4. Make sure to include links in the video description. A video without links to your site is an opportunity wasted. You want the viewer to become a fan, so be sure it's easy for him to find more information by including a link to your website and/or social media.

***TIP**: Make sure that your description contains the same phrase as your title. Using our example above, that would mean "Recording basic tracks at La Grange Studios."*

Figure 9.4: The video description

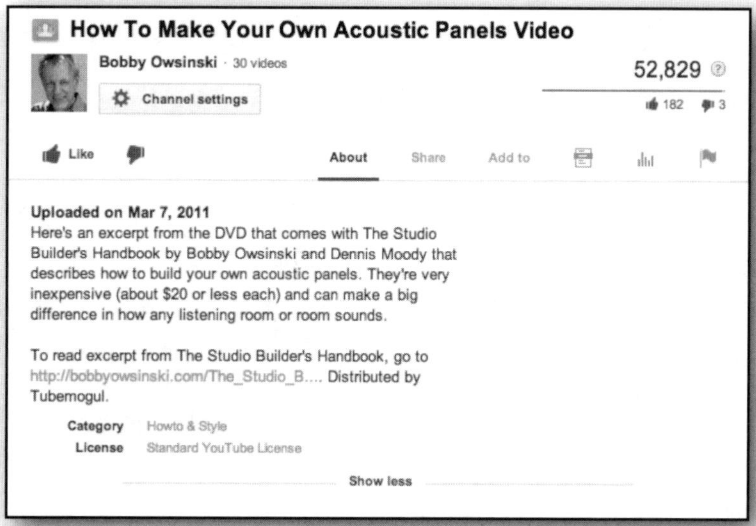

5. Add the proper tags. All of the keywords that you used in the title and description can be used as meta tags, although it's best to try to limit these to between five and seven. More tags aren't necessarily better, as these tags generally don't have that much effect on search ranking anymore anyway. One thing to remember is to make sure that all the major characters in the video are properly identified with tags. That said, misleading tags can cause YouTube to consider the video SPAM, which is something you don't want. You can add or edit tags by clicking on the *Info and Settings* icon (the first one) on the video viewer.

***TIP**: YouTube now also makes tag suggestions, which you can select by just clicking.*

---

6. Create custom thumbnails for your videos. One of the easiest ways to get more views is by having an appealing thumbnail image. When you upload a video, YouTube usually selects three screen grabs from which you can select the thumbnail. The problem is that it's likely that none of these provide an image that instantly tells the potential viewer much about your video. A customized image can now be used as the thumbnail instead of the selections made by YouTube. Here's what to do:

- **Find the perfect still shot.** Search through your original video (the one you had before you uploaded it to YouTube) until you find that one shot that perfectly describes what the video is all about. This might be an action shot, or it could be a close-up of a face or product, or it could be anything that grabs the viewer's attention. Whatever it is, make sure that it's relevant to the video. When you've found it, export it as a jpeg or PNG image.

- **Add text.** Use an image editor like Photoshop or GIMP to add text to identify the video. Make sure that the text is large enough to read easily on a small screen found on a smartphone. The file size should be less than 2MB.

- **Click on the *Custom Thumbnail* icon and upload.** This can be found on the *Info and Settings* page, which is accessible from the first icon (the first one) at the bottom of the video viewer. Viewers will now see your custom thumbnail.

7. Add a link. I'm sure you've seen videos that have embedded links to websites, social media and affiliate stores and wondered how that was achieved. Links can actually be added to a video in a number of ways. The first involves the Annotations feature of your movie, and the other involves using a third party app.

Annotations are the lines of text that show up over the viewing pane of a video. On the bottom left of the video viewer you'll see five edit icon. Go to the fourth one, which is *Annotations*. Once you click on it, you'll see the Annotations editor, which will provide a timeline of your video. From there you can select the exact time, type and duration of the annotation, and then program your annotation so it appears at the exact right spot in the video. At the bottom of the window there's a *Link* selection that will open up the Link window where you can program exactly when that link will appear and the duration it stays on the screen.

The big problem with adding a link this way is that you're limited to links within YouTube, such as a link to another video, a channel, playlist, subscribe, Google+ profile or fundraising project, unless you've selected what's known as an "associated website." The associated website is the only external site that you can link to from within your videos without a third party app.

In order to designate an associated website:

1. Click on the *Channel Settings* icon below your channel name. It will take you to the *Advanced* settings tab.
2. Insert the URL of your associated site, then click verify.
3. After YouTube verifies that your site is real, the green "Success" button will light. You can now link to your associated website.

***TIP**: It's best if you use your website as the associated site, since that's usually where you want to send viewers.*

In order to program a different external link you must use one of the various third party apps available. Not only will these allow you to embed a link, but some can include your RSS or Twitter feed, or create chapters in the video. Some of these include:

- Linkedtube.com
- Viewbix.com

These are pretty easy to use and have free versions that should work just fine for most applications. Note that these third party apps don't work if you want to run ads on your videos to monetize them.

8. Post socially. When you upload a video (or even after it's been uploaded), you can choose to share your video along with your comments to Google+, Facebook and Twitter directly from YouTube. That said, sometimes customized post to your social networks have a much greater affect, so that's something that you might want to consider. Sharing is done on the lower right side of the video's *Info and Settings* page below *Post to your subscribers*.

9. Don't forget the contact info. Always be sure to add your contact info to the end of the video. Even if it's just a website URL, you can't always be sure where someone will view the video, so it's best to have that additional info at the end so that the viewer can get more info if he wants it.

10. Embed your videos. Why have a link that takes people away from your blog or site when you can easily keep them there in the first place? With YouTube, it's so simple to embed a video these days. Just click on the *Share* button beneath the video, then the *Embed* button, copy the code, then paste it into the HTML of your blog or website. It's easy and almost no hassle, since you don't have to worry about uploading a video or any bandwidth limitations that might be imposed by your ISP.

TIP: *Make the video for yourself first. If you're not having fun and enjoying the process, it will come through the camera to your viewers.*

In-Video Branding

YouTube now allows you reinforce your channel branding by placing a custom thumbnail watermark on every one of your videos. Go to the YouTube *Video Manger* link, then click on *InVideo Programming* and you'll find in-video branding under *Channel Settings*. If you want it to look like the logo bug that you see on television, the watermark should be transparent and 800 pixels by 800 pixels. The file format can be JPG (remember that JPG doesn't support transparency), GIF, BMP or PNG, but make sure that it doesn't exceed 1MB.

In the same window you can also select the ability to feature a video within the other videos of your channel. This might work well to alert viewers to your latest release, for example. in this area you're given the ability to select where the video is placed and for how long it will be on the screen during the video.

While these branding features might work in some cases, other times your viewers might think they're excessive. They are convenient though, in that you're able to apply either feature to all your uploaded videos at once.

The Key To Viral Videos

Everyone would love for their video to be like Psy's "Gangnam Sytle" and go viral with millions of views overnight, but that rarely happens. That said, there are a number of generally accepted principles for creating a video that has a chance to go viral:

- **Keep it short.** It seems pretty obvious, but videos have a much better chance of going viral if they're short, mostly because that's what our attention span demands these days.

- **Provoke a response**. You'll see that most viral videos cause you to laugh or gasp. Anything else and your viewers probably aren't going to want to share it with their friends.

- **Be timely.** You have a greater chance to go viral if your content is about something currently popular, although there are perennials like cats and babies that never seem to go out of style.

- **Try humor to keep your viewer's interest**. That said, don't force it since that can be most unfunny.

- **Avoid asking for comments.** One thing that turns people off is asking them to like, share or comment on the video. If they enjoy your video they'll do all of these things naturally and won't need to be cajoled.

- **Don't create a commercial.** Viral videos are hard enough to create, but they're even more difficult if they're constructed like ads. It's true that you're creating a video to promote either an album, a song or your band, but being subtle works best.

- **Avoid Copyrighted Material.** Copyrighted material can stop a video dead in its tracks due to a take-down notice from the content owner's attorneys. You might get away with it; then again, you might not.

- **Seed your content.** Before your video can go viral, you've got to get it in front of influencers. Consider using a viral seeding company such as Sharethrough or Unruly Media to do that for you. Be aware that these services usually charge a per view fee so the costs can rack up, but it's measurable and effective with the right video.

- **Don't create a video because you think it might get views.** Create content that you really care about.

- **Watch other videos for inspiration and tips.** You can learn a lot about what to do, and maybe more importantly, what not to do, from other artists, bands and brand's videos.

- **But be yourself.** You're better at being you than anyone else.

Don't Believe The Half-Life

Even though we'd all like the next huge viral hit, having a viral video isn't the key to promotion after all. Sometimes a clever promotional video that isn't viral in the slightest can be just as effective (or even more so) in getting the word out.

While a study by video distributor TubeMogul found that a typical YouTube video gets 50% of it's total views within the first six days and 75% of the total views after 20 days, the study mostly applied to DIY "novelty" videos, and not to those that are meant to extend your brand. The fact is, many videos gradually gain an audience and continue to build over time, especially after a mention on a blog or social network. Many of the videos on my own YouTube (youtube.com/polymedia) channel are good examples. They'll have a slow first week or month or even a number of months, then they gradually pick up steam.

Optimizing Video For Mobile

Mobile viewers watch videos a lot longer than they do on their desktops. In order to maintain that attention, it's important to observe the following:

1. Avoid using tiny text. Make sure that any text you use is readable on any screen that the video might be viewed on, especially a smartphone.

2. Make sure the audio is clear. Great audio is always a plus, but even more so when viewing on a phone. Remember that the speakers are small, so you're not going to hear many of the low frequencies, but that's okay as long as everything is intelligible. Also remember that there's always a lot of ambient noise around a phone if the user isn't wearing earbuds, so make sure that the audio is able to cut through it.

3. Use lots of close-ups. Close-up shots work great on small screens - wide shots don't.

4. Test the video on your own phone before you upload it. What good is the video if it doesn't get the point across? The only way you'll know for sure is if you test it, and your personal phone is a great place to start.

These are all good tips to keep in mind the next time you create a video. Remember that it's more than likely that a great number of your viewers will now be watching on their phone, so compensate for the small screen right from the beginning.

People Watch Longer On Tablets

While most people watch at least a couple of YouTube videos on their laptop or desktop during the day, it turns out that tablet users actually have the longest video engagement. Video distributor Ooyala did a study that determined that tablet users watched 28 percent longer than the desktop average. They also found that tablet viewers are more than twice as likely to finish a video than on a desktop, which was about 30 percent higher than that of mobile devices.

The study also found that desktops and laptops are more likely to be used for short video clips, whereas videos that are 10 minutes or longer make up 30 percent of the hours watched on mobile devices, 42 percent on tablets, and nearly 75 percent on connected TV devices and game consoles.

The bottom line is, if you make a video, be sure that it plays well on a tablet.

Making Money From Your Videos

Many artists, bands, brands and videomakers are using YouTube to generate income. The majority of the time this is done through a version of Google's Adsense program, which allows publishers in the Google Network of content sites to serve automatic text, image, video, and rich media adverts that are targeted to that particular site's content and audience. YouTube's monetization features are very easy to apply, so let's take a look.

Enabling Your Account

The first thing to do is enable your account for monetization. This is done under the *Channel Settings* link and then clicking *Monetization*, at which point you'll be lead through the registration process (see Figure 9.5). After your application for Adsense is confirmed, click on the *Start Monetizing Your Videos* link and you'll be taken to your video manager, where you'll be able to see a list of your uploaded videos.

Figure 9.5: Monetizing your account

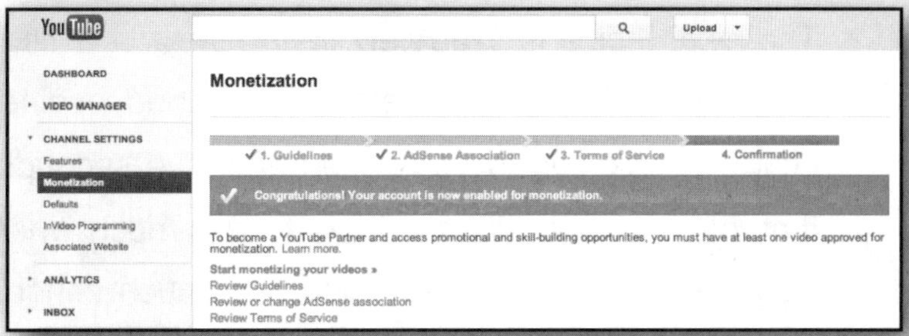

To the right of each video in the Video Manager you'll see small three tabs; the first selects whether the video is available to the public or only private viewing, the second shows when the video was published, and the third (the one with the dollar sign) will allow you to monetize the video. When you click on the monetize tab a new window with your video will load with a selection box at the bottom that says *Monetize my video*. Once that's selected, a new set of selections appear.

***TIP**: Be sure your video has at least a PG-13 rating if you want to appeal to advertisers to make monetization possible.*

Selecting The Ad Type

Now you're able to select the type of ads and the way they show up in your video (see Figure 9.6). The first is *Overlay in-video ads* which loads a transparent ad bar on the lower portion of the video. This is usually the most unobtrusive type of ad, since it allows the user to instantly play your video without having to wait for a commercial to start.

Figure 9.6: Ad type selections

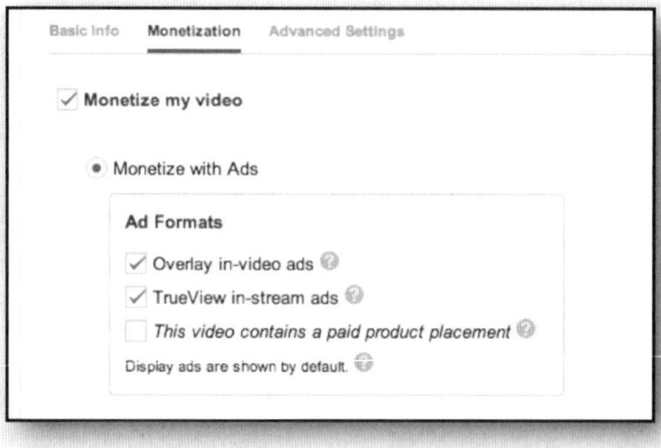

The next choice is *TrueView In-stream ads*. This is the dreaded pre-roll commercial that occurs before your video begins. The viewer has the choice of skipping to your video after five seconds, but that also means that the advertiser doesn't have to pay much when that happens, which also means you don't get much paid much either. In videos longer than 10 minutes, a mid-roll ad may appear around the seven minute mark.

The ads in your video are chosen automatically based on the context of the video, which includes the demographic of the viewers, the title and metadata, and how you categorize your video. This means that if you have a music video, the ad is probably going to relate to the person who likes music. You're not able to manually select the type of ads that are inserted at this time.

What's more, once you've been selected to be an Adsense partner, banner ads sized at 300 pixels x 250 pixels will also appear on all pages but your channel homepage. This may or may not be related to the ad in the video. It's possible to filter or block Adsense banner ads that appear next to your video though, and you can block either by advertiser URL or by category. To do this you have to log in to your Adsense account and visit the *Allow and Block Ads* tab, which is beyond the scope of this book.

One of the things about ads is that they appear even if you or someone else embeds your video on another site, which allows you to still generate income even if the video isn't on a site that you control.

***TIP**: Don't expect to make a huge amount of money from ads in your video. The average ranges from between $5,000 to $8,000 per million views. On top of that, YouTube may ask you to prove that you own or control the copyright of the material on the video before monetization can begin.*

How Content ID Can Earn You Money

In 2007 YouTube created the technology used to detect uploaded videos that infringe on copyright called Content ID. This creates an identification file for copyrighted audio and video material and stores it in a database. When a video is uploaded, it's checked against the database and flags the video as a copyright violation if a match is found.

When this occurs, the content owner is alerted, and then has the choice of blocking the video to make it unviewable, allowing the video to be viewed while tracking the viewing statistics of the video, or adding advertisements to the video and collecting the revenue.

To qualify for Content ID, you must own or control the exclusive online streaming rights for the content you upload. To sign up, go to youtube.com/content_id_signup.

Creating Online Video Contests

Artists, bands and musicians are always looking for ways to increase their fan engagement and contests can be a good way to do that. A white paper from Launchpad6, a site that specializes in conducting all kinds of online contests, had a number of suggestions regarding conducting a successful one with video. The following three ideas from the paper are worth considering.

1. You need a premise. A premise is the basic idea of the contest itself. Here are some ideas to ask yourself first:

- Is content for the contest readily available or easily created?

- Is that content interesting?
- Is the content shareable?
- Is there enough passion for the idea?
- Is an element of voyeurism involved?

2. You need a prize. Cash is always king when it comes to attention, but sometimes smaller more niche prizes can be more alluring to your target audience. Ask yourself the following questions:

- Does the prize appeal to my target market?
- Will my market find the prize valuable?
- Are there any other smaller prizes that I can offer?

3. You need promotion. Your contest won't get any traction if it's not promoted and you get people to enter. Here are a few ideas to consider:

- Create a video for the contest and seed it around the web
- List your contest in directory sites
- Don't forget social media
- Try partnering with a blog or industry publication or anything that has more reach than you do.

Video Analytics

One of the best things about YouTube is that it has extensive analytics that allow you to measure the engagement of videos. These can be accessed either from the *Views* button located on the navigation bar at the top of your channel (see Figure 9.7) or through the Video Manager. Among the measurements that can be found are:

- The number of total channel views
- The estimated total number of minutes watched
- The total estimated earnings (provided that you've signed up for Adsense)
- The number of likes, dislikes, shares, shares, comments and favorites and subscribers added
- The location in the world where people are watching your videos

- The gender of your viewers
- Where people discover your videos
- The top traffic sources

Figure 9.7: Typical YouTube Analytics

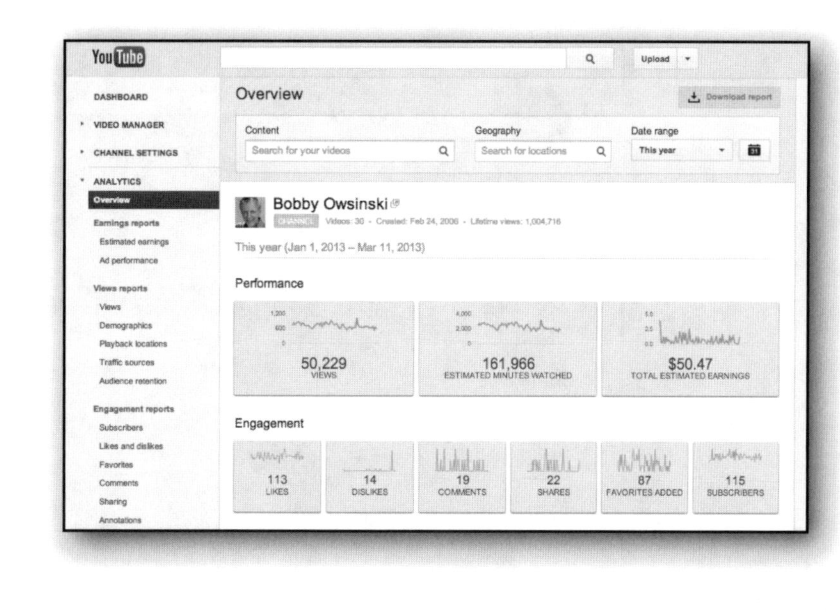

Each one of the above is available in a separate report that allows you to look at a particular period in time, from a single day to the entire history of your channel. You can also look at these metrics for each single video as well.

Some of the most useful metrics are buried deep within the analytics. In fact, a number of advanced metrics can be found under the *Compare Metric* menu on the upper right of the line/map chart (see Figure 9.8). At the bottom of the menu you'll find a *More Metrics* link that reveals another entire list of analytics (see Figure 9.9). You'll find some interesting metrics such as *Average View Duration* and *Click Through Rates* that can be very useful in determining just how effective each video is when it comes to engagement or making money.

Figure 9.8: The link to advanced metrics

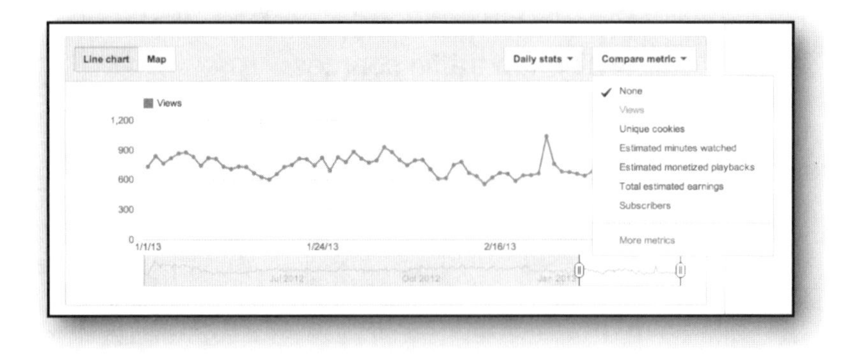

Figure 9.9: The advanced metrics

***TIP**: Use all the analytics and metrics available, not just views. Remember that it's the quality of views (meaning the length of time spent watching), not the quantity that's important.*

The YouTube Trends Dashboard

YouTube has come up with a new analysis tool call the Trends Dashboard that lets you see exactly what people are viewing and sharing across YouTube in multiple ways (see Figure 9.10). The Dashboard also gives you a picture of some of the gender and age demographics of the views. Here's what it allows you to see:

- Views by gender
- Sharing
- Views by age group
- Views by city, country, or globally

- Comparison of any of the above

Figure 9.10: YouTube trends for 18 to 24 year olds in New York, Los Angeles, and South Korea

A downside of the Trends Dashboard is that the trend information only portrays viewer habits over the last 24 hours, or for the last 28 days on individual videos, so it's mostly short term. That said, for many purposes that's more than enough data.

The Trends Dashboard can be a great informational tool if approached from the right perspective. If you want to learn what's working in a particular location, you can dial it up to take a look. Even better is that you can then analyze the top 10 videos to gain an overview of the production techniques that worked in those particular cases.

Because the timeline is only over the last 24 hours, it's best if you watch the trends for at least a week just to be sure that you're not getting any false impressions. Also keep in mind that many videos are viral because of their cuteness (cats and babies), weirdness, or just plain outrageousness, which is difficult to duplicate. That being said, YouTube Trends is a pretty cool tool.

The Online Video World Is Bigger Than You Think

While you may think that YouTube is the only game in town, you'll be surprised to find that there are over 50 online video networks in the US alone. Most of them are very targeted and specialized, but there are a few that are clear competitors for Youtube's throne (although there's not much chance of any of them overthrowing the king anytime soon). Here are four Youtube alternatives that are definitely worth checking out.

Blip.tv: Blip encourages regular content and as a result has a lot of serial videos and web series. It features a pro account that provides additional storage space and a suite of tools to create, manage and promote your work, and also provides a split of any ad revenue generated. What's more, it also distributes through other video platforms, including YouTube.

Vimeo: This service features high-quality content instead of the user generated videos that are so popular on YouTube, so it's mostly aimed at the serious user. It has a pro account that bumps your weekly upload capacity, and even has a video school to help you make better videos.

Veoh: This is the place for long-form videos like movies since Veoh doesn't have an upload size limit and has few upload restrictions. It doesn't have as large of an audience as YouTube but it's growing all the time, especially since the platform has attracted some top-quality videos and shows.

DailyMotion: DailyMotion's strength is its organizational tools, allowing the user to easily find a category of interest. Like some other platforms, it restricts storage capacity to 150MG and less than 20 minutes of video, but emphasizes its community features. That said, it also has a pro account which takes the features up a notch. Many viewers swear by the platform.

Make sure to take a look at these video platforms, because there's lots of life beyond YouTube. You might also want to check out the complete list of video sites at all-video-sites.com, which has up to date info on nearly every video site worldwide.

Using OneLoad

One of the reasons why YouTube has become the de facto standard for online video is the fact that it can be such a hassle to upload to any of the other platforms such as the ones mentioned above. As good as the other sites may be, it's a time consuming process to have to log on and upload to each service separately, not to mention converting the video if a particular resolution and format is recommended or required. That's why a service called OneLoad is so valuable.

OneLoad allows you to upload your video just once, and the service automatically formats it and distributes it to multiple video sites at the same time (see Figure 9.11). It will log on and provide your password to each individual site, and if you've not registered on a video site previously, will even allow you to do that quickly and easily. From there all you do is upload the video and OneLoad does the rest.

Figure 9.11: OneLoad upload page

Video Upload Status [refresh status]

sites	login credentials (username or email / password)	
YouTube	Using YouTube authentication token.	[more options]
DailyMotion	Using DailyMotion authentication token.	[more options]
Metacafe	User	[more options]
Blip.tv	User	[more options]
Veoh	User	[more options]
Viddler	User	[more options]

More sites

MySpace	Requires Myspace token. [Get token]	[more options]
Brightcove	read token / write token	[more options]
Vimeo Plus/Pro	Requires Vimeo token. [Get token]	[more options]
Sevenload	username	[more options]
IFoodTV	username	[more options]
Facebook	Requires Facebook token. [Get token]	[more options]
Flickr	Requires Flickr token. [Get token]	[more options]
Photobucket	Requires Photobucket token. [Get token]	[more options]
Travel Sites:		
TripTV	Based on the category selected, this video is not relevant to TripTV. email address	[more options]
General Sites:		
Bing	email address; Additional Bing Information:(Bing Supplier / Bing Source) bing supplier / bing source	[more options]
Humor Sites:		
StupidVideos	username	[more options]
Sports Sites:		
GrindTV	Based on the category selected, this video is not relevant to GrindTV. username	[more options]
SportPost	Based on the category selected, this video is not relevant to SportPost. email address	[more options]
Auto Sites:		
StreetFire	Based on the category selected, this video is not relevant to StreetFire. username	[more options]
CarDomain	Based on the category selected, this video is not relevant to CarDomain. username	[more options]

Another advantage of OneLoad is that it also supplies an interesting amount of analytics, showing not only how each individual video that you've uploaded is doing across all platforms, but how it's done on each video site as well (see Figure 9.12). You can also check your total number of views for each of your videos across each video site, or all of them.

Figure 9.12: OneLoad analytics page

As with most services online, there are both free and paid tiers, but the free one is more than enough for most artists or bands since it offers up to 100 video deployments a month as long as the total file size is less than 500MB.

10

Using Google+ For Marketing

Google+ may be the new social kid on the block but it's rising fast in terms of user numbers, with over 500 million total users and 350 million active users. It has some unique features that separate it from its competitors (namely Facebook), which makes it an excellent tool for connecting with fans and clients.

Google+ Overview

Many social media users are still doubters about Google+, but the network is growing like a weed, which mans that if you're an artist or a band, you just can't ignore it any more. While Facebook still has about double the users, at the rate G+ is growing it may not take long for it to catch up. As a matter of fact, as of the writing of this book it has over 550 million users, of which about 350 million are active on a monthly basis; and all this from a service that only launched in September of 2011. To put it into perspective, it took Facebook more than five years to get to the number of users that G + put up in only 18 months.

It's for that reason that Google+ is now a must for any band or artist and here's why:

- **Google+ pages rank high in Google searches.** Of course they would, G+ is owned by Google.

- **Circles**: This is one of the main reasons why people love G+. Essentially, Circles is your list of friends and followers, but it goes a step further by allowing you to categorize them (see Figure 10.1). Facebook has something similar with its Lists, but Circles are much easier to use.

Figure 10.1: Google+ Circles

- **Hangouts On Air**: This is another killer feature of G+. It's basically like video conferencing in that you can connect with up to 9 fans at once, but now you can broadcast it to the world on YouTube as well.

- **+1:** This is G+'s version of the "Like" button, the difference being that it will help your page rank higher in Google searches. Be sure to include it on your website and your blog.

- **Privacy**. unlike Facebook, people can add you to their circles, but that doesn't mean that you'll be getting any of their posts.

Google+ is now an essential part of an artist's social strategy. It's easy to use and offers a number of useful features, so sign up now and take advantage of them. One thing to be aware of is that G+ has been blocked by both the People's Republic of China and the Iranian government, but it's available just about everywhere else in the world.

Other Google+ Features

Beyond the above features, Google+ has a number of others as well. Many of these are similar to what can be found on other social networks, but some are unique. Let's look at them.

- **The Band Page:** This is like your Facebook Fan Page in that it's only for artists and bands. Ideally it would have a similar URL name to your other online entities to keep your branding consistent.

The Stream: Your stream occupies the middle column of the G+ page and shows updates from people in your Circles. There's also an input box that you can use to post new updates and share photos, events and videos.

- **Messenger**: This is a feature available to iOS, Android and SMS devices enabling instant messaging within your Circles.

- **Hashtags**: Google+ uses hashtags in a similar way to Twitter, with each one hyperlinked to the most recent or highest-trending search result within G+ that contains the term.

- **Ripples**: This is an interactive diagram that shows how a Google+ post spreads as it's shared by users (see Figure 10.2). You can find the Ripple of any public post using the dropdown to the right of the post as long as it has +1s or reshares (see Figure 10.3).

Figure 10.2: Google+ Ripples

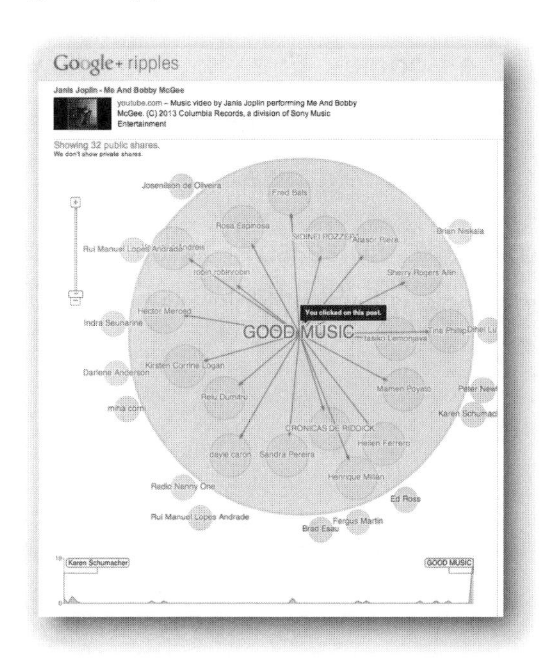

Figure 10.3: Accessing a Ripple

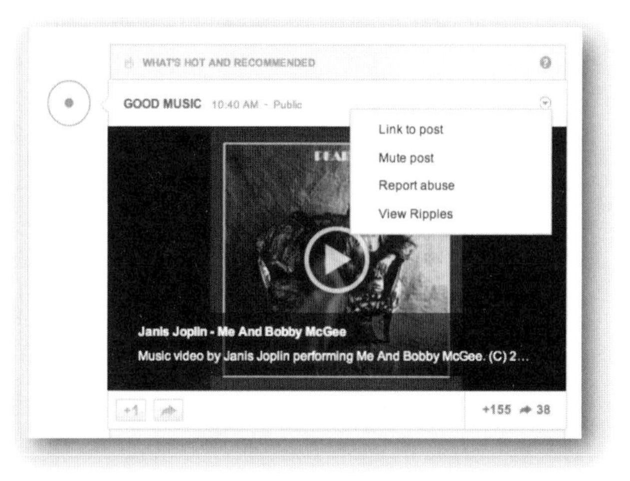

- **Google+ Badges:** Badges are sidebar widgets which embed "Add to Circles" buttons and drop-down lists into external (to Google+) websites and blogs. These are very similar to Facebook's “Like” widgets.

- **Google+ Local**: Google+ Local is another selection on the left side of the home page that allows users to post photos and reviews of locations and services, and is a replacement for the old Google Places. It now also features detailed reviews and ratings from Zagat as well.

- **Google+ Events:** This allows users to add events, invite people, and then share photos and media in real-time during the event (see Figure 10.4). The program is integrated with Google Calendar and is posed as a direct competitor to similar features offered by Facebook

Figure 10.4: Google+ Events

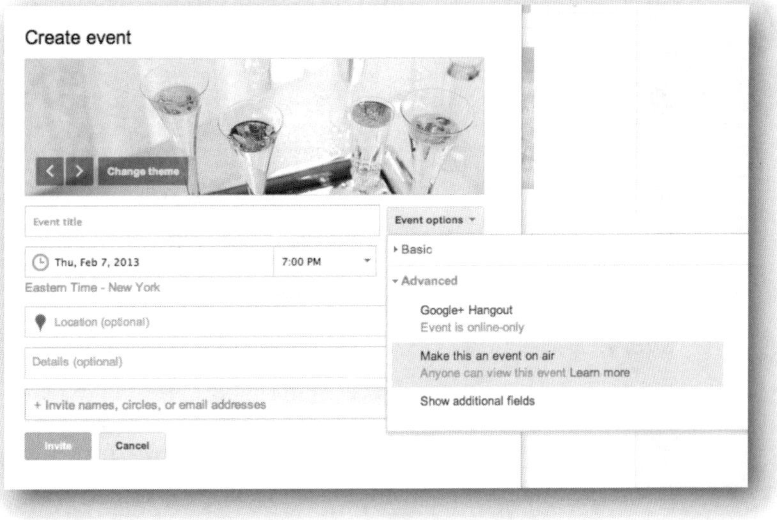

- **Google+ Communities:** This feature allows users to create ongoing conversations about particular topics, similar to what might happen on Twitter or the comments on a blog (see Figure 10.5).

Figure 10.5: Google+ Communities

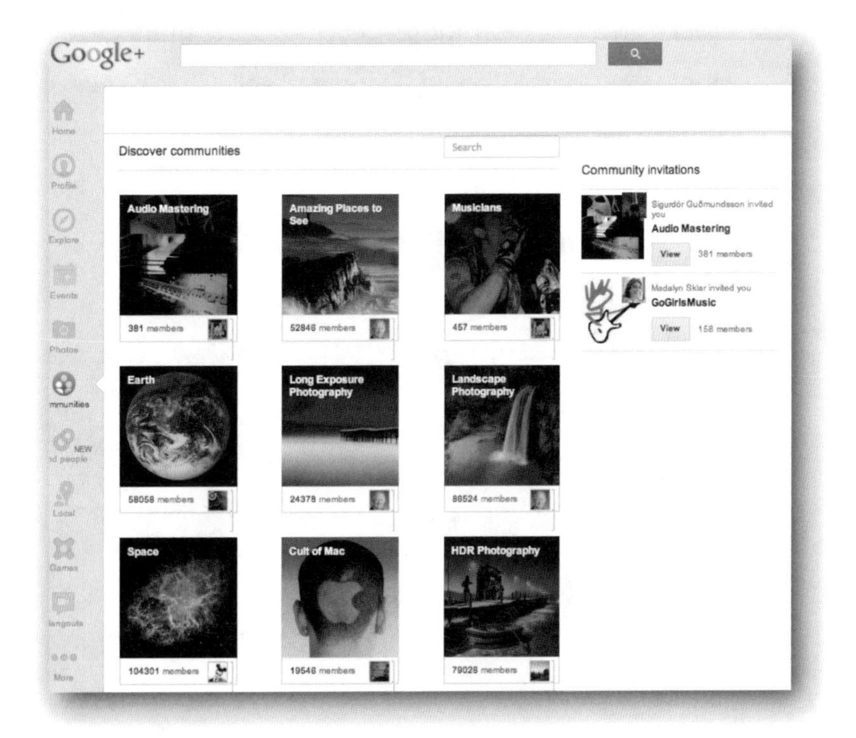

As you can see, Google+ has quite a number of features that make it worth checking out. While not everyone that's signed up actively uses it, those that do on a regular basis are profuse in their love, and it looks like it will only get bigger as time goes on.

Setting Up An Artist Or Band Page

Google+ makes it possible to set up a dedicated page specifically for an artist, band or brand. This isn't as cool as it could be, since the customization possibilities are still limited, but it's evolving just like everything else on G+. Here's what to do to get started:

1. Sign in to your Google account and then go to google.com/+/business. If you use Gmail, then you already have a Google account, but you're not obliged to use it. You can also create a new account by going to accounts.google.com.

2. Pick a category. You now have to select which category you fit into. This one might be a little difficult in that most artists, bands, engineers and producers find many categories that seem to work (see Figure 10.6). To make the decision more difficult, each main category has subcategories that conceivably could work as well. Don't over-think this and just pick *Arts, Entertainment and Sports.*

Figure 10.6: Google+ Page categories

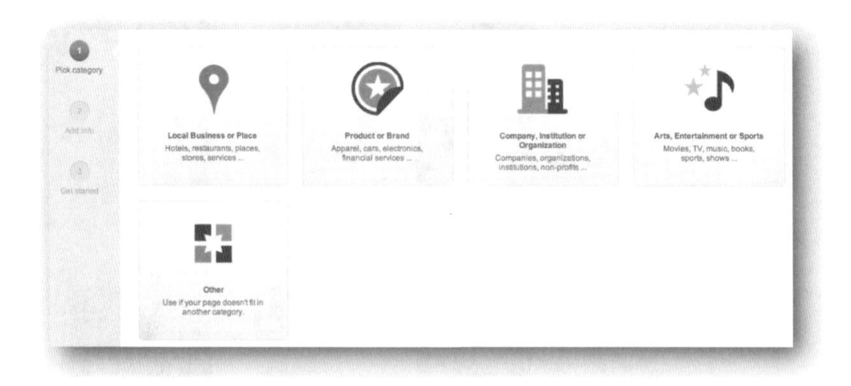

After you choose the primary category, then select the subcategory that suits you best. These sub-categories are dependent on the main category you choose. If you're a band, you can use "Music Band" under the *Entertainment* category. On the other hand, you might want to be classified under "Celebrity", "Arts and Entertainment" or "Music" under the

Product or Brand category. It's not yet known if this selection ultimately makes much difference in your traffic, so don't fret over your choice.

3. Add info. Now enter your band or business name and website info. On the same page, select who can view your Google+ profile. The default is any Google user, or you can restrict it to 18 and older or 21 and older. Click *Continue*.

4. Add a tagline and photo. You have only 10 words to summarize your music, business, or what you do, then you can add an image. Doing this in so few words is actually a pretty good test of nailing the true essence of who and what you are.

5. Get the word out. At this point, Google+ offers you the ability to tell your personal circles about your new business page.

On your new welcome page, Google generates a link to your G+ page (which unfortunately is a string of random characters instead of a vanity URL), and generates the code for a Google+ button to put on your site. It's now up to you to start adding people to your Circles and get posting. There are a number of things that you should know about brand and band pages though:

- You can +1 a page to show your support or add them to a Circle.
- Other Google+ pages can't mention you until you're connected.
- Other Google+ pages automatically unfollow you if you unfollow them.

Having your own Google+ brand page is cool, but remember to show the love to others as it's the only way to get it back.

Setting Up Your Circles

Google+ Circles is considered by some to be the killer app of the network, and it's one of the features that makes it unique in the social networking world. Circles are really just lists, but what makes them notable is that you can follow anyone you'd like without needing their approval. This is cool because you can create different Circles for different groups of people or resources that you'd like to follow closely.

1. In order to create a Circle, **first find some people that you want to add.** Use either the *Find People* icon on the left side of the page or the *Find people and pages* link at the bottom of the right-hand column under *Interesting On Google+*.

2. After you've found people you'd like to add, **scroll over the circle that says *Drop here to create a circle*, then click on *Create a circle***.

3. **Enter a title for your circle, then follow the instructions to add people.** Brand pages are different from personal pages in that the default Circles include "team members," "customers," and "VIPs," but you can rename them anything you want (see Figure 10.7).

Figure 10.7: Naming a Circle

***TIP**: You can also create a new Circle by dragging people into the blank circle that reads Drop here, then click Create circle that appears in the center of that circle.*

Once you're done, your new Circle will appear among the rest of your Circles. You can continue to add people by dragging and dropping them into the new Circle. If you add someone to a Circle they're already in, they won't be added again.

***TIP**: You can put the same person into as many Circles as you like. When you add people to multiple Circles, that doesn't mean that you remove them from other Circles you've previously put them in, and they'll only be notified once that they're in one of your Circles.*

If you want to see which of your Circles a person is in:

1. Mouse over their name tile, and the circles they're in will illuminate at the bottom of the page.
2. Mouse over their name tile, and a pop up box will appear which includes the names of the circles they're in (see Figure 10.8).

Figure 10.8: Seeing what Circles a person is in

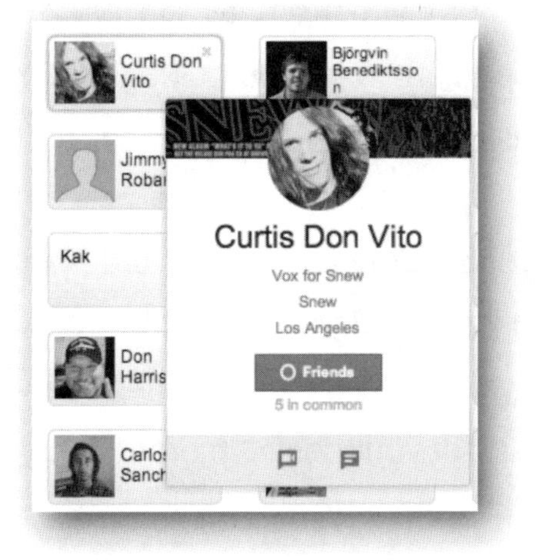

It's also possible to share a Circle. That means that a list of the people who are in that circle at that time are shared, but not the name of the circle. To do so:

1. Click the circle that you'd like to share.
2. Click inside the circle.
3. Choose who you want to share with.
4. Under the *Actions* menu on the left of the page, click *Share*.

Removing Someone From A Circle

There may come a time where you'd like to remove someone from a Circle. Here's what to do:

1. Click the Circle to open it.

2. Select who you'd like to remove from the Circle and click on the *X* at the top right of their name tile.

***TIP**: You can also remove people from Circles by clicking their photo in the circle and just dragging them out.*

It's also possible to remove a person from all of your circles at once. Here's how:

1. Click on the person's name.
2. Go the the *Actions* menu on the left of the page and click *Remove*.

A confirmation will appear at the top of the page indicating that the person selected was removed from all circles. You'll also have the option to remove this person from your Google Contacts address book, but be aware that this could affect other devices that are using Google Contacts.

Sometimes you don't want to remove a person from a circle but you want to block them instead. This means that you won't see their content in your stream, they won't be able to comment on your posts, and they won't be able to view any of your posts. In order to do this:

1. Select the person you'd like to block.
2. Click *Actions*.
3. Select *Block* in the drop down menu.

You can see the list of people you've blocked by selecting *View blocked* from the gear icon on the Circles page.

Wading Into The Stream

The primary screen of Google+ is called the Stream, just like with many other social networks. Updates from people that you follow show up in boxes in your stream, which appear in a multicolumn view that expands or contracts depending upon the size of your browser window. You can change from a multicolumn to a single column by clicking on the "More" button on the top of the screen, the selecting “Stream Layout” from the drop-down menu.

If there’s a post in your stream that you don’t like, just hover your mouse over the post and click the arrow icon that appears in its upper right corner. You can then choose “Mute the post,” unfollow the poster or report him for spam or unseemly content.

Also notice that many posts also use hashtags like you’ll find in Twitter and other social networks. When you click on a hashtag, you’ll see more public posts that are related to the topic.

Posting On Google+

Posting on Google+ is similar to posting on Facebook, but with a few more variations. When you click on the “Share What’s New” box, it will move to the center of the screen and your profile picture will pop up next to it. From there you can:

- Select whether to attach a photo, link, video or event
- Select who to share the post with

You have a number of options of who you want to share your post with. You can select:

- The public, which will allow anyone to see the post
- One or more of your circles
- An individual from one of your circles

You can browse your circles and the people within them by clicking on the “Browse People” icon to the right of the “To:” box.

Hangouts On Air

One of the more intriguing features of Google+ is Hangouts On Air, a video conference that although limited to yourself and 9 others, allows you to stream what could be considered your very own TV channel through YouTube. Of course, this is also possible with services like Ustream, Justin.TV and

Livestream, but Hangouts On Air has a terrific video codec and a lossless audio codec available, so the quality of the broadcast can be great.

With Hangouts On Air, you can invite your Circles or individual fans to join you in a hangout, then broadcast it to the world. A live version of your hangout is posted to your Google+ Home page and your YouTube channel. Your hangout is then recorded as a public video on YouTube and will be available on your Home page once your hangout has ended. You'll also be able to edit the recording when the hangout is over. If you edit your video, your post (including the video URL) will automatically be updated to show the edited version. You have to link your Google+ account to your YouTube account to do this, but Google's made this pretty easy.

Hangouts On Air now defaults to full screen mode, and includes a pan and zoom feature for photos. It stitches participants together into a single stream with seamless camera switching, or you can use the Cameraman app to put the main speaker in the background and focus just on another participant. All in all, it's a very sophisticated technology available for free as part of the G+ service.

Things You Can Do With Hangouts

Hangouts On Air is extremely versatile, with far more to offer than what on the surface seems only like video chat. You can:

- **Broadcast your video on YouTube as well as Google+.** Your video streams live both on your YouTube account and on your Google+ stream, which means you can share your YouTube URL with anyone who wants to watch your broadcast live.

- **Live-stream your Hangout on any website.** While in your Hangout, you can grab the YouTube video embed code and paste it into your blog or website to make it available live to more viewers.

- **Incorporate Google+ apps.** Right now, you can use a number of applications like Google Docs, SlideShare and

Cacoo to help you collaborate or present your ideas in the video. This gives you the functionality of hosting your own webinar at no cost.

- **Chat on a sidebar.** Simply click on the *Chat* button on the top left to chat with others during your Hangout. If you're doing a presentation, invite others to leave questions or comments as you're talking or playing.

- **Screen share.** To share different parts of your screen, simply click *Screen Share* to select which window you want to show everyone else. This is helpful if you want to talk about a website, application, program or anything else on your desktop.

- **Edit your hangout when complete.** When your Hangout is complete, you can edit the video in your YouTube account. Go to your Video Manager page and click on the *Video Editor* link at the top of the page.

- **Share Your Recorded Hangout**. Once you're happy with your video, you can then share it just like any other YouTube video.

Starting A Hangout

Even though Hangouts can seem like they're pretty sophisticated (and they are), they're actually pretty simple to set up. Here's how to organize an HOA.

1: Log into Google+ and click on the Hangout button. Simply log into your Google+ account and click on the *Hangout* button on the right side of your stream.

2: Name your Hangout and invite people. You'll be prompted to invite your friends or circles before you enter the Hangout On Air (see Figure 10.9). If you invite fewer than 25 people, they'll receive an instant message with a link to join, but if you invite more than 25 people, the Hangout invite will only be shown in their stream, which they might not see. Someone that you've invited can either join the hangout or not, but if they don't join they'll only be able to watch it on YouTube when you start broadcasting.

Figure 10.9: Starting a Hangout

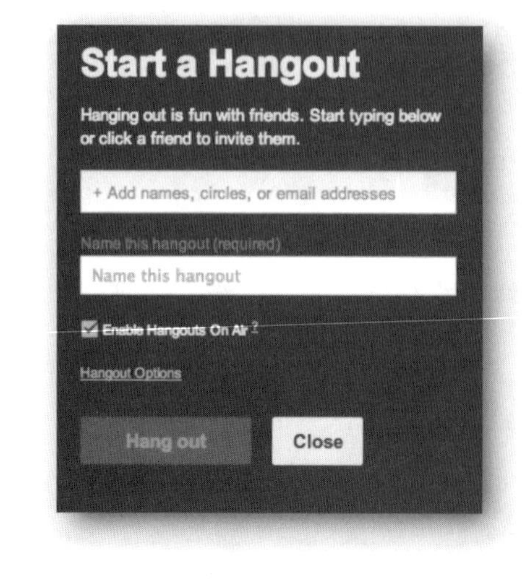

TIP*: You can also invite people to join in by phone if they're not available online.*

Please note that while you can't invite the public to join a Hangout on Air as a participant, you can open the hangout for public viewing by clicking *Start broadcast* from within the hangout window. You can then share the URL of the Hangout, and whoever you shared it with will be able to watch the hangout even if you didn't explicitly invite them.

3: Check *Enable Hangouts On Air.* After naming your Hangout and clicking on the *Enable Hangouts On Air* box, you'll get a pop-up informing you that the hangout session will be streamed on your YouTube channel and on your Google+ stream. Once you click on the blue *Okay, Got it!* button, you'll need to agree to Google's terms of service.

4: Agree to Google's terms. You only need to agree to the terms during your first Hangout, but the main gist of it is that any content that's being broadcast must be owned by you. Any music or videos played in the background that you don't own should be avoided, including those from others that join your hangout. YouTube uses Content ID to detect whether or not a Hangout On Air is broadcasting copyrighted content.

Once you click *Continue*, your first Hangout session will begin. You can then either wait for others to join your Hangout or start broadcasting live without them. Anyone else you invite to join your Hangout will also receive a note to inform them the Hangout will be live-streamed on YouTube.

TIP: *Only users 18 years and over can participate in Hangouts On Air.*

5: Press *Start Broadcast*. Click on the red *Start Broadcast* button to begin broadcasting, where you'll get a message informing you that the broadcast will be public. After clicking OK, the red button will give you a 10-second countdown before going live.

6. Use the Cameraman app to make participants part of your broadcast. After loading the app, choose a default action for when participants join. To bring the participants "on stage" or to remove them from the live Hangout On Air, hover over their thumbnail and click the video icon (see Figure 10.10). Their thumbnail will be greyed out when they're off stage.

Figure 10.10: The Cameraman app

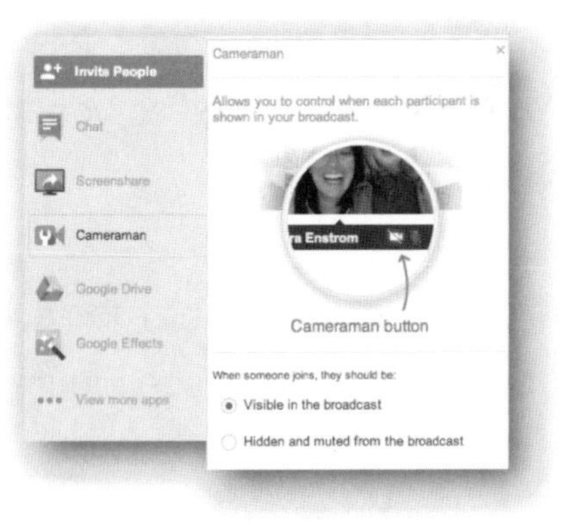

TIP: *You can see the video during the broadcast by clicking the Home page post. Please note that when clicking on the post you should mute your audio to avoid hearing an echo.*

---

7. **Embed the live player of your Hangout On Air in another website.** Click *Embed*, copy the YouTube HTML code, and paste it into your blog or website. Once It's embedded, viewers can watch the Hangout directly from that site.

Optimizing The Audio

Hangouts On Air offers two audio settings, one for voice, and one with a higher fidelity that's intended for music. You can optimize the audio for the type of Hangout you're broadcasting by going to your Hangouts' settings and choosing one of the following:

- **Voice**: This setting optimizes your audio for voice conversation and is the best for most broadcasts that don't feature music.
- **Studio**: This setting provides higher fidelity audio and is intended for music broadcasts.

***TIP**: The Studio setting is stereo, so be sure to provide a stereo input or your guests will only hear one side of the audio broadcast.*

How to Record Longer Hangout Sessions

YouTube allows videos of longer than 15 minutes only if you get their permission. Since a Hangout might last longer than that, verify your account with YouTube beforehand so your recorded video doesn't get cut. Here's how that's done:

1. After you've logged into your YouTube account, go to your Upload page and click on Increase *Your Limit* (see Figure 10.11).

Figure 10.11: Increasing your YouTube upload time limit

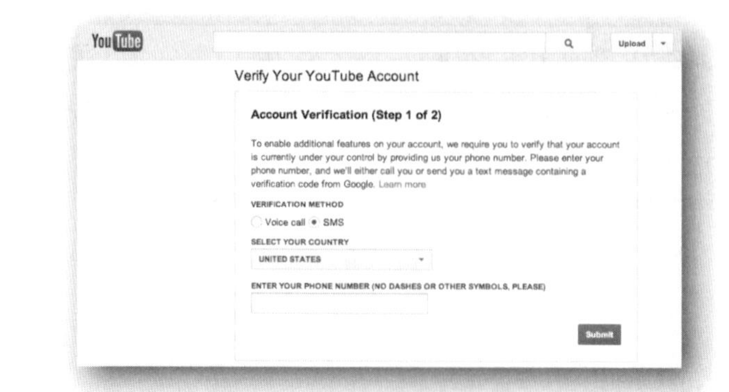

2. You'll then need to verify your account by submitting your mobile phone number.
3. Google will then text you a code that you'll need to type in to verify your account.
4. After your account is verified (which happens almost instantly), you'll receive a prompt notifying you that you're able to upload a video longer than 15 minutes.

Hangout Tips

Here are a few other tips you should know before starting your first Hangout:

- **Avoid using Wi-Fi.** In order to get a stable connection, it's best if you use a wired Ethernet connection instead of Wi-Fi.

- **Leave lots of headroom.** Even in Studio mode, the audio codec can be unforgiving if overloaded. Be sure to leave at least 6dB or more of headroom if possible.

- **Block inappropriate people**. If you're hosting a Hangout, you're able to block anyone that you think is acting inappropriately, but remember that the other participants in the Hangout can still see or hear him. You can force someone out of your Hangout by hovering over their video thumbnail and clicking *Eject*.

- **Admins only.** All Hangouts are automatically associated with the page administrator's YouTube account. That means that if you want it on your artist or band page, you'll need to download the video from your personal account and upload it there afterwards.

- **Mute your audio to avoid hearing an echo if you want to watch your broadcast live.** During a Hangout you can go to your Google+ profile page to watch the video streaming, but there'll be a delay in the audio feed as a result. Make sure to mute the audio so you don't hear an echo.

Use a unique name for your Hangout. Try not to make the title too generic so you don't have people unfamiliar with what your doing joining by mistake.

Try a Hangout by yourself first. Take some time to get a feel for what it's like doing a Hangout by starting one with just yourself. Learn the interface, switch back and forth between video of you and your screen, and generally get comfortable with it before launching your first real Hangout.

***TIP**: Check the settings every time you join or start a Hangout as they'll sometimes return to their default selections.*

After Your Hangout

After you've finished your Hangout, it could take up to an hour before the video appears in your YouTube account, depending upon the length of the Hangout. When the video is ready, it will appear in your YouTube Video Manager page where you can then place it into a playlist, share it or make any necessary edits.

Editing Your Hangout Video

You can also edit your Hangout video. Go to your Video Manager page and click on the *Video Editor* link on top of the page (see Figure 10.12). This will then allow you to:

- Add music or sound effects
- Trim clips
- Integrate video from other video clips that you've uploaded
- Share your Hangout
- Embed the YouTube code on your website

Figure 10.12: The YouTube video editor

Practical Ways For Musicians To Use Hangouts

The first thing that any artist thinks of when presented with Hangouts On Air is "live concert." While it may be true that HOA is used for that more than anything else where artists are concerned, that's not all that it's good for. Here are a few other ideas:

- **Live Q&A with fans:** Do your fans ask you the same types of questions all the time? Well then host a weekly Hangout On Air to address those common questions live. You can ask fans to tweet questions to you during your presentation, then post the video on your website for those who missed it.

- **Behind the scenes:** Fans love anything behind the scenes, no matter how mundane it might be for an artist or band. What's it like in the van or bus, backstage at the gig, soundcheck, during rehearsal, writing a song, in the studio, or during mixing? There's a host of wonderful video opportunities to share at your fingertips every day.

- **Gig Meet And Greets:** You can easily set up a virtual "meet and greet" either before or after one of your gigs using

Hangouts On Air. Even if your fans can't be there in person, they can still share in some of the experience.

- **Live interviews:** The broadcast doesn't always have to center around you. The people that you work with can be just as interesting. How about interviewing your road crew, the soundman at the club, the bus driver, the merch people, the bartenders, the club manager, your producer or engineer, or any of the countless others that cross your path every day? You can also easily do a panel discussion with some of the other musicians that you love and respect.

- **Vlogging:** Vlogging is a "video blog." All the rules to blogging apply (see Chapter 8), but Hangouts On Air gives you everything you need to host a regular show.

Google+ SEO

Since Google+ has come on the scene, just about everyone has wondered if there's a way to optimize your G+ posts to help your search engine ranking. Just like with every other social network, there are a number of things that you can do to help those posts get noticed. Here's a good place to start.

- **Post fresh content frequently.** A G+ profile with no posts within the last 72 hours won't show up in the "Related People/ Pages" section of Google's search results. In fact, posting a few times a day is a good strategy. Reshares and links work just as well for this since your posts don't all have to be original to count.

- **Pages can matter more than profiles.** Brand pages with a few thousand followers or circlers can appear in "Related

People/Pages" of the search engine rankings ahead of individual profiles with more than a million followers or circlers.

- **+1s matter.** Profiles and pages that get a lot of +1s on their posts tend to show up more often in "Related People/Pages" results than those that get a similar number of comments and reshares.

- **Circle influential people with big Circle followings.** It pays to circle people in your area of expertise. You're not so much expecting them to follow you back (though some will) as much as looking to interact with the content they produce. That engagement can translate into more people circling you.

- **Make your Google+ posts as readable as possible.** Optimize the format of your Google+ posts by creating a title for each post using bold formatting. You do this by placing a * at the beginning and end of what you want in bold (i.e. *This is the title*). When you share that post the * will disappear and the text between will be in bold (i.e. **This is the title**).

- **Always post to the public.** By not doing so, you limit the ability of others to find you and your content.

- **Respond to engagement.** If someone +1s your post, make sure you circle them if you haven't already. If they comment, reply to that comment using their @name. If someone shares your content, be sure to +1 that share and add a thank you comment if appropriate.

- **Cultivate engagement.** Keep track of the people who engage your content most frequently by putting them in a Circle. From there you can share directly with them thereby increasing the probability of more engagement.

- **Monitor real time searches.** You can quickly find, monitor and engage specific content by searching by keyword and jumping into the real time stream of results.

- **Never spam.** It sticks out like a sore thumb on G+ and you can bet that Google will penalize you for it as a result.

Don't overlook Google+ when it comes to your online presence. It's extremely powerful with a lot of unique features and will only grow in importance in the future.

✦

11

Using Pinterest For Marketing

Pinterest is a social network site that allows you to collect and share photos of your gigs, events, meet and greats and tours by posting images or videos to your own or other's pinboards (a collection of pins with a common theme). Unlike other social networks, Pinterest revolves around the user's lifestyle (which in this case would be music), which is reflected in the pinboards and images that are selected.

Unbelievably, Pinterest is now the third-largest social network behind only Facebook and Twitter, with users pinning images just as much as they're tweeting. Unlike other networks though, Pinterest is equally popular with different age demographics. Although at one time it had a larger gender mix difference than any other of it's social counterparts with five times more women pinning than men, this is changing rapidly as men, businesses, and brands and bands discover its features and reach.

Pinterest is growing, and it's the perfect place to serve up a variety of rich media that fans just love. From backstage pictures to tour videos to outtakes of your latest song, Pinterest can do it all. Let's take a closer look.

Pinterest Overview

Pinterest allows you to save and categorize images of things that you like (called "pins") even when you're browsing (see Figure 11.1). This process of selecting or uploading a pin is called "pinning." You don't have to log onto Pinterest in order to pin something that you like from a site, as this can be handled using a browser applet.

Figure 11.1: Pinterest pins

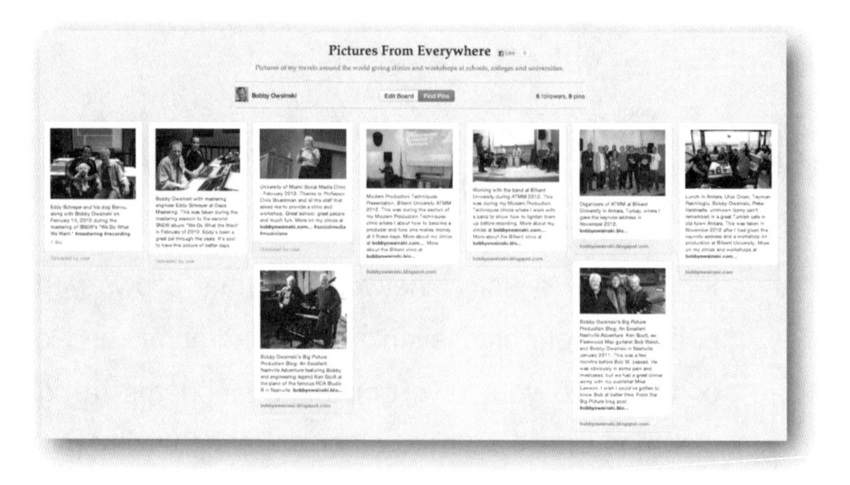

You pin things to folders that have a common theme called pinboards or "boards." Every time you pin something, it shows the link of where the pin came from, which can be a good way to get traffic if you pin your own site's graphics.

Boards can be either public or secret, which means that anything you post there won't show up anywhere else on Pinterest. This means you can use a secret board for collaboration, planning events, strategizing, or just keeping things to a limited number of people.

Just like other social networks, you can follow people and use keywords and trending item hashtags like on Twitter, Facebook and Google+. You can also link your account to both your Facebook and Twitter accounts so that when you pin something, it simultaneously publishes to those networks as well if you desire.

Creating A Personal Account

Like Facebook, Pinterest features two different types of accounts; personal and business. The business account is a slightly better way to go because it allows you to fill in more information in your profile, but you can still do quite a bit of that in a personal account as well. Here's how to set up a personal account.

1. Go to pinterest.com and register by using either your Facebook account or email address. It will then take you to a page where you can create your account.

2. Fill in the personal info. Enter an email address and password, then your first and last name, then finally your gender. The *Create An Account* button on the bottom of the page will then turn blue. Click on it and you're almost finished.

3. Select some people to follow. The next page will provide you with a number of categories to choose from, with a variety of popular people to follow underneath each one. Select five, then your account is established and you can begin pinning.

4. Fill in your profile. Just like in other forms of social media, your profile is important, but in order to complete it, you have to take an extra step and click on your picture on the top right of the page and go to the *Settings* selection in the menu (see Figure 11.2). Go to the *Profile Into* section and add a short bio, which will show up right under your photo. You only have 200 characters so you must be succinct.

***TIP**: Be sure to add links to your website, blog or social networks.*

Figure 11.2: The complete profile page

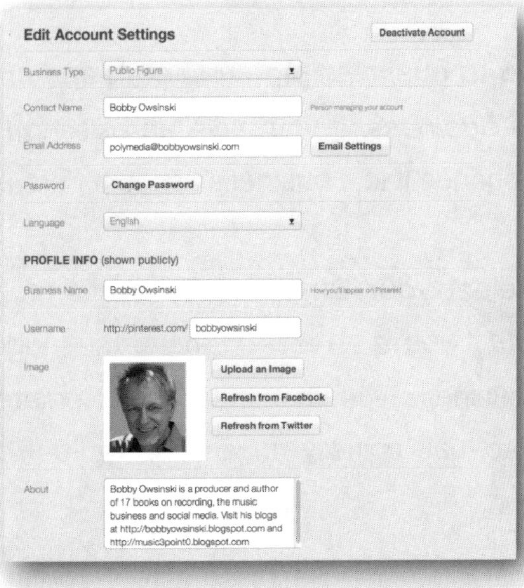
Edit Account Settings
Deactivate Account
Business Type
Public Figure
Contact Name
Bobby Owsinski
Person managing your account
Email Address
polymedia@bobbyowsinski.com
Email Settings
Password
Change Password
Language
English
PROFILE INFO (shown publicly)
Business Name
Bobby Owsinski
How you'll appear on Pinterest
Username
http://pinterest.com/
bobbyowsinski
Image
Upload an Image
Refresh from Facebook
Refresh from Twitter
About
Bobby Owsinski is a producer and author of 17 books on recording, the music business and social media. Visit his blogs at http://bobbyowsinski.blogspot.com and http://music3point0.blogspot.com

5. Upload a profile picture. Pinterest is personality driven so it's best to use a headshot or band shot instead of a logo. Remember that people are more likely to follow individuals rather than bands or brands, unless the brand is very well-known.

6. Tie your profile to your Facebook and Twitter accounts to quickly share pins in both social networks. Not only will this help you gain followers, but making this connection adds social media icons under your profile picture that link to your Facebook and Twitter profiles.

7. Click the red *Save Profile* button on the bottom of the page and your finished.

After you've completed your profile, add a *Pin it* button on your browser to help you quickly pin an image that you like, then add the Pinterest social media button to your website and blog and your Pinterest signature to your email (more on this in a bit). This will help you in promotion and in building your fan base.

Creating An Artist, Band, Or Business Account

Setting up an artist, band or business account is almost as easy as establishing a personal account, except that you have the ability to supply a lot more information about you, your band, or your business. Here's how it's done:

1. Go to business.pinterest.com and click on *New to Pinterest? Join as a business*. If you have an existing Pinterest personal account, you can change it to a business account here as well.

2. Select your Business Type. It's probably best that you use *Public Figure* if you're an artist or band (see Figure 11.3). After you've selected the business type, then enter your *Contact Name* and *Email Address*. The contact can actually be anyone in your organization, as it's not publicly shown.

Figure 11.3: The business type selection

3. Enter your band or business name. On a personal account you have to use both a first name and last name, which can be awkward for some artists and bands, for example "The" (first name) "Unsigned" (last name). With a business account you can set up your account with your band or business name just as it is without having to worry about dividing it in half.

4. Fill in the profile info. You have 200 characters to tell the world who you are and what it is that you do, like your genre of music and anything that sets you apart from other artists or bands.

5. Upload a profile image. While you can use a logo if it's strong, Pinterest users respond to something more personal, so a head or band shot works best.

6. Read the terms of service agreement, then accept the terms by clicking the box at the bottom, and press *Create Your Account.*

7. Follow five boards. In order to begin, you need to follow five boards, but Pinterest gives you a wide range of categories to choose from. You can't move on until you do this, but after you pick your first five, you'll see a blue *Next* button to click on the top right of the page.

8. Verify your site. You can do this in two ways, either by downloading a file that you upload to your website's folder on your hosting site, or by placing a piece of custom metadata on your site's index file (see Figure 11.4). Both are fairly easy to do, but if you're unsure of how it's inserted, speak with your webmaster or someone who knows their way around the files and folders that make up a website. After this is finished, click on the *Verify* button, and if all went well with your install, your site will be verified. Why is this important? Because your website doesn't show up in your profile as a link until it's verified, which means you can lose the opportunity for more traffic since visitors won't have a direct link back to your site.

Figure 11.4: Verifying your site

9. Verify your email address. Pinterest will send you an email at the address that you entered to make sure it's real, which then asks you to verify that address. When you click on *Verify*, you'll be taken to your Pinterest page where you can begin creating boards and pinning photos.

10. Select *Edit Profile* and complete your profile by adding your location, and link your Facebook and Twitter accounts. When you do, Facebook and Twitter icons will appear next to your website link at the top of your page. As with a personal account, this is the final step to complete your profile that you don't have to do immediately, but it's a good idea to get out of the way.

Pinterest is serious about business pages and has provided lots of useful marketing and educational materials specifically for businesses to learn how to market themselves on the network. This can be found on the section on business.pinterest.com called Pinning, which covers four areas:

- How to tell your story
- How to build a community on Pinterest
- How to send traffic to your site

- How to analyze your Pinterest presence

Although it's best to get right into using Pinterest to get a feel for how it works, take a moment to look this information over as soon as you can for some great ideas on getting the most from the network.

Creating A Board

A board is a short name for the analog world equivalent of a cork board that we literally use a pushpin to stick photos to. Since we're talking digital domain here, you can think of a board as sort of a file folder that you put images of the same category into.

Creating a board is easy. Select one of the blank *Create a Board* boxes on your page, then enter a name and select a category (see Figure 11.5). You can also have others contribute to your board by inviting them, which you can do by entering in their name if they're on Pinterest, or their email address if they're not. You can also create a board while you're pinning an image, as you're given an option to create and name one at that time. Yet a third way is to click on *Add +* on the right hand top of the page and select the *Create a Board* option.

Figure 11.5: Creating a board

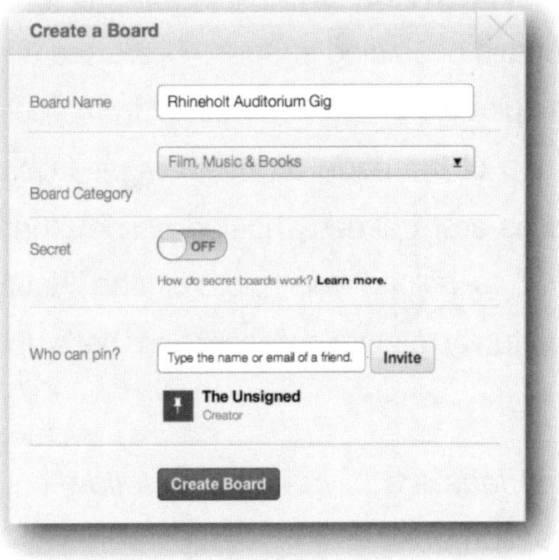

Secret Boards

A secret board is one that doesn't show up anywhere on Pinterest, even in the activity feed that shows your latest pins. You can create up to a maximum of three secret boards, but if you'd like to create another, you'll either have to delete one or make a current secret board visible to everyone to clear some space. That said, if you're invited to contribute to someone else's secret board, it won't count against your three board limit. You can also create a secret board on the bottom of your profile, which is where they'll always reside in the future.

While your instinct might be to broadly name these with something like "Gigs," or "Rehearsal," board names are very much like keywords in that if the name is too broad, then you don't get any SEO value from it, nor does it make anyone want to check it out. It's better to get specific and call it "A Day In The Studio" or "Rhineholt Auditorium Gig," or even "The Funnest Gig In The World." In fact, Pinterest users are usually curious about boards that are crazy and unusual, and just like YouTube, anything that makes people smile or laugh is often a hit. That said, getting more specific and unique in your board descriptions is critical to helping you get discovered on the network.

Pinning An Image

Now that we've taken care of the preliminaries, we can get down to business of pinning images. There are two ways to pin an image. First, you can upload a photo to Pinterest from your computer by clicking on *Add +* at the top of the page on the navigation bar (which you'll need to do if your images aren't already hosted online), then select the middle option, *Upload a Pin*, to upload your picture (see Figure 11.6). You'll then be given the opportunity to enter a description that's up to 500 characters long.

TIP*: Pinterest fans are more likely to follow your boards if they feature at least some original content.*

Figure 11.6: Uploading an image

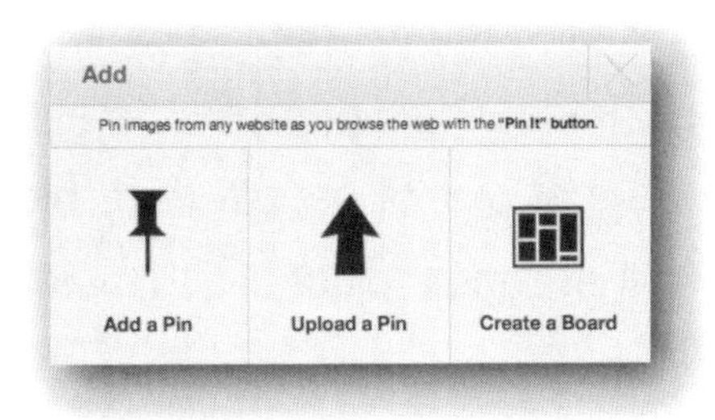

The second way is to pin an image that you find on a website or blog. Rather than saving the image to your computer and then uploading it to Pinterest, you can simply click the "Pin It" button on your browser, which Pinterest makes available to you on their bookmarks and buttons page along with an easy install for all browsers (see Figure 11.7).

Figure 11.7: The *Pin It* button on a Chrome browser toolbar

***TIP**: Pinterest expects you to be careful that any content you pin from a website doesn't violate any laws or infringe another's copyrights.*

When you click the *Pin It* button, you're given the option to pin any of the images embedded on the webpage you're currently visiting. You'll also have the opportunity to choose which board you want to pin it to and describe your new pin, as well as to let your followers on Facebook and Twitter know that you've just pinned something if you want. Remember that any pinned image automatically retains its original URL, which is displayed over the photo.

***TIP**: Pin from lots of different sources, instead of just from one or two sites. Variety is important on Pinterest.*

Refusing To Allow Pinning On Your Site

Some people would prefer that images on their site not show up on Pinterest. If that describes you, be aware that Pinterest has created a "No Pin" code that blocks people from pinning images from your site. Here's the code that can be placed with the other metadata of the site:

```
<meta name="pinterest" content="nopin" />
```

When the code is inserted in a site, if someone tries to pin an image they'll get this message:

"This site doesn't allow pinning to Pinterest.
Please contact the owner with any questions. Thanks for visiting!"

I'm not sure that restricting Pinterest pinning is a good idea unless you have specific images that you want to protect. If that's the case, use the code and your images won't be found on Pinterest.

Pinterest Shortcuts

There are a number of shortcuts that you can take from your Pinterest page. Although the design may seem rather stark, everything on it has a purpose. You'll find a shortcut for virtually everything on the page, like:

- Click on Pinterest logo to go to the feeds of people that you follow, as well as your own profile feed. From there you can also go to the *Categories, Everything, Popular* and *Gifts* categories located next to *Following* on the navigation bar.

- You can choose to unfollow someone by clicking on *Following* on the navigation bar on your Pinterest page, then clicking on the *Unfollow* button. Remember that you must follow at least five people at all times.

- Utilize the search box in the top left hand corner to search for other people on Pinterest with similar interests.

What Pinterest Can't Do

While Pinterest has a wide variety of features and benefits, there are a few things that it can't do yet that you should be aware of. These include:

- **The inability to pin posts from Facebook or Twitter.** It's also difficult to post pins to Facebook without cutting and pasting a link, unless you use the Pinterest iPhone app. You can, however, "tweet" your pins very easily.

- **The pinning function online only works with image files and videos.** This means that text files can't be pinned to your page, which is bad for bloggers.

- **Pinterest may use the wrong thumbnail picture from a site during the pinning process.** This can be a drag if it picks up something that's far from what you wanted, like an advert.

Pinterest Marketing Strategies

Marketing on Pinterest revolves around a strategy of quality posts and interaction, just like many other social networks. In this case the difference is that your interaction is meant to directly drive traffic much more than with other networks. Our strategy revolves around the following points:

1. Only add compelling high-quality pictures. In order to get the most traffic, you want to at least have some pictures that can't be found anywhere else. Regardless of which pictures or graphics you use, make sure they are at least 500 by 500 pixels in size. Also remember that image resolution should match the screen at 72 pixels per inch. The file size is pretty much unlimited, but it's still best if you keep it below one meg or smaller so it loads quickly.

***TIP**: Tall images get more interest on Pinterest than square or horizontal images.*

2. Make your images shareable. There's a running debate as to whether you should ad copy or watermarking to your images. While a watermark with something like "Property of The Unsigned" over it probably will keep people from sharing your image, having a logo and/or website address inconspicuously inserted in a corner might work okay. Remember that if you're trying to sell merch, let the product sell itself by its appearance. You might be able to get away with a price tag on a merch picture on a "Gifts" board, but for the most part, Pinterest users frown on anything that feels too much like a promotion.

***TIP**: A big thing to remember is that the content you post on Pinterest will be used by other Pinterest users, which means not only can they repin it, but they can also modify it, reproduce it, display it, distribute it, or do whatever they want, but only within Pinterest.*

---

3. Be sure the image has a proper name. Many pinners make the mistake of uploading photos that use their default names. For example, an image named "DX90315.jpg" doesn't help you in a search, while one that's clearly named, like "Rhineholt Auditorium Gig.jpg," is a lot more searchable. Furthermore, if you pin an image from your website, make sure it has a completed alt tag. Finally, don't forget to use keywords in your image file name if you can.

***TIP**: Pin content continually instead of in huge bursts to maximize your exposure and engagement.*

---

4. Size your pictures correctly. Pinterest doesn't place any restrictions on the height of an image, but it does constrict the width to 554 pixels. Anything wider than that will be resized or if it's beyond 2000 pixels, might even be rejected. Dan Zarrella's analysis shows that taller images are also more repinnable because they take up more space in Pinterest feeds, so use that to your advantage and create an image that's tall, visually interesting, and aptly named using appropriate keywords.

5. Add compelling descriptions to your pictures. Pinterest pictures are just like YouTube in that a detailed description can help the SEO immensely. There are 500 characters available for your description, but research has found that the most repinned items had descriptions that ranged from 200 to 310 (see Figure 11.8). Too much text can actually be a turnoff here! Also be sure to use plenty of keywords in your description, as that's how people find your images, which hopefully means that more traffic will make its way back to your website. Remember that a description will stay with the picture even when it's repinned over the Pinterest world, so be sure to include your band or site name in it.

Figure 11.8: A pin with a typical description

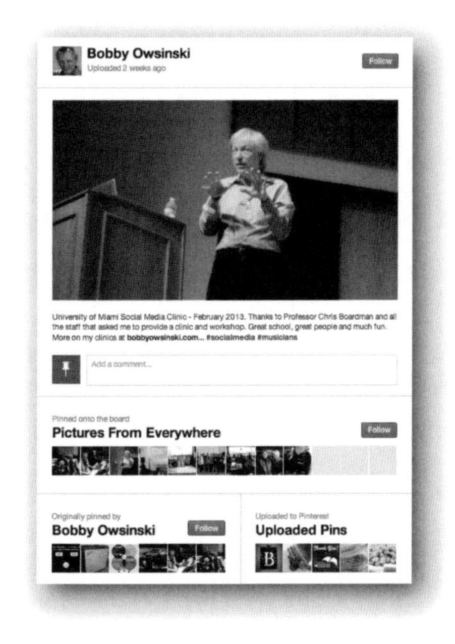

***TIP**: Add a link to your blog or website in your description to increase traffic and SEO leverage.*

---

6. Repin other images. When you repin someone's pinned picture, they'll be notified via email, which is an opportunity to have them check out your site. Since Pinterest is so community oriented, you can be sure that most will follow the links to your account to see where you pinned their picture, giving you an opportunity to have them look through your boards. Obviously it's important that they find your boards interesting enough to follow your links back to your website as well. Also remember that if an image is too small, pinners can't share it, and if they can find a larger version somewhere else, you'll lose out on the traffic opportunity.

***TIP**: Highlighting text on a page before clicking the Pin it button will bring that text into your pin description.*

---

7. Make some comments. When you hold your cursor over a pinned picture you see the *Repin, Like,* and *Comment* tabs. When you make a comment it stays with the picture, so whatever you write has the potential to catch people's attention and drive traffic to your boards. Pinterest also notifies the person who pinned the picture that a comment has been made and gives them a link to respond to your comment, which once again provides a chance to drive traffic to your board, and therefore your site.

8. Follow others. Following others is another way for you to drive traffic to your boards. Once again, whenever you follow someone they get an email notifying them, which provides a link to allow them to go to your account and follow you.

9. Tag others. You can also tag other Pinterest users in your pins by using "@username" in your descriptions. This allows you to network with other professionals and vendors in your field by using this feature. Not many people are doing this yet, so it's a great way to build your following and stand out.

***TIP**: Avoid excessive self-promotion. Pinterest is all about community and how your images contribute to it.*

---

10. Watch for trends. Click on the *Popular* link on your Pinterest home page to research what's trending on the network, then integrate those trends into your content strategy.

11. Follow users who are pinning or repinning your products or images. Also make sure to follow the top Pinterest users, which encourages them to follow you back. Here's where to find a list of the most prolific pinners to follow here.

If you take notice, Liking wasn't included in the above points because it has the least value from a marketing standpoint. Unlike the above methods, a Like doesn't provide a notification with a link back to you, so it's an empty endorsement marketing-wise.

Optimizing Your Website Or Blog For Pinterest Sharing

There are a number of ways that you can optimize the content on your website or blog to be shared on Pinterest. Every blog or site update is another opportunity to cross-promote if you do the following:

- **Use images in every post you write or on every page of your site.** This allows the post to be shared on Pinterest. If you don't use an image, then no one can pin it. The images that appeal to Pinterest members are ones that are powerful and emotive, so keep that in mind when choosing your pictures.

- **Add a prominent Follow Me on Pinterest button to your website** to advertise that you're a pinner.

- **Feature your recent pins in a widget in your blog's sidebar** by using a Pinterest widget.

Buttons And Widgets

- Pinterest offers a number of button and widget options that you can plug into your site or blog on the Buttons and Widgets section on business.pinterest.com (see Figure 11.9). These include "Pin It" and "Pinterest follow" buttons that have a number of configurations, which when selected, will create the HTML code that can then be inserted on your site. The profile widget lets you embed code on your site that shows your 30 most recent pins, while the board widget lets you embed code on your site that shows 30 of your favorite board's latest pins.

Figure 11.9: The buttons and widgets section of business.pinterest.com

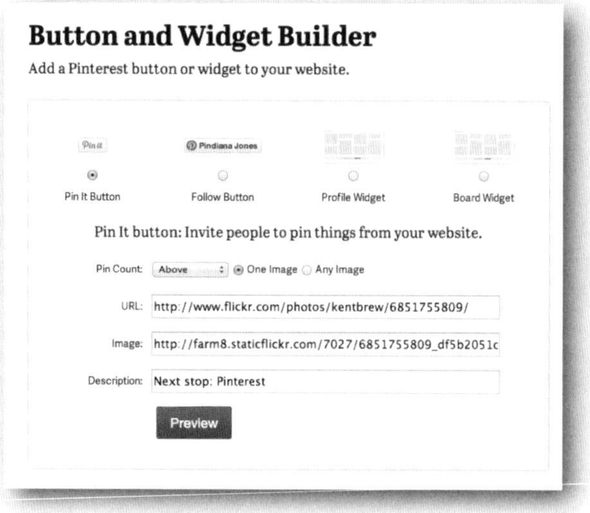

Pin Chats

A pin chat is a unique event that works in conjunction with your Twitter followers. Ask your followers to tweet links, pins and videos around a particular theme like pictures of your last gig, images of their favorite artist or album, artist you remind them of, or even one about their favorite guitars. Repin the tweeted items to one of your boards, then notify everyone who contributed, and even those that didn't, to see the collection. A pin chat can be a unique way to build your community faster than any other avenue.

Pin Contests

Pinterest contests are a great way to attract new followers and drive traffic, and the company makes it easy, thanks to some of the least restrictive terms in all of social networkdom. In fact, the only restriction is that you can't run a contest where whomever gets the most likes or repins wins, which is what's known as "pin to win." Other than that, everything's on the table.

One of the most popular types of contest is a "follow me" contest. To enter, the pinner must do the following:

- follow you.

- create a board with a specific theme, like "The Best Fan Pictures" or "Fan Merch Ideas."
- pin at least five items to the board which tell the story.
- add a designated hashtag to each pin, like #fanpictures, #TheUnsigned, #merchideas or #dreamgig.
- share the URL of their board either on a special contest submission page on your website or blog, or by making a comment on the contest pin.

Obviously in order to make this work you must create both a board and a pin specifically for the contest, then either you or your fans must pick a winner.

***TIP**: In any contest, make sure to include a hashtag with your name so it ends in a search for the contest subject.*

Other simple contest ideas include:

- creating a board about your pictures, album, songs or videos, then asking participants to leave a comment on which one is their favorite and why.
- asking participants to create a board and name it with your band name, then pin their top five favorite items from your website.
- creating a board that asks your fans to upload a photo of themselves either wearing your merch or holding your album
- creating a board where your fans can upload a video testimonial.
- asking participants to create a board with pins that best represent your music.

Contest Elements To Keep In Mind

Holding a contest is more than just the contest itself. Here are a number of things that you must consider before beginning:

- **Offer a worthy prize.** It has to have a high enough value to make someone want to enter. In fact, it's always a great idea to be sure that everyone who enters wins something.

- **Establish clear guidelines** about what entries will be legal, how the contest will be run, when it will end, how the winners will be picked, when the winner will be notified, and how the winner will redeem his prize.

- **You must promote the contest.** Add a link to the contest on your site and blog, mention it in your newsletter, and promote it on Facebook, Twitter, LinkedIn, YouTube and your other social media networks.

- **You need contest materials.** Be sure to create at least a pinnable image for your contest as well as a special web page on your site or blog if necessary.

- **Choose a winner.** Is the winner going to be picked at random (you can use a service like www.random.org), will you select a winner based on responses, or will you have a panel of judges determine the winner based on certain criteria?

- **Check out Pinterest's Terms and Conditions** (which are constantly changing) to make sure you abide by their rules before beginning a new contest.

- **Don't spam or ask contest participants to spam** on your behalf.

As with everything, setting up a Pinterest contest is a little more work than it seems, but after the first one, you'll find that you'll be able to repeat it over and over, each time with better efficiency.

Pinterest SEO

While the above marketing ideas are simple ways to use Pinterest for promotion, it's also possible to take that a step further using a number of simple SEO techniques.

1. Choose an optimized username. The first thing to do to optimize your Pinterest business account for search is to make sure your username name is straightforward. The field for the name has no character limit, but the real challenge often comes with your *username*, which is confined to 15 characters. If your full artist or band name fits, then you're in business, but if it doesn't, choose something that's memorable, keyword-conscious, and easy to spell that is also clearly associated with your music.

2. Optimize your page's *About* section. The Pinterest *About* section provides you with 200 characters of prime keyword real estate, so use this space wisely. Two hundred characters is plenty of space for a keyword-rich overview that covers the who, what, and where of what you do. Don't forget to add your website URL in the space provided.

3. Include links back to your website. Always include a reference link back to your website with your pins, and if you repin a post that features your content or products, edit the description to include a full link instead of a one using a link shortener (see Figure 11.10). Including a link back to your website will not only reinforce the fact that the image is associated with your brand, but it also makes it possible for the pinner to purchase something or learn more about you.

Figure 11.10: A link and hashtags in a description

***TIP**: Pinterest has been known to mark pins that have shortened links in their description as spam.*

4. Incorporate hashtags. Hashtags on Pinterest not only allow you to organize pins by a specific theme or campaign, but they also make your pins a lot more searchable (see Figure 11.11). Use hashtags that pertain to your band, brand or type of music, but also check to see if there's a popular trend that you can associate with.

5. Stay within a niche. Get granular with your descriptions and consider adding your location, gig and merch details, or the audience you'd like to target.

6. Use commonly searched keywords. Use common keywords people use to search for things.

Ideas For Using Pinterest

There's a lot more about Pinterest than meets the eye. Here are some additional hints and ideas for using Pinterest.

- **Pin pictures of your fans and then paste their testimonials in the pin's description.** People love seeing faces with testimonials because it seems more credible and friendly.

- **Your Pinterest page has its own RSS feed!** Your RSS feed can be found by going to the your Pinterest URL and adding /feed.rss to the end of the link. Here's an example using my username "bobbyowsinski:"

  http://pinterest.com/bobbyowsinski/feed.rss

- You can also view a specific board feed by going to the board URL and replacing "feed" with the board name, like in this example where my board name is "Pictures From Everywhere."

http://pinterest.com/bobbyowsinski/pictures-from-everywhere.rss

Use the RSS feed anywhere that a feed is appropriate (Facebook, LinkedIn, for syndication on other sites, etc.). Alert your fans and readers to your feed and ask them to add it to their RSS feed readers.

- **Create a special board to highlight your band or album project team members.** Use the description area under each photo to write a bio of each person.

- **Show behind-the-scenes photos of your gigs, rehearsals or studio recording.** People love knowing the back story of what you do.

- **Become an information curator.** Gather the last news and resources regarding your type of music on a board or boards. If you become a trusted source for information on Pinterest, your following will grow by leaps and bounds.

- **Highlight old content on your blog** so that people can repin your archived posts.

- **Schedule your pins using Viraltag.com.** It provides some analytics as well.

- **Create a board that tells the story of the band and communicates your core values.** A "History of the Band" board is the perfect way to show your evolution.

- **Consider creating "thank you" boards for fans that send special messages.** Pin their pictures to the board and thank them in the description.

- **Have a blog?** Create a board for it.

- **Going to a conference like SXSW?** Create a board for it.

Pinterest Audio And Video

It's now possible to pin audio and video to your boards as well as images, which allows you to share them on your page. The process is exactly the same as pinning images if you use the Pin It widget in that the video will show up as one of the selections. Select it and proceed just like when pinning a photo.

Pinnning A Video

In order to pin a YouTube video, you need to make sure you use the video's URL rather than the embed code. Navigate to the video you want to share on YouTube and do the following:

1. Click on the *Share* button.
2. Click on the Pinterest widget.
3. Select the board and proceed just like with a photo.

Now the video will show up on your board and actually play within Pinterest when you click on it even though it's not embedded. People can Like and repin it just like any other pin. You can also pin a video by using the *Pin it* widget on your browser, if you inserted one (see Figure 11.11).

***TIP**: Don't copy the YouTube URL at the top of your browser screen because it's different from the one under the Share menu and won't pin the video to your board.*

Figure 11.11: Pinning a video using the browser widget

Remember that many of the view options in YouTube, like choosing a specific start time, aren't supported by Pinterest. If the pertinent part of a video is beyond the start point, use the description to tell your viewers to jump forward to the specific time.

Optimizing Videos For Pinterest

While you can pin a video without thinking too much more about it, there are ways to optimize it for life on Pinterest. Try the following:

1. Customize the thumbnail image. As outlined in the YouTube chapter, it's now possible to upload custom thumbnails for each video, which are perfect for Pinterest use as well. If you've not done that, it's up to you to find or create an eye-catching image that properly represents your video. Just make sure that the thumbnail is inviting and nothing important on it is obscured by the default *Play* button

2. Keep videos short if possible. Pinterest is designed for quick browsing and pinning and people probably won't end up watching a long video to the end.

3. Be sure to describe the video. Just like with an image, a video benefits greatly from a keyword-rich description.

4. Include "Pin This" annotations. When you're creating a video that you know will land on your Pinterest page, include annotations with a "Pin this video to Pinterest" call-to-action, or provide a link to your Pinterest profile as a way to connect. You can also add "Follow me at pinterest.com/

[pinterest name]" in your video outro to encourage your viewers to engage with you there.

5. Place a *Pin It* button next to your video player. Make sure that the button is embedded under the video player on your website and blog pages.

Pinning An Audio File

It's now possible to also pin an audio file, but there are far more limitations than with video. That's why it probably makes more sense to pin a video of your song rather than the audio-only file at this time. If audio of the song is all you have, be aware that the only audio that Pinterest will pin is from Soundcloud.

There are three ways to pin a sound:

1. Click the *Share* button below the song's Soundcloud waveform and then click the *Pinterest* button.
2. You can also use Pinterest's *Pin It bookmarklet,*
3. Copy the URL of the sound you want to share onto the site as with a video file.

When you pin a sound on Pinterest, it's artwork will automatically be displayed alongside your other pins, and the SoundCloud HTML5 widget will automatically launch when the pin is clicked. The sounds are also fully attributed with a link back to their page on SoundCloud, so its creators will always be credited.

✦

12

Using Bookmarking Sites

A social bookmarking site is an online service that enables users to add, edit, and share bookmarks of websites and blogs. Online bookmarking is similar to bookmarking a real book where you might stick a piece of paper between a couple of pages to easily find your place later, but adds a social twist in that those bookmarks can be tagged with keywords and shared with communities set up around categories and subcategories.

Social Bookmarking is free, easy to use, and effective in building website and blog traffic and backlinks, but only if you frequently update your blog or site with new posts. A user selects a bookmark either through a browser widget, plugin, or extension that is readily available and easy to install. Many bookmarking services also offer pro packages that allow ad campaigns as well.

There are dozens of social bookmarking sites, but we'll be looking at the top five: StumbleUpon, Digg, Reddit, Delicious, and Technorati.

Bookmarking Benefits

It's easy to either dismiss or overlook social bookmarking as a necessary part of your online marketing, but the fact of the matter is that search engines pay a lot of attention to these sites. None of the bookmarking sites have rules against bookmarking your own blog or website, which means that you're free to bookmark your URLs so others can discover them. This can be important because they can:

- drive traffic to your blog or website.
- improve its SEO.
- speed up page indexing by the search engines.
- increase the reach of your content.
- help you to discover content that you might want to curate.

- provide new ideas for a blog post.

The Disadvantages

As with most things online, there can be disadvantages to social bookmarking as well, especially if you rely on them as your main source of building traffic.

Sometimes the quality of the traffic drawn to your site from social bookmarking is low because the people drawn to it stay only briefly then leave, since what you've posted might not be exactly what they're looking for. It's also not uncommon for a link to make it to the front page of social bookmarking site that results in thousands of visitors to your site, which ends in a server crash that makes it inaccessible to your high quality visitors.

Another disadvantage is that some social bookmarking sites tag all of their stored and shared links with a "nofollow" tag that tells the search engines not to include the links in their search results. This degrades the value of any link that you might have there. Of the five major bookmarking sites that we'll look at, only StumbleUpon does this.

StumbleUpon

StumbleUpon is a great social site for artists, bands and musicians because it features a diverse crowd that spans hundreds of topics and thousands of tags, and it continues to accumulate 50,000 new pages every day, all handpicked and endorsed by real people, many of which can be your fans. As a result, it can definitely be a valuable addition to any social media marketing strategy.

Go to the main StumbleUpon page and register either with an email address or through your Facebook account. Fill in the details of your profile, add a picture, and link your account to other social networks if you'd like for your bookmarking activity to show up there. Like with many other social sites, you'll be asked to select at least four categories of interest before you get started.

***TIP**: It's better to not link your account to your other social media accounts, since you don't want to exceed the strategic number of posts on those services. Keep your posts custom to the social network, if possible.*

The best and easiest way to use StumbleUpon is to have the Firefox Add-On or the Chrome Extension installed on either browser (see Figure 12.1). Once installed you're presented with a range of selections below the icon, although the two most useful ones for most stumblers are the *Stumble* and *Thumb* buttons. Hitting the *Stumble* button takes you to a page in a category that you're interested in or have liked previously, and if you like the content you can give it a thumbs up, and if you don't, a thumbs down.

Figure 12.1: The StumbleUpon Toolbar in Chrome

•

StumbleUpon sends visitors to a site based on a number of factors, although the most important one is how many times people thumb up the content. The more thumbs up, the more people StumbleUpon will send.

The site also has a personal score called a StumbleDNA, which is a representation of your Likes and a quick way to see what you and other Stumblers have in common. Every page a stumbler likes belongs to an interest, and all of the interests on StumbleUpon map to one of fourteen larger categories like Health, Sci/Tech, Art/History, and dozens of music genres. The number of Likes a stumbler has per category determines the amount of the category's color in the stumbler's DNA on the profile page. As you Like more content, your DNA will change to reflect what you Like.

***Tip**: Although stumblers can comment about a site, a thumb up is much more powerful in terms of potential traffic to your site.*

Submitting To StumbleUpon

Submitting your sites to StumbleUpon will give them the opportunity to be seen, liked, and shared at no cost to you. Pages that are submitted get assigned to certain categories and potentially can reach thousands of people. If your site does particularly well among a particular interest group and receives a lot of Likes as a result, it can spread across other interests and be seen even more.

In order to submit your website or blog, go to the Submit Page (see Figure 12.2), which can be accessed from the drop-down menu next to your picture by selecting *Add a Page*. There are a number of things to remember when you submit:

Figure 12.2: The StumbleUpon Submit Page

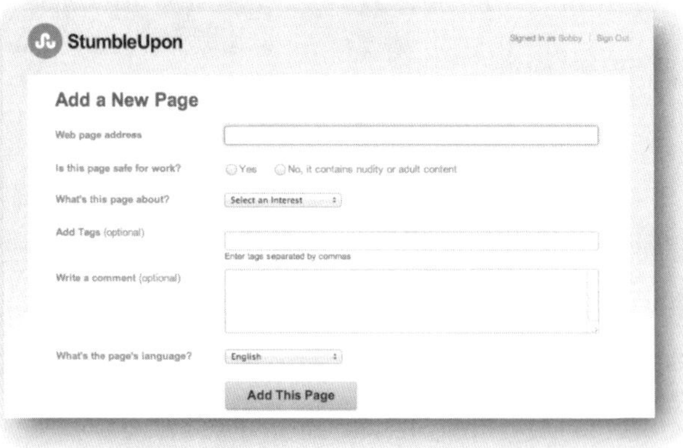

- **Use the correct tags.** Tagging allows you to label your content so it's easily recognized by others. If, for example, you use the tag "EDM," others who are fans of that category are more likely to find you. The tags page shows tags that are recently hot as well as the most popular all time.

- **Use multiple tags.** You can give your content a much higher chance of getting traffic if you use more than one tag. For instance, if you posted about recording at the famous Record Plant studios and the fact that Beyonce was in the studio next you, you might use keywords like:

recording studio, Record Plant, Beyonce, record production

- **Submit to the proper topic.** Don't submit to a topic just because it has a large following or is extremely popular expecting to get the most exposure as a result. Submitting to an incorrect category will most likely result in a lot of thumbs down, which is not very helpful for increasing your traffic.

- **Share with your fans and friends.** You can use the *Share* function to send your stories directly to your fans and friends. After you select *Share*, the recipients will then be notified that they have a new item to be stumbled.

- **Don't spam.** Like any social site, spamming the site by submitting Digg or Reddit links, using incorrect categories, or sharing every story that's on your site or blog will be frowned upon. Remember that if you aren't adding value, you probably won't see much traffic coming back to your sites.

- **Use StumbleUpon lists.** Follow relevant StumbleUpon lists that are already popular, like your genre of music. Many times these groups have active discussions where you can talk to fellow members and moderators, who can also post links to sites.

StumbleAds

StumbleAds is a way that you can pay to have your sites show up during viewer stumbles and have stumblers give a thumbs up or down on it. It's a pay-per-click service where you set the limit that you'd like to spend and the promotion stops when the money runs out.

To apply, go to stumbleupon.com/pd, submit your site's URL, then choose your target category. With your StumbleAds account you can also view the number of users who are subscribed to different categories, which means that you can make sure that a few of the tags with large subscribers are included with all your submissions.

Digg

For the average user, Digg is a place where you can find the most interesting news and online content on just about any given topic. Its users help find the content by "digging," or voting on, interesting articles that are then featured on the site's main page. For artists, bands and musicians with websites or blogs however, Digg provides the possibility of gaining a huge audience in a flash. Stories that are submitted to Digg that make it to the front page can cause what's known as the "Digg Effect," which is a huge influx of traffic as a result.

Digg's main page consists of three parts: *TopStories, Popular* and *Upcoming*. By default you'll see the *Top Stories* first when you visit Digg because it's at the top of the page. These are the stories that have been ranked high because of the nature of their importance. The *Popular* section shows the most-shared stories on Digg in the last 18 hours, while *Upcoming* covers the most recently shared stories.

A "digg" is a thumbs-up, or positive vote, for a story. Any Digg user can digg a story, and every digg helps to determine where that story appears on the Digg homepage. A Digg Score is the total sum of the number of diggs, Facebook shares and tweets for a story. Roll over any Digg Score to see a breakdown of the votes. Commenting is not allowed on Digg at the moment.

***TIP**: You can sign in to Digg by using either your Facebook or Twitter Account, and Digg will use that profile info to create a new Digg profile for you. If you decide to sign up for Digg with Facebook, all of the stories you digg will be shared to your Facebook Timeline, although that can be disabled at any time by visiting the Digg Settings.*

Submitting To Digg

There are two ways of submitting your content on Digg: either submit a story or use a bookmarklet. To submit a story, copy the URL of the webpage, go to the bottom of the Digg main page and click on *Submit a*

Link (see Figure 12.3). Paste the link and click *Submit*. You can also share a story by navigating to a Digg button/bookmarklet located in the social share section of a website or blog.

Figure 12.3: Submitting to Digg

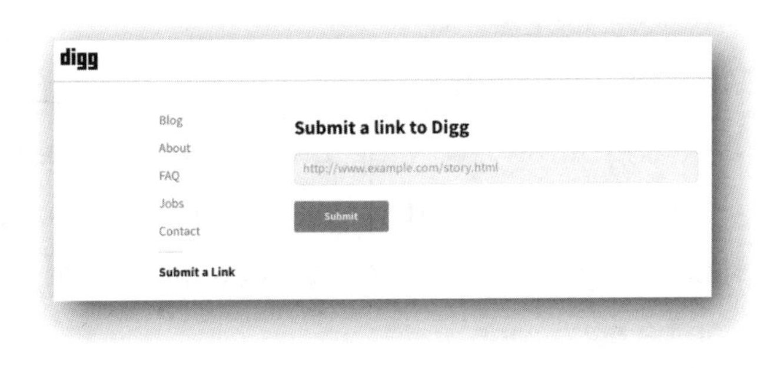

***TIP**: The key to making lots of people look at your submitted link is to write an interesting description for it.*

Although Digg's influence has slightly fallen off recently, any presence on the site is still powerful. By consistently submitting your content to Digg, you might strike gold and be included on one of the categories on the main page. Still, even if your site gets only a few "Diggs," its authority will slowly aggregate and you'll have an opportunity to have your story in front of the eyes of many additional interested readers and potential fans.

Reddit

Reddit is a very powerful social site and unlike Digg, ranking isn't determined as much by your social influence, but by a submission that the community really wants.

Like the other social bookmarking sites, Reddit users provide the content and then decide through voting what they like and what they don't. Links that receive community approval bubble up towards #1, so the front page is constantly in motion and filled with new and fresh content.

With over two billion page views a month, the potential for major traffic from Reddit is huge, even if you barely make it on the front page of a small subreddit that only has a relatively small number of readers (like 20,000).

***TIP**: You don't need a huge amount of positive votes to drive heavy traffic, as that can sometimes occur with as few as a hundred positive votes.*

The Subreddit

A Subreddit is a category on Reddit and the reason why the site is a breeding ground for viral content on the web. Why are they so important? Subreddits allow you to follow very specific areas of interest (like your music or genre of music), are easy to create, can be about anything, and can be public or private.

The Subreddit finder and subreddits.org are great places for finding the exact one that you're looking for, although the list of music related Subreddits is also a good place to start. If you have an account, you can add Subreddits to your front page in a feed that shows the top stories from each of your selected categories.

Submitting To Reddit

If you plan to use Reddit in an effort to increase your backlinks and traffic, you need to register for an account. It's fairly easy to do as you'll find the *Register* button in the upper right hand corner of the home page. You can submit to Reddit by going directly to the Submit page or selecting the links at the top right of the homepage called *Submit a new link* or *Submit a new text post*. If you want to submit a link to your blog, enter the title, URL ,and the Subreddit (see Figure 12.4).

Figure 12.4: Submission to Reddit.

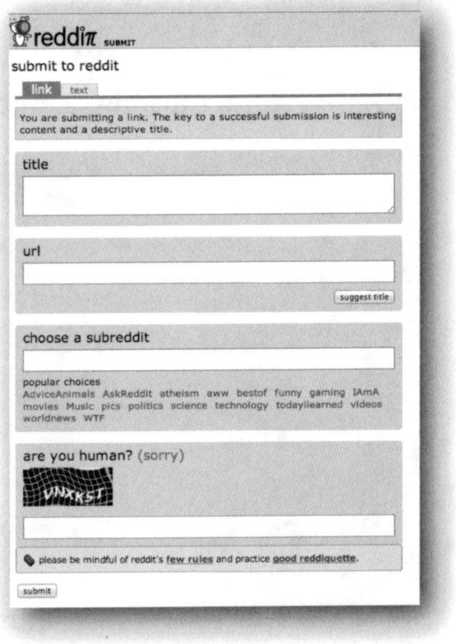

Delicious

Although its popularity has been stagnant in recent years, Delicious is still one of the larger social bookmarking sites currently on the web. Since all bookmarks posted to Delicious are publicly viewable, pages of your site that are posted can force Google to crawl it faster and more often, which then gives it the opportunity to make the Delicious "Hotlist" if it's popular enough, which can help drive traffic back to your site.

To get any real traffic from Delicious your posts have to be repeatedly bookmarked (called "tagged") and given the same or similar tags (keywords) by the many people tagging you (this is a good way to get fans involved). To help this along, add a "Tag this to Delicious" plug-in for your blog or news section of your website, or choose to activate that option on your blog software (most have it available as part of the platform).

Submitting To Delicious

The easiest way to add links to Delicious is with the Delicious bookmarklet, which is a button on your browser that you use while viewing any page, image, video, or document on the web (see Figure 12.5). You can also select *Add a link* from toolbar menu on the top-right corner of any page to open the *Add-link* box so you can directly enter a

URL. Finally, clicking the "+" icon associated with any link you see on Delicious will instantly add it to your own collection.

Figure 12.5: Delicious submission tools

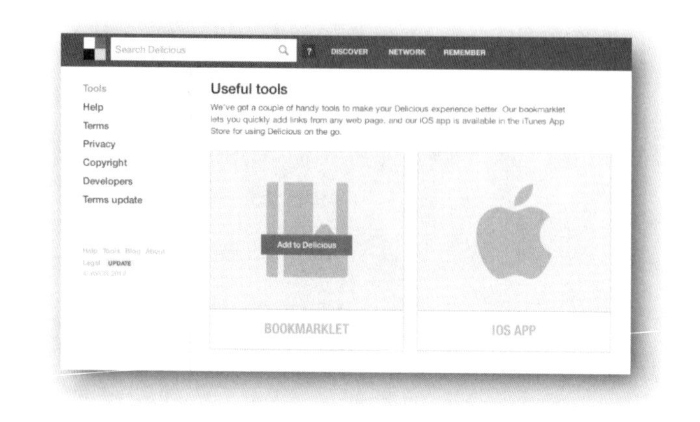

***TIP:** Use popular tags and a great description. Popular tags ensures more people will see the link. The tag cloud feature can help you to find the most popular tags and to understand people's likes and dislikes.*

Technorati

Technorati is an Internet search engine that has more than 110 million blogs indexed and over 250 million pieces of tagged social media. It tracks not only the authority and influence of blogs, but also has the most comprehensive and current index of who and what is most popular in the Blogosphere. It now also publishes high quality, fully edited original content daily on a wide range of topics written by hundreds of member writers.

Technorati is built around tags, and tags used properly can vastly improve your chances of getting exposure. The site looks at those tags to categorize search results, with the most recent results coming first, then rates each blog's "authority," which represents the number of unique links to the blog over the previous six months. Technorati has also been known to go out and find your tags even if you don't register, although it's still best if you do.

Submitting To Technorati

In order to use Technorati you first have to tell it who you are by registering and creating a profile. The most important step is claiming your blog so that it can be added to the Technorati directory (see Figure 12.6). To do that:

Figure 12.6: Claiming your blog on Technorati.

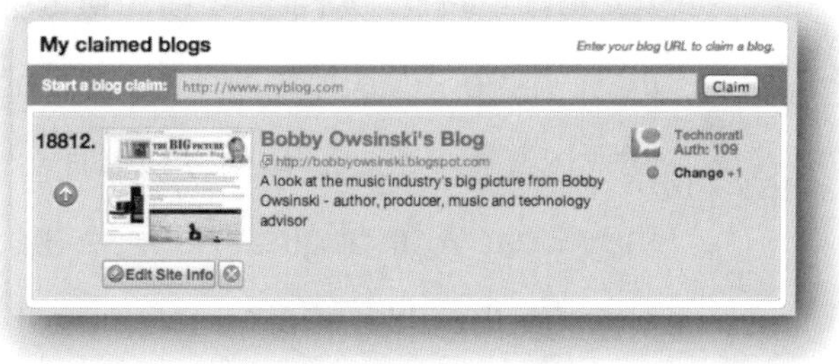

1. Scroll to the bottom of your account page and **enter your blog URL** in the *My claimed blogs* section and click *Claim*.

2. **Enter your blog details,** including the title, the feed URL, and up to three blogs that link to your blog.

3. **Enter a description** for your blog.

4. **Select up to three categories** that best describe your blog's content.

5. **Enter the tags that describe your blog**.

6. **Copy the claim token** from the email that's sent to you and paste it into a new post on the blog you are trying to claim.

After that, Technorati will be following your blog.

General Submission Tips

There's a lot of similarity between the major bookmarking sites, so here are some general submission tips to consider that will help fans using the sites find you more easily.

- Use helper sites to post to multiple bookmarking sites. If using more than a few bookmarking sites is a pain, you can opt for tools like OnlyWire or Socialmarker to post links across multiple social bookmarking sites. Socialmarker also provides bookmarking buttons for your website and blog.

- Avoid multiple versions of the same post, as search engines then have a tough time deciding which is the original and which is the copy. If the search engine bots get confused, they may treat your original post as the duplicate. It's best to slightly change the title and description if you're submitting to multiple bookmarking sites in order to avoid any duplication penalties.

- Generally speaking, a band or brand account tends to look too promotional. Use an individual account instead.

- The use of shortened links is sometimes seen as spam.

- An attractive image goes a long way in obtaining a response from both readers and bookmarkers.

- Submit only a few pieces of content per day per site. If you overdo it, your account risks being blocked.

- Submit varied content, including blogs, infographics, videos, articles, cartoons, and anything that you think your fans might find interesting.

- Submit third party content to build your credibility and make you look unbiased.

- Make submissions consistently week after week. If you stop submitting for a week or two, your authority, and therefore your traffic, could decrease.

- Have members of the band all use social bookmarking. Ask them to view your submissions, vote and post comments, which will make your content more popular.

- Connect with other users and fans interested in your musical niche. They may read your content and help make it more popular.

- Make it easy for your fans to bookmark your content. Place social bookmarking icons on all your content assets.

- Go for paid models if you have the budget. In StumbleUpon's Paid Discovery, your content automatically gets served in user's streams. 5% of all stumbles are reserved for paid discovery.

Social bookmarking isn't usually a route to instant traffic. You have to be patient and think long-term. That said, it's a powerful way to increase your marketing reach if you're willing to spend the time working it.

TIP*: It's best to begin with only one or two services that you feel the most comfortable with and concentrate on them until you see some results, then add the others one at a time.*

Posting Frequency Strategy

You've read about post frequency throughout the book, but it's such an important concept that it deserves a chapter of its own. A musician using any kind of online promotion risks drawing the ire of his fans by posting too much, and lowing the marketing opportunities by posting too little. Obviously a balance must be struck, but posting frequency is not a one-size-fits-all situation; it must be tailored for each application. Here's the game plan for posting not only on social media, but for content sites like your website and blog, as well as the latest strategy for releasing your videos and songs.

Posting On Social Media

While many have the opinion that you can never post too much on a social media network, research shows that there's definitely a threshold after which additional posts begin to feel like spam. That point varies for each network however. Let's look at the different points in all the major networks.

Facebook

Posting on a personal Facebook page has a different post limit than on a fan page. You've most certainly had friends that shortly after being introduced to Facebook felt that their every action during the day was of the utmost interest to their friends and as a result would post incessantly. Luckily, just at the point where you make the decision to block them they begin to realize that posting that much during a day is a lot of work and inherently back it off to a reasonable four or five times a day or less. Still others never quite get the message and end up being blocked by even their friends.

The limits on a fan or band page are far lower however, since fans expect only quality posts, and have a much lower post tolerance. Studies have found that the more you post, the less effective each post becomes. This is definitely a case of less is more. ***Limit your posts to one per day; two at most.***

***TIP**: Play close attention to the number of unfollows or unlikes relative to your number of posts.*

Twitter

Twitter is another case where a higher number of tweets on a personal account can be tolerated by your followers because the lifespan of each post is short (about an hour). There have been studies that have found that the average number of personal tweets range as high as 22 per day, and there are certainly circumstances where that many can be effective, like during a news event. Under most circumstances, more than four per hour lowers engagement considerably, and the possibility of a copy miscue that incites a flame war increases with each additional post.

As with Facebook, the frequency landscape for a brand account changes as well. Studies have found that the sweet spot is ***between two and four per day***, with engagement dropping as the posts increase beyond that number. That said, don't be afraid to thank anyone who either retweets a post or comments, although more than five to ten per day in your Twitter stream can also be deemed as excessive, in which case it's best to do a direct message instead.

***TIP**: Be sure to space out your posts throughout the day. Too many tweets at once can clog up your follower's Twitter streams or may even be considered spam by some.*

Google+

Google+ is similar to Facebook in that posts have a longer lifetime than Twitter at about four hours each, but not as long as other types of online media. Just about all the same parameters apply in that engagement falls after four posts per day, and too many in a concentrated period of time feels like spam to your readers.

An advantage for G+ is that you can target your various Circles with posts specific for that group. That means that you'll probably have fewer posts that will apply to your full audience as a result. Still, the **two to four post limit** still applies.

Yet two other advantages for G+ is that Events and Hangouts both require multiple posts as part of the feature. Since your followers expect and even desire these posts, the volume that's generated usually isn't an issue. On a day with a Hangout or Event, it's a safe practice to cut down on your general posts, perhaps to only one, to balance out any other posts generated as part of the other features.

Pinterest

Pinterest is a somewhat different animal when it comes to post frequency in that the quality of the image is much more important than the quantity. As a result, your followers can sustain more pins per day if what you post directly pertains to them.

That said, there's less noise on Pinterest than on Twitter, so there are times when an artist or brand can post *too* much in that the posts become very obvious. As a general guideline, an artist, band or brand should post **several times throughout the day**, staggering your posts daily so that they aren't posted at the same times every day. Studies have shown that mixing up the times that you post increases the chances that your pins will be seen by your followers.

Posting On Blogs

As stated in Chapter 8, Blogging is all about the commitment to post in a timely fashion, but choosing that time can be somewhat daunting at first, especially if you've not blogged before. As someone who posts every weekday, I can tell you that doing it well does take time, so the amount of time that you have to spend on creating a post is a big part of the decision on your posting frequency.

That being said, if you want to build a reputation and an audience you should post at least once a day. A generally accepted amount for a "power blogger" is between three and five times per day. This is reserved more for the likes of a blog that's built as an news aggregator or source like MacDailyNews, Hypebot or TechCrunch, where the blog receives the blogger's full attention.

I believe that posting once a week is just barely enough to sustain an audience, but twice a week can be sufficient enough to grow it. As said before, more so than any other communication type online, blogs require a specific time and frequency to be successful. Once those have been determined, you must stick to that decision.

Updating Your Website

While it's true that research has shown that websites with a high update frequency generate more repeat visits per month, we all know just how difficult that update process can be, especially if your site is built traditionally off-line by a web designer and not as part of a blogging platform. While your site update frequency by itself doesn't directly effect your rankings, it does affect the user experience, and that's one of the major criteria that search engines rely on today when determining search ranking.

Google's spiders regularly crawl the web to rebuild its index, and the frequency that they crawl your site is a determining factor in how often your site needs to be updated. For instance, if you update your site every week but it's only crawled every month, then one of the reasons for updating it in the first place is negated. Of course, if you don't really care about your page rank and just want to concentrate on the user experience of the site, then a more frequent update makes sense. You can have both though, since there are many ways to improve Google spider crawling frequency, such as:

1. submitting a directory and sitemap to Google (Google allows you to submit a sitemap once per hour).
2. using social bookmarking sites.
3. adding fresh content to the website on a daily basis.

4. using a signature that has your site address on forums where you comment to get your website crawled.
5. modifying your meta tags regularly.

That said, a site should ideally be updated **once a quarter** if for no other reason than to add a new look or new content to attract returning visitors, although another criteria to use is any drop in traffic.

Newsletter Frequency

The frequency that you mail your newsletters is extremely important to the open rate, length of engagement, and click throughs. Email too frequently and those measurements will fall, email not enough and you lose the advantage of the newsletter, which is for keeping your fans informed. Ultimately, the ideal frequency rate comes down to your business, your audience and your content quality.

Even if you're a musician, the type of business that you run can vary widely. For instance, if your major priority is to inform your fans about your upcoming gigs, then once a week might seem about right. If the newsletter is more to keep in touch about major events like song and video releases, then once every four to eight weeks could be sufficient. If your merch business is strong and you have new items constantly coming available, then once a week could work. Some sales sites like eBay Deals, Woot and DealMac, or news sites can mail every day without the fan feeling intruded upon.

The tolerance of your audience for email is something that you'll have to gauge. Do you promise a certain frequency when they first subscribe? Do you see more than 5% unsubscribes with each mailing? These can indicate that either you're mailing too frequently or your content quality isn't high enough.

Content quality is probably the most important criteria. If you have news that your fans look forward to that doesn't feel like a constant bombardment of promotion, they can probably stand a frequency rate of once per week. If you're not sure what to include or are searching for material, then it's probably best to wait until there's no question that you have enough quality material.

All that said, for an artist or band, the sweet spot frequency for a newsletter mailing is **every four to six weeks**, which is just long enough from the last one that it's welcome, yet not long enough that you're forgotten. It's possible to push the time between posts to 12 weeks if you're in a dormant period and don't have much that's newsworthy, but any longer than that and you risk being ignored.

Posting Videos

Videos are different from the above networks in that a polished music video can't be produced quickly, but what's off-the-cuff and behind the scenes shot from your smartphone can. In fact, sometimes these impromptu videos are the ones that are the best received precisely because they're not slick and show your human side.

That said, when it comes to video, less is more. If you're doing just a quick smartphone movie, then **once every two to three days** is optimum, but more often can be possibly tolerated if you're shooting something that's newsworthy. If you're at a trade show, for instance, and keep running into celebrities that are willing to speak to you on camera, more frequent posts can be acceptable. Even in that case though, the best strategy is to save them for later and space their releases out, either over the course of a day, or even better, over a longer period of time.

Releasing Music

A new strategy in releasing music is beginning to take place, even within the major labels. In almost a return to the early days of records, the single song is king rather than the album, and that requires an entirely new look at the timing of when your material becomes available.

Back in the 1950s and '60s, the music world revolved around the single. Many artists we're signed for only a single or two that would have to be successful before the label would commit to making an album. If they finally got to that point, recording the entire album could be done in only a day or two back then. As technology evolved and recording track counts increased, overdubbing became possible so artists were able to not only perfect their performances, but also be a lot more creative as well, and this led to the creation of an album taking more and more time.

There was a lot more money in albums than there were singles, and as music sales took off, the record labels were more apt to spend more time making an album because of the potential profit involved. Slowly but surely, the two album per year norm of the '60s became one per year, then one every two years, then even longer. As far as the consumer was concerned, the wait for an album was hard enough, but what if there were only one or two good songs on it? Even a hit artist's fan base could actually dissipate if the product didn't come at regular intervals and feel like it was worth the wait.

Digital music turned that thinking upside down in that the fan could now cherry pick only the songs he wanted. As a result, music returned to the singles world that it is today, which brings about a new philosophy regarding recordings and how they are released, since albums are no longer the focus of the fan or audience.

Fewer Songs More Often

The basic premise of the new release philosophy is to release fewer songs but have more frequent releases. In other words, it's better to release a song or two every six, eight, or twelve weeks than to wait a year for one album release of ten songs as was once done. This benefits the artist in the following ways:

- The artist keeps their fans happy with a constant supply of new music. New music keeps the buzz and dialog going about the artist on the social networks.

- Each release is a separate marketing event. With the release of an album, you have one single event to publicize with a long period of time until the next one is produced. With individual releases, you have the potential for 11 separate releases (ten plus the album), which means that there's constantly new music in your fanbase's ecosystem, and increased potential to reach new fans as a result.

- The artist gains increased exposure for every song. In a ten song album release, it's easy for a fan, reviewer or radio programmer to focus on just one or two of the songs while the others fall in priority. With individual releases, each song gets equal attention and has the ability to live and die on its own merits.

- An album can still be compiled after all the songs have been individually released. At the end of the year, or at the end of the artist's creative cycle, the songs are then put into an album that can be released in any format. The advantage is that the album has much advanced exposure and publicity thanks to previously released singles. Plus it can be treated as a marketing event to the artist's advantage.

Make no mistake, the album format is not dead in Music 3.0 (although sales continue to decrease), but the emphasis has shifted to the individual song. Not only that, the tastes and attention span of audiences today are shorter and shorter, which makes multiple releases an ideal fit with the lifestyle. No one is saying that you can't release an album; just that multiple singles at regular intervals before the album release works better in today's marketplace.

Remember that in our Music 3.0 world, your music is your marketing, not your product. Your social world is ultimately built around it, so the more frequently its available benefits you greatly by providing more chances for fans hear it, and for potential fans to find it.

✦

Glossary

+1: Google+'s version of Facebook's "Like" button.

above the fold: the upper half of the front page of a newspaper where a headline, important news story or photograph is often located. On a webpage, the text on the screen before you scroll down.

Adsense: a Google service for supplying advertisements to a website based on factors such as the website's content and the user's geographical location.

alt attribute: alternative text that's rendered when an element like a graphic on a web page can't be displayed. Also used by screen reader software so that a blind person listening to the page understands the element.

Arbitron ratings: a measurement of the number of people listening to a radio station.

art: a creative endeavor that you do for your own personal satisfaction.

autoresponder: a program that automatically answers emails sent to it.

avatar: a graphical representation of the user's alter ego or character.

B2B: business to business.

B2C: business to consumer.

backlink: an outside link on another website that's connected to your page.

banner: a form of Internet advertising.

barcode: a series of vertical bars of varying widths in which the numbers 0 through 9 are represented by a unique pattern of bars that can be read by a laser scanner. Barcodes are commonly found on consumer products and are used for inventory control purposes and, in the case of CDs, to tally sales for the purposes of chart position.

bashtag: the use of a person or company's Twitter hashtag to bash them or their products.

blip: a cross between a song and a tweet.

blog: a discussion or informational page on the Web consisting of discrete chronological posts.

Blogosphere: all blogs, their connections and communities.

bootleg: an unauthorized recording of a concert, a rehearsal, an outtake, or an alternate mix from an album.

brand: a name, sign, or symbol used to identify the items or services of a seller that differentiates them from their competitors. A brand is a promise of quality and consistency.

branding: the promotion of a brand.

brick and mortar: a physical retail store, which is usually composed of building materials like bricks and mortar.

catalog: older albums or recordings under the control of the record label.

Circles: on Google+, a list of connections, which could be fans, friends, brands, or any other category that a user creates.

click-through: the number of times a link is clicked

co-branding: two firms working together to promote a product or service.

codec: a device or algorithm dedicated to encoding and decoding a digital stream. Usually used in audio and video.

collectible: an item (usually nonessential) that has particular value to its owner because of its rarity or desirability.

conglomerate: a multi-industry company or a large company that owns smaller companies in different businesses.

craft: a creative endeavor that you do for someone else's approval.

crowdfunding: a method of raising money for a project by offering incentives for fans to pool their money.

distribution network: The various retail sales outlets or, in the case of Music 3.0, digital music download sites.

DIY: do it yourself.

Edgerank: a news feed formula that Facebook has created to determine which stories are the most relevant to a user.

ESP: Email Service Providers.

flame war: hostile or insulting interaction between blog or forum commenters.

Flash: a program by Adobe used for creating short-form animation with a small enough file size that it can be used on the Web.

frames: an outdated method of displaying multiple HTML documents on a single webpage.

Google Alert: email updates of the latest relevant Google results (web, news, etc.) based on a set of criteria chosen.

Google Voice: a phone service offered by Google.

Hangout: a Google+ feature similar to video conferencing in that you can connect with up to 9 other people at once.

hashtags: the pound symbol (#) placed directly in front of a word in a tweet so it acts as a keyword.

heritage artist: a superstar act that is still active. Madonna, Tina Turner, The Rolling Stones, and The Eagles are examples of current heritage acts.

image map: an easy way of adding hyperlinks to various parts of an image.

ISP: Internet Service Provider.

kbps: kilobits per second, or the amount of digital information sent per second. Sometimes referred to as "bandwidth."

keyword: a word or phrase that is closely linked to, or describes, a subject or website.

keyword stuffing: when a page is overloaded with keywords in an effort to be recognized by a search engine.

landing page: the home page or page that a user lands on after clicking on a link from a search engine.

Like: a button that allows Facebook users to show their support for a specific comment, status, picture wall post, or fan page.

Like-gating: an attempt to increase Likes more quickly than otherwise possible by providing exclusive content or prizes in exchange for Liking a page.

lurker: one who reads a blog but doesn't participate or post himself.

meet and greet: a brief meeting with an artist to say hello, answer a few questions, and take pictures.

metadata: data about other data or content.

meta tags: html page data, which can typically include the Title, Description, and Keywords.

micropayment: a means for transferring very small amounts of money in situations where collecting such small amounts of money is impractical or very expensive using the usual payment systems.

millennial: a member of the generation of children born between 1977 and 1994.

MP3: the contraction of MPEG-2 Audio Layer III, which is the de facto standard data-compression format used to make audio files smaller in size.

Music 3.0: the current generation of the music business, in which the artist can now communicate, interact with, market and sell directly to the fan. Record labels, radio, and television have become less relevant in Music 3.0, and many more single songs are purchased instead of albums.

opt-in: when someone provides permission to receive an email.

paid download: a downloadable song that you buy and own.

pay-per-click: an Internet advertising model used by search engines, advertising networks, and content sites such as blogs, in which advertisers pay their host only when their ad is clicked on.

paid search: a type of contextual advertising in which website owners pay an advertising fee to have their website shown in the top placement on search-engine results pages.

peer to peer: a type of transient Internet network that allows a group of computer users with the same networking program to connect with each other and directly access files from one another's hard drives.

P2P: see the entry under "peer to peer."

pirating: an illegal copy of a digital file, CD, CD artwork, or any other creative product, that is sold for a profit, but the record label, artist, and songwriter never takes part in the profit or provided royalties.

pop-ups: a form of advertising where unwanted and unexpected browser windows open automatically.

pull-down menu: also called a drop-down menu, where the item you select is at the top of the display, and the menu appears just below it when moused over, as if you had pulled it down.

QR Code: a graphic code similar to a bar code that provides a link to a website when scanned. An analog web link.

relevance: the manner in which keywords are related to the content of a page or search engine query.

record: a generic term for the distribution method of a recording. Regardless of whether it's vinyl, a CD, or a digital file, it's still known as a record.

RSS: Real Simple Syndication is a family of Web-feed formats used to publish frequently updated works such as blog entries, news headlines, audio, and video in a standardized format.

SERP: Search Engine Results Page.

sentiment: determining the attitude of a page visitor with regards to the content.

SEM: Search-Engine Marketing.

SEO: Search-Engine Optimization.

skin: a custom graphical interface.

smartphone: a mobile phone with advanced features such as Internet access, GPS tracking, and a camera.

spam: unsolicited advertising messages.

splash page: an introduction page of a website that sometimes features animation and appears prior to the home page.

superfan: a fan that is more passionate than the average fan.

swag: another name for merchandise, such as T-shirts, that is sold at a concert or on a website.

tag: a word or phrase that conveys the most important aspects of a product or website to help users search for content.

tag cloud: a box containing a list of tags with the most prominent or popular tags receiving a darker and bigger font than less popular tags.

troll: someone who posts inflammatory off-topic messages with the intent of provoking a response.

tweet: a Twitter posting.

Vine: a 6 second Twitter video using the Vine platform.

widget: a small application with limited and specific functioning.

watermarking: a recognizable image or pattern that's encoded into digitized music, video, or a graphic.

Bobby Owsinski Bibliography

The Mixing Engineer's Handbook 3rd Edition (ISBN #128542087X - Thomson Course Technology): The premier book on audio mixing techniques provides all the information needed to take your mixing skills to the next level, along with advice from the world's best mixing engineers.

The Recording Engineer's Handbook 3rd Edition (ISBN #1285442016 - Course Technology PTR): Revealing the microphone and recording techniques used by some of the most renowned recording engineers, you'll find everything you need to know to lay down great tracks in any recording situation, in any musical genre, and in any studio.

The Audio Mastering Handbook 2nd Edition (ISBN #1598634496 - Course Technology PTR): Everything you always wanted to know about mastering, from doing it yourself to using a major facility, utilizing insights from the world's top mastering engineers.

The Drum Recording Handbook *with DVD* [with Dennis Moody] (ISBN #1423443438 - Hal Leonard): Uncovers the secret of making amazing drum recordings in your own recording studio even with the inexpensive gear. It's all in the technique, and this book/DVD will show you how.

How To Make Your Band Sound Great *with DVD* (ISBN #1423441907 - Hal Leonard): This band improvement book and DVD shows your band how to play to it's fullest potential. It doesn't matter what kind of music you play, what your skill level is, or if you play covers or your own music, this book will make you tight, it will make you more dynamic, it will improve your show and it will improve your recordings.

The Studio Musician's Handbook *with DVD* [with Paul ILL] (ISBN #1423463412 Hal Leonard): Everything you wanted to know about the world of the studio musician including how to become a studio musician, who hires you, how much you get paid, the gear you must have, the proper session etiquette required to make a session run smoothly, and how to apply these skills in every type of recording session regardless if it's in your home studio or at Abbey Road.

Music 3.0 - A Survival Guide To Making Music In The Internet Age 2nd Edition (ISBN #1423474015 Hal Leonard): The paradigm has shifted and everything you knew about the music business has completely changed. Who are the new players in the music business? Why are traditional record labels, television, and radio no longer factors in an artist's success? How do you market and distribute your music in the new music world - and how do you make money? This book answers these questions and more in its comprehensive look at the new music business.

The Music Producer's Handbook *with DVD* (ISBN 978-1423474005 Hal Leonard): Reveals the inside information and secrets to becoming a music producer and producing just about any kind of project in any genre of music. The book also covers the true mechanics of production, from analyzing and fixing the format of a song, to troubleshooting a song when it just doesn't sound right, to getting the best performance and sound out of the band and vocalist.

The Musician's Video Handbook *with DVD* (ISBN 978-1423484448 Hal Leonard): Describes how the average musician can easily make any of the various types of videos now required by a musical artist either for promotion or final product. The book will also demonstrate the tricks and tips used by the pros to make it look professionally done, even with inexpensive gear and not much of a budget.

Mixing And Mastering With T-Racks: The Official Guide (ISBN 978-1435457591 Course Technology PTR): Learn how to harness the potential of T-RackS as well as the tips and tricks of using it's processor modules to help bring your mixes to life, then master them so they're competitive with any major label release.

The Touring Musician's Handbook *with DVD* (ISBN 978-1423492368 Hal Leonard): Answers all the questions regarding becoming a touring musician, regardless of whether you're a sideman, solo performer, or member of a band. As a bonus, individual touring musician guides for guitar, bass, drums, vocals, keys, horns and strings as well as interviews with famous and influential touring players are also included.

The Ultimate Guitar Tone Handbook *with DVD* [with Rich Tozolli] (ISBN 978-0739075357 Alfred Publishing): The definitive book for discovering that great guitar sound and making sure it records well. The book outlines all the factors that make electric and acoustic guitars, amplifiers and speaker cabinets sound the way they do, as well as the classic and modern recording and production techniques that capture great tone.

The Studio Builder's Handbook *with DVD* [with Dennis Moody] (ISBN - 978-0739077030 Alfred Publishing): While you might think that it costs thousands of dollars and the services of an acoustic designer to improve your studio, the *Studio Builder's Handbook* will strip away the mystery of what makes a great sounding studio and show how you can make a huge difference in your room for as little as $150.

Abbey Road To Ziggy Stardust [with Ken Scott] (ISBM - 978-0739078587 Alfred Publishing): The memoir of legendary producer/ engineer Ken Scott, who holds a unique place in music history as one of only five engineers to have recorded The Beatles, and producer and/or engineer on six David Bowie records, among many others. Funny, poignant, and oh, so honest, Ken pulls no punches as he tells it as he saw it, as corroborated by a host of famous and not-so famous guests who were there as well.

The Audio Mixing Bootcamp *with DVD* (ISBN - 978-0739082393 Alfred Publishing): If you're creating your first mix and don't know where to begin, or your mixes aren't as good as you'd like them to be, *the Audio Mixing Boot Camp* is here to help. Built around a series of hands-on mixing exercises designed to show you how to listen and work like a pro, the book reveals the tips, tricks, and secrets to all the different facets of mixing, including instrument and vocal balance, panning, compression, EQ, reverb, delay, and making your mix as interesting as possible.

Audio Recording Basic Training *with DVD* (ISBN - 978-0739086001 Alfred Publishing): If you're new to recording and don't know where to begin, or your recordings aren't as good as you'd like them to be, *Audio Recording Basic Training* is a great place to begin. Built around a series of hands-on recording exercises designed to show you how to listen and work like a recording pro, the book reveals the tips, tricks and secrets to all the different facets of recording - including miking a drum kit, recording vocals, and miking just about any kind of electric or acoustic instrument.

The Music 3.0 Guide To Social Media. *Tips and Tricks for using Facebook, Twitter, YouTube and Google+.* (ISBN - 978-0988839106). An ebook derived from the archive of over 800 posts on the Music 3.0 blog that date back to when the blog first started in 2009 until the end of 2012. This first volume primarily looks at social media concepts for musicians, and examines the various tips and tricks for using Facebook, Twitter, YouTube and Google+ as a promotional tool.

You can get more info and read excerpts from each book by visiting the excerpts section of bobbyowsinski.com.

Bobby Owsinski Lynda.com Video Courses

The Audio Mixing Bootcamp Video Course: Over 8 hours of movies outlining the various steps, tips and tricks of mixing like the pros.

Audio Recording Techniques: Discover the industry secrets to recording crisp, rich vocals and instruments tracks, as renowned audio engineer Bobby Owsinski walks through the process of miking and tracking a complete song using A-list session musicians in a top-of-the-line studio.

Mastering For iTunes: Best practices for mastering music and audio destined for sale on Apple iTunes with their new Mastered for iTunes high-resolution audio program.

Audio Mastering Techniques: Explore essential mastering concepts and techniques used by experienced audio engineers to create a cohesive album from a set of mixed tracks.

Also Available From Bobby Owsinski

Delay Genie iPhone App: Time your delays and reverbs to the track with this easy to use app. Also has a live mode for delaying speakers or delay towers. And it's FREE!

Bobby Owsinski's Social Media Connections

Bobby's Music Production Blog: bobbyowsinski.blogspot.com

Bobby's Music Industry Blog: music3point0.blogspot.com

Bobby on Facebook: facebook.com/bobby.owsinski

Bobby on YouTube: youtube.com/polymedia

Bobby on Linkedin: linkedin.com/in/bobbyo

Bobby on Twitter: @bobbyowsinski

About Bobby Owsinski

A long-time music industry veteran, Bobby Owsinski started his career as a guitar and keyboard player, songwriter and arranger, eventually going on to become an in-demand producer/engineer working not only with a variety of recording artists, but on commercials, television and motion pictures as well. One of the first to delve into surround sound music mixing, Bobby has worked on over a hundred surround projects and DVD productions for a variety of superstar acts.

Combining his music and recording experience along with an easy to understand writing style, Bobby has become one of the best selling authors in the music recording industry with 18 books that are now staples in audio recording, music and music business programs in colleges around the world.

A frequent speaker at universities and industry conferences the world over, Bobby has served as the longtime producer of the annual Surround Music Awards, and is one of the creators and executive producers for the "Guitar Universe" and "Desert Island Music" television programs.

Bobby's blogs are some of the most influential and widely read in the music business. Visit Bobby's production blog at http://bobbyowsinski.blogspot.com/, his Music 3.0 music industry blog at http://music3point0.blogspot.com, and his website at http://bobbyowsinski.com.

BO
MG
Publishing